SPIRAL GUIDE

GW01003584

VIENNA

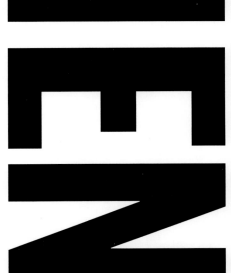

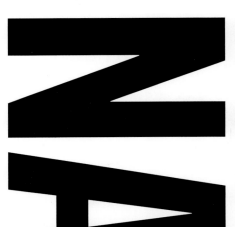

AA
Publishing

Contents

Written by Hanne Egghardt and Katharina Kunz
Copy edited by Katrin Wampula
Picture research by Gabriele Forst
Page layout by Cyclus · Visuelle Kommunikation

Translated by Christopher Wightwick and Sylvia Goulding
English text copy edited by Silva Editions Ltd

ISBN-10: 0 7495 4540 2
ISBN-13: 9780 7495 4540 6

Published by AA Publishing, a trading name of Automobile Association
Developments Limited, whose registered office is Southwood East, Apollo
Rise, Farnborough, Hampshire, GU14 0JW. Registered number 1878835.

© Falk Verlag, Ostfildern, 1. Auflage 2005
Maps: © MAIRDUMONT / Falk Verlag 2005

Cover and design © Automobile Association Developments Limited
This Spiral guidebook was produced with Falk Verlag in agreement with
Automobile Association developments Limited, owner of the
"Spiral guide" series
English translation © Automobile Association Developments Limited

Cover design and binding style by permission of AA Publishing

Printed and bound in China by Leo Paper Products

Find out more about AA Publishing and the wide range of services the AA
provides by visiting our website at www.theAA.com.

A02225

the magazine

A few years ago Austrian opinion was sharply divided over a character in the TV series *A echter Wiener geht net unter* (Your true Viennese will never be beaten). There were indignant cries of "We're really not as vulgar as that!", while others thought it "really great, a slice of life". However you take it, though, you can learn a lot about the Viennese from the TV series.

The character, Mundl Sackbauer, is a loud-mouthed primitive, never without a bottle of beer in his hand and fond of letting go with strong language. He is a lovable, ungainly rogue who always manages to avoid giving offence despite his dubious dealings. So he is on a par with Helmut Qualtinger's legendary Herr Karl, a character taken straight from the malicious world of lower-middle-class Vienna, who became the image of the archetypal Viennese opportunist and malcontent.

the past, stereotyping has centred on three traits above all. The first was quibbling: very rarely, it was said, can you get it right for the Viennese – they find fault with

A "true Viennese"?
Does a "true Viennese" exist? Go and find out for yourself that there's no such thing. In

everything. The second was more positive: they have a "golden heart", especially for animals, it was believed. The third and last was their predilection for "Viennese Schmäh", a unique sort of sarcastic humour.

These three age-old stereotypes no longer hold true today – if, indeed, they ever did. The young people of today, especially, are modern-thinking and open to the world. Perhaps the only thing you will genuinely come across is the Viennese Schmäh, since many places

Page 5: The Pallas Athene fountain in front of the Parliament building

Above left: Cabbies at their favourite pastime

Above right: Occasionally you can scale the Rathaus-platz walls have their own and local sense of humour – if you can understand the dialect, that is. Ask about the building works in Vienna or any other universal topic for complaints, and you'll hear the typical mixture of "Schmäh" and grumbles. Talk about the hotly disputed "poo-bags", which in July 2004

Multiethnic Vienna

The fact is, of course, that there is no such thing as a "true Viennese" and probably never has been. From its earliest days through to its rise as a city at the end of the 19th century, people of

won't be beaten

were imposed on cab-horses, to catch droppings even before they have a chance to foul the streets, and you'll hear a passionate plea for the dignity of the horse. But is that "Schmäh" so different from what you would hear in other cities?

the most varied origins have lived in this city on the fault-line between East and West. Even around 1900 it was still a requirement that higher-grade civil servants should speak six to eight languages. And if you look in the Vienna telephone book you'll see that names like Swoboda and Cerny, Kovacs and Arslan fill

Above left:
A quiet moment in the café

Above centre:
Business doesn't stop for shopping

Above right:
Naughty but ice – the ice-ream parlour

What is "Viennese Schmäh"?

Scholarly dissertations have been written on the subject of what "Viennese Schmäh" really is, but there is still no precise explanation. Whatever its definition, it is certainly composed of a number of elements: a curious sort of humour, a trenchant way of talking, and a dash of bragging. Its home base is above all at cafés, in wine bars with their earthy locals, and late at night by the Wiener sausage stall, where the chat, and with it the Schmäh, flows so freely that the Viennese say "Schmäh's on the run".

UN Headquarters

Since 1979 Vienna, together with New York and Geneva, has been a headquarters of the United Nations. This venue was chosen because Vienna was to be the mediator between the great power-blocs. UNO City, with an area of 180,000sq m (over 44 acres), six concave office towers and a conference and congress centre, is home to the International Atomic Energy Authority (IAEA) and the UN Industrial Development Organisation (UNIDO), among others.

many columns. In fact, immigrants have always shaped Vienna with their cultures, their cuisines and their lifestyles. Long before the idea of multiculturalism was common currency, people from every corner of the empire were drawn to the city on the Danube, which became a melting-pot for the multiethnic state. And later, when Vienna was the over-large head of a shrunken realm, the influx continued. Thousands came from Hungary after 1956, joined from the 1970s on by people from the former Yugoslavia and from Turkey, who were known as "guest-workers".

Immigrants created

A taste of the Caribbean on the Danube

Vienna's unique atmosphere for the city's cultural development. Around 1900

Facts & Figures

Vienna, with an area of 415sq km (160 sq miles) and a perimeter of 133km (82 miles), has 1.6 million inhabitants, of whom 18% are foreigners. In population terms, Vienna is the seventh largest European capital.

his fertile background allowed the sciences, architecture, decorative and ine arts as well as music to flourish. Writers such as Arthur Schnitzler and Robert Musil, Heimito von Doderer and Hermann Broch, Alfred Polgar and Egon Friedell drew their creative inspiration from the diversity of Vienna's roots.

In recent years Vienna has begun to rediscover its old strength and creativity. There's a strong sense of urban revival, the city is renewing itself, with a vibrant life seldom felt before. "Your true Viennese will never be beat." On the contrary!

Multicultural music in Stephansplatz

Vienna and the Danube

To say that Vienna lies "on the beautiful blue Danube", as the text of the Strauss waltz has it, is pure nonsense. The Danube is murky and grey, and always has been. The 280-m (300-yard) wide river was certainly always important as a transport artery, but its flooding posed equally great dangers. In the 1970s the construction of the New Danube, an additional river channel 21km (13 miles) long, brought some relief. As an additional benefit, it also created the Donauinsel (Danube Island), a vast recreation area.(► 153).

HIGHLIGHTS AT A GLANCE

Once Round the Ringstrasse

It's not the most luxurious form of transport, but taking trams D or 2 round the Ringstrasse is the simplest and cheapest way to see the elegant buildings either side of Vienna's famous boulevard from close up. You can start your circular route wherever you want, at Schwedenplatz, by the Staatsoper or at Schottentor, and then stay put until you arrive back to your starting point. The Ring isn't just a name, it really is a ring.

The Most Exciting Musical Experiences

Nothing beats a visit to the Staatsoper (➤ 98). But performances of classical music in the Konzerthaus (➤ 136) or the Musikverein (➤ 131) come a close second. Recently Vienna has also caught up with the world of jazz. Joe Zawinul's *Birdland* (➤ 158) in the newly refurbished Hilton Hotel is truly sensational, and *Porgy and Bess* (➤ 68) also sounds good.

The Most Exciting Museums

"Art and enjoyment" is the motto of the new Viennese museums. In the museum district (➤ 103), art and urban

Background: The traffic jam at Schottentor

Above: From the terrace of the Haas House you can almost touch the Stephansdom

The Staatsoper, Vienna's most famous temple of music

A sweet place to go: Demel's café in Kohlmarkt

flair can be enjoyed in many venues. The lavishly renovated Albertina (► 82) is an imposing new temple of the arts, and the splendid Palais Liechtenstein (► 26) really is a "place of baroque joie de vivre". But it would be a mistake if these marvellous new museums led you to neglect the Kunsthistorisches and Naturhistorisches Museums (Museum of Art History and Museum of Natural History), not only because of their fascinating exhibits but also because of the fine architecture of both buildings.

Leisure in the Open Air

In summer the opera and film festival in Rathausplatz (► 18) is the favourite free open-air event of the Viennese. Other popular shows for cool entertainment on hot summer nights include Copa Cagrana on the Danube Island, the Summer Stage by the Danube Canal, and Campus in the inner courtyards of the old AKH (► 19). The Schweizerhaus in the Prater (► 155) is also great fun.

The Finest Views
• the north tower of the Stephansdom (► 52)
• the roof terrace of the Haas House (► 5)
• the cafeteria in Leiner's furnishing store (► 105)
• the great Ferris wheel (► 146)

Splendid butterflies feel at home in the butterfly house

The Best Torten
The very best Viennese *Torten* – gâteaux, flans, cakes – are to be had at Demel's, the court confectioner's in Kohlmarkt (► 90), but you're also guaranteed top quality in the world-famous Café Sacher (► 110) and many other patisseries such as Kurkonditorei Oberlaa (► 111), Café Landtmann (► 111) and at Sluka's (► 111).

The Finest Viennese Coffee-houses
Sperl's (► 134) is the most romantic of all Viennese coffee-houses, Landtmann's (► 111) the liveliest and the Bräunerhof (► 89) the most traditional. In any case: don't just take a look, but set aside at least an hour to enjoy the ambience.

The Best Places for Children
• ride bumper-cars in the Wurstlprater (► 150)
• admire butterflies in the Palmenhaus (► 86)
• watch the animals in the Schönbrunn zoo (► 121)

Coffee and croissants, lilacs and doner kebabs: everywhere in Vienna you'll find traces of the city's Turkish past. To see the Islamic crescent standing on the top of the Stephansdom was for a long time a Turkish ambition, which was almost achieved in 1529 and 1683. In fact, they didn't conquer Vienna until much, much later.

Vienna's
Turkish Past

Sultan Suleiman II the Magnificent, sultan of the Ottoman Empire, had the ambition to extend his realm and set his sights on Vienna. In 1529 he laid siege to the city with 150,000 troops. 20,000 camels brought reinforcements and supplies. At that time Vienna was not well fortified, and the defending general, Count Niklas Salm, had only 20,000 troops. Virtually at the eleventh

Background: The First Turkish Siege, 1529

Above: The Second Turkish Siege, 1683–9

hour, though, the city was saved, winter arrived earlier than usual, in early October, and the invaders were forced to withdraw.

In 1566 Sultan Suleiman II was again marching against Vienna. He besieged the town of Szigetvár in Hungary and put it to the torch on the night of 5 September. On that same night he died of a heart attack, so he never got his second look at Vienna. All the same, he gave something to the city's image. It was he who presented an emissary of the emperor, Ogier Ghislain de Busbecq, with a few tulip and hyacinth bulbs, and some lilac plants. Since then Vienna has been at its most beautiful each year in May, when the lilacs bloom all over the city.

The Kipferl – a Giant Crescent

In 1683 the Turkish forces besieged Vienna a second time. Once again the situation was desperate. Within the city dysentery was rife, and supplies were running low. To prove that they had enough flour, the Viennese are said to have baked a *kipferl*, a pastry shaped like a giant crescent and hoisted it in defiance above the city walls. Vienna's fate was on a knife-edge, but the relief army under the Polish king Jan Sobieski came to the rescue. The attackers were put to flight – they even left their coffee-making gear behind (► 28)!

Peaceful Conquest

By the 18th century Turkey posed no further threat – in fact all things Turkish became the fashion. Painters and composers produced works "alla turca", people wore orientally inspired clothing and used harems as the backdrop to operas, as in Mozart's *Die Entführung aus dem Serail*. Few contemporary composers could do without instruments such as cymbals, triangles and glockenspiels.

At the end of the 1950s the first Turkish immigrant workers came to Vienna. Since then 52,000 of them have settled in the city. Sometimes they joke that "now we have conquered the city after all". And in the meanwhile the Viennese themselves have taken to döner kebabs and heatedly discuss the pros and cons of Turkey's entry into the European Union.

(► 28)

Turkish Footsteps

• **Wien 1, Am Hof 11:** a gilded Turkish cannon-ball
• **Esterházykeller, Wien 1, Haarhof:** a plaque commemorates the fact that during the Turkish siege of 1683 the city's defenders took wine at this cellar.

ur Zeit der Belagerung Wiens durch die Türken im Jahre 1683 tranken hier in diesem Keller schon die Verteidiger der Stadt den vom Fürsten Esterházy verabreichten Humpen freiwein.

• **Neustädterhof, Wien 1, Sterngasse 3:** the largest Turkish cannon-ball in this district.
• **Galerie des Michaelertors, Wien 1, Michaeler-platz:** Turkish trophies

Above: An actress in Mozart's opera *Die Entführung aus dem Serail* – all very Turkish

the magazine **13**

In places as diverse as Schönbrunn, Hofburg, Kapuzinergruft you find traces of Maria Theresa. That's hardly surprising, as the Empress is the ancestral mother of Austria. During her reign (1740–80) the state was reorganized.

The Baroque
Empress

May 2, 1750, was a fateful day. It was when Empress Maria Theresa made a radical change to the constitution: she brought together the hereditary provinces of Austria and the lands of the Bohemian kingdom to form a single state. This act made the capital, Vienna, the centre of an empire, and in consequence the city needed a royal residence appropriate for its increased importance. And so Maria Theresa had the palace of Schönbrunn enlarged.

"Thou, happy Austria, marry!"

Although Maria Theresa fought and lost wars, she married off her 16 children to all points of the compass, following the motto "Bella gerant alii, tu, felix Austria, nube" (Let others wage war, thou, happy Austria, marry). Marie Antoinette had the worst luck. At the tender age of 15 years, she was married to the French King Louis XVI and ended up on the scaffold in the French Revolution.

Maria Theresa, Holy Roman Empress and Queen of Hungary and Bohemia

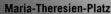

Maria-Theresien-Platz

Since 1888 "Europe's mother-in-law" has gazed from her place of honour between the Kunsthistorisches Museum and the Naturhistorisches Museum towards the city centre. At the empress's feet stand the men who came to fame during her reign. Among the 16 high-relief figures you can find Mozart, Haydn and Gluck.

Everywhere in Vienna you feel the imperial splendour and the elegance of the "k.u.k." era, short for "kaiserlich und königlich" (imperial and royal) and nostalgia for the "good old days". The great symbol of that time is Franz Joseph I. The emperor with the paternal look and the long sideburns ruled for 68 years and he oversaw Vienna's transition to an important city.

"It was very beautiful ...

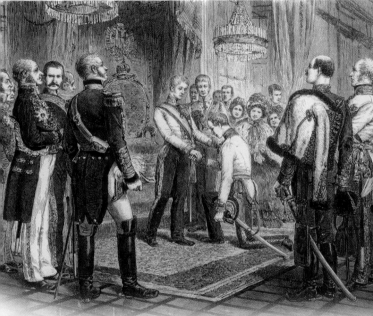

Franz Joseph ascended the imperial throne in 1848, the year of revolutions, at the age of only 18. Always true to the advice of his counsellors and his mother, Sophie, whose cool and unbending nature he had inherited, he remained conscientious and dogmatic throughout his rule. In 1854, in Vienna's Augustinerkirche,

he married the very young Elisabeth, known as "Sisi". She soon began to suffer from the distant manner of the emperor and his mother. The emperor found solace with his soulmate, the actress Katharina Schratt.

"It was very beautiful, we were very pleased": this was one of the courteous, but

The emperor's ascent to the throne, December 2, 1848

... we were very pleased"

meaningless phrases which the emperor liked to use. A more appropriate phrase might have been "I have been spared nothing", for he had to endure a whole series of blows. In 1867 his brother Maximilian was executed in Mexico; in 1889 his son, Crown Prince Rudolf, committed suicide in Mayerling (► 166); in 1898 his wife Elisabeth was the victim of an assassination; and in 1914 the heir to the throne, Archduke Franz Ferdinand, and his wife were murdered.

The Construction of the Ringstrasse

When Emperor Franz Joseph came to the throne, Vienna was still encircled by broad ramparts and fortifications, which had long lost their function and were really just a tight corset hemming in the city. The proposal to raze them provoked violent dispute – anyone with the time and leisure to read the *Wiener Zeitung* for Christmas Day 1857 would have been astonished. With the words, "It is my will", the emperor gave the official order to start the demolition of the fortifications and the construction of the Ringstrasse, and thus an era of urban expansion. Vienna developed from its idyllic Biedermeier period (early 19th century) into a cosmopolitan city, a metropolis whose architecture was designed to show

In Franz Joseph's day the imperial army was a significant force

with precious objects, but lived in a modest, even spartan manner in Schönbrunn. Grown cautious as a result of various political mistakes, he increasingly became the symbol of political inactivity and opposed any innovations or reforms, also refusing to abdicate in favour of his nephew Franz Ferdinand. In 1914, at the age of 84, he signed, in Bad Ischl, the declaration of war on Serbia, the start of World War I. The Austro-Hungarian empire collapsed under the strain of war. The emperor was spared seeing that happen: he died in 1916, two years before the end of the war.

its dominance over every town in the kingdom. (►93)

(►93)

Heyday and decline

Under Franz Joseph's rule cultural and intellectual life ourished, though the mperor himself had little iterest in the fine arts. He id not surround himself

Poor Unhappy Sisi

What had begun as a great romance ended in loneliness and sorrow. The young empress (1837-98) suffered under the ceremonial protocol of the Hofburg and the strict regime of her mother-in-law, Sophie. She took refuge in illness, isolation and extensive travel. Her beauty became a obsession. She spent hours each day tending her ankle-length hair, rode, exercised and followed strict diet regimes – on some days she ate only a few oranges. Fate was unkind to the empress: in 1857 her two-year-old daughter Sophie died and her soulmate and good friend King Ludwig II of Bavaria drowned in mysterious circumstances in Starnberger See. When in 1889 her son Rudolf and his lover Mary Vetsera committed suicide, her melancholy deepened. "Would that death would surprise me", she wrote in her journal. Her wish was fulfilled when she was assassinated in Geneva by the Italian anarchist Luigi Lucheni who stabbed her with a file.

Totally Cool

The Outdoor

Gone are the days when the Viennese spent summer and winter entirely in smoke-filled coffee-houses. Outdoor living is now all the rage: streetlife, ethnic food in the open air, cinema beneath the starry sky and impromptu parties. A fresh wind is blowing through the streets of Vienna, and not only in summer.

Vienna's open-air cinemas

- **Arena**, Wien 3, Baumgasse 80, tel: (01) 798 30 77, www.arena.co.at
- **Filmarchiv** (Austrian avantgarde and feature films), Wien 2, Obere Augartenstrasse 1, tel: (01) 216 13 00, www.filmarchiv.at
- **Kino unter Sternen** (classics OV), Wien 2/20, Augarten-Schlüsselwiese, tel: (01) 585 23 24 25, www.kinountersternen.at
- **Rathausplatz** (opera and classical music films), Wien 1, Rathausplatz, tel: (01) 400-81 00, www.wien-event.at
- **Schloss Neugebäude** (box office hits, entertainment), Wien 11, Meidlgasse, tel: (01) 74 03 41 11 18, www.schlosskino.at
- **Tribüne Krieau** (cult, classics and music), Wien 2, Südportalstrasse 231, tel: (01) 52 21 07, www.krieau.com
- **Volxkino** (repertory and box office hits), Wanderkino, tel: (01) 219 85 46, www.volxkino.at

ife

"Happy Hour 20 Uhr -50% Cocktails"

"Schani, get the garden ready" – as soon as the boss spoke these words, Schani the apprentice waiter knew that spring had arrived. On the first warm sunny days he carried tables and chairs outside – and the "Schani-garden" was ready. That's how it used to be.

Nowadays Vienna has been totally transformed. Practically the whole of the city centre is one huge Schani-garden. From Graben to Kohlmarkt, Lugeck to the inner courtyard of the Museumsquartier, it's one café and restaurant after another. Almost every week new bars and meeting-places open. Chic and modern, with all the flair and the freshness of up-to-the-minute gastro-culture.

The Whole of Vienna in Party Mood

Throughout the summer a regular party mood reigns in the numerous Copa Cagrana bars on the Danube Island (► 158) and in Summer Stage at the Rossauer wharf on the Danube Canal. There the fashionable bars set up "open-air branches", with live music and amusements such as trampolining. The university campus pubs in the inner courtyards of the old AKH (the former general hospital) are also always crammed full (Wien 9, Spitalgasse2). So the question is: who in Vienna really spends the evenings in front of the television? There are obviously not many couch potatoes who want to miss the open-air party.

The outdoor life, however, isn't just a summer thing in Vienna. In the run up to Christmas time streams of people go to the Advent markets, and the mulled wine stalls are the coolest place to meet your friends. Austrians celebrate New Year in a big way and party on the street all night. And if it's a really icy winter, Rathaus-platz becomes a skating rink.

bove left:
here's always
lively scene in
tephansplatz

entre:
ummer Stage
olds many
vents

eft: MQ is
favourite
eeting-place

bove right:
iverside bars
re great for
ot nights

ight: Nina
roll on the
anube Island

the magazine **19**

Death must be

To say that Vienna has a special relationship with death is a cliché, but there is some truth in it. Traces of the liaison are everywhere. It extends from the reverence paid to memorials and tombs, last resting-places and grave-yards, which is almost a cult, to the Viennese songs sung at the wine-harvest: sad, melancholy and beautiful.

The Viennese and death go back a long way: to the 17th century, when "der liebe Augustin" (dear Augustin), a famous minstrel, was accidentally thrown into a mass grave for plague victims. Even there he did not lose his sense of humour, but went on clowning around to the tune of his bagpipes, to keep his courage up. And

so he survived, among all the plague-riddled corpses.

The story culminates in the notion that a "fine corpse" (a splendid funeral) is the highpoint of life. And there is a scholarly side to this preoccupation with death: in Vienna, Sigmund Freud (1856–1939) researched the death-wish and Erwin Ringel (known in the trade as Mr

a Viennese

The plague column at the Graben is a reminder of horror and death

Suicide) founded Europe's first crisis intervention centre in 1948; and in Vienna Professor Tomáš Masaryk (1850–1937), who was later to become the President of Czecho-slovakia, wrote his doctoral thesis on the topic of suicide.

Europe's Largest Cemetery

The Central Cemetery, which the Austrian multimedia artist André Heller called the "aphrodisiac for necro-philes", is at 2.4 sq km (about one square mile) the largest cemetery in Europe. The custodian at the main gate has a guide to the last resting-places of great personalities: here lie the musicians Johannes Brahms, Johann Strauss father and son, Wolfgang Amadeus Mozart (memorial) and Franz Schubert; as well as the actors Curd Jürgens and Helmut Qualtinger, who coined the marvellous words: "In Vienna you have to die before they'll say 'Long live ...!', but then you'll live for aeons."

Melancholy and Happiness

The waltz kings Johann Strauss father and son, themselves often shaken by fear of death, wrote music whose surface gaiety is always tinged with a touch of melancholy and pain. That goes also for the Heurigen (wine taverns) music. When the waves of gaiety are at their peak, enter Death. Not inspiring fear, though, but as a friend. "When it's all over, with music and wine ..." – that's a reminder of death, easy to sing ...

the magazine **21**

JOSEPH HAYDN
*1732 ROHRAU
†1809 WIEN

Street performers won't play the "Blue Danube" waltz in the U-bahn, but you'll still see throughout the city that Vienna is the world capital of music. The cornerstones of this elite art are the Staatsoper, the Philharmoniker, the Konzerthaus and the Musikverein.

Vienna Plays First

Vienna has been home to more musicians than any other city in the world. On the "Walk of Fame" between Naschmarkt and the Stephansdom the recently installed 70 marble stars commemorate great musicians of the world (see above left for Haydn's). Most of them did not have an easy life. The cabaret artist Georg Kreisler once put it thus: "Vienna has always been hostile to music,

W. A. Mozart

Mozart has often been treated badly in Vienna. The Figaro House was a disgrace until renovation finally started in 2004. Steffl's department store now stands on the site of Mozart's last residence, and the room he died in is commemorated by a bust and a plaque sitting among toys, children's clothing and antique furniture. And "Mozart's grave" in the Friedhof St Marx (➤ 179) is empty: the greatest musical genius of all time was buried in a mass grave, no-one knows where.

The House of Music

To hear, see and feel music – the Haus der Musik (House of Music), a super-modern musical theme park with seven separate experience zones, makes it all possible. You can even take the baton yourself and conduct the Philharmoniker (Wien 1, Seilerstätte 30, tel: 01/516 48, www.hdm.at).

Fiddle

doing its best to frighten off any significant musician." In many cases they succeeded. Franz Schubert was destitute. Hugo Wolf starved. Anton Bruckner was valued as teacher and organist, but never as composer. Gustav Mahler had to get himself baptized before he could become director of the opera, and Webern, Schönberg and Berg were simply ignored. And as for the fact that Haydn, Beethoven and Gluck, whom Vienna likes to boast about, were not even born here – well, nobody mentions that.

The Vienna Waltz Conquered the World

All the same, no-one can deny that musical history has been written in Vienna. Twice, in the classical era and at the end of the 19th century, more pioneering musicians were working in Vienna than in any other city. And from the banks of the Danube the strains of the Strauss Family's waltzes went round the world. Nowadays, Vienna is equally famous for its musicians and instrument-makers as for its first-class centres of training and performance. The Wiener Sängerknaben (Vienna Boys' Choir), the Philharmoniker and the Bösendorfer grand-pianos are synonymous with the highest standards in the whole world.

The New Year Concert

Many people love Viennese music as a vibrant and cheerful start to the year. The New Year Concert from the Golden Hall of the Musikverein is broadcast around the world and watched by millions.

Background: Violins are on sale in markets as well as music stores

Above: Bliss in three-four time, that's the Vienna waltz

Left: Mozart spent his best years in the Figaro House

Far left: The three "Viennese" stars: Haydn, Beethoven and Mozart

VIENNESE JUGENDSTILL

Viennese Jugendstil (art nouveau) is more than an architectural style. A way of life, it combines graphic design, architecture, commercial art and traditional crafts into one great and very elegant synthesis.

It all began with a youthful rebellion. In 1897 Gustav Klimt and his comrades-at-arms left the "Genossenschaft", the artists' association, and founded a new artists' group, the "Secession", a name which was later applied to the style itself. The artists Josef Hoffmann, Joseph Maria Olbrich, Koloman Moser, Otto Wagner and Adolf Loos now had one main aim: to protest against meaningless ornamentation, such as that used to excess on the buildings of the Ringstrasse.

The Secession Style
The floral art nouveau style, which flourished at that time in other countries, foundered in Vienna on the conservative attitude of the emperor. And when eventually the new style did reach the city it developed its own identity

"A golden titbit" is what the Viennese call the Secession movement

---

Where to See Jugendstil
- **Majolikahaus**, Otto Wagner's house with decorative iron balconies and a façade of majolica tiles (Wien 5, Wienzeile 40), and next to it the apartment block at Linke Wienzeile No 38.
- **Postsparkasse** (Post Office Savings Bank) Otto Wagner's milestone in architectural history (Wien 1, Georg-Coch-Platz 2)
- **MAK** (Museum of Applied Arts). Craftwork from Gustav Klimt's Stoclet frieze design to Thonet's bentwood furniture and work from Viennese workshops (Wien 1, Stubenring 5, www.mak.at)
- **Backhausen-Wiener-Werkstätte-Museum**, the Backhausen Vienna Workshop Museum holds 3,500 original designs (from the period 1860–1950) from the textile firm Joh. Backhausen & Söhne (Wien 1, Schwarzenbergstrasse 10, www.backhausen.at)

A FLIGHT OF FANCY

marked by clear, severe forms. The Viennese Jugendstil was characterized by a return from curves to straight lines, from organic to geometric forms. Vienna Jugendstil's favourite shape was the square; verticals were also important to them. Ornamentation was used sparingly and always set against large empty surfaces. Vienna Jugendstil should be seen as a late phase of the art nouveau movement, a style which already anticipates the Bauhaus style of the 1920s.

movement. And in the Sanatorium Purkersdorf, which has a flat roof and glass walls, Josef Hoffmann explored new directions towards functionalism.

Decorative Art

The Secessionists did not stay together for long. In 1905 Klimt, Wagner, Hoffmann and Moser left the group. Art, they declared, must penetrate into every area. With this in mind, Hoffmann and Moser took over the direction of the craft association "Wiener Werkstätte" (Vienna Workshops), in order to devote themselves to the reform of domestic culture and to bring their aesthetic standards to bear on every aspect of daily life. They created fabrics, furniture, clothes and other everyday items; typically handmade and of immense beauty their aesthetic quality still fascinates today.

On the Way to Modern Architecture

From this point of view, the Jugendstil works of Otto Wagner, such as the Stadtbahn (Urban Railway) and its stations (► 125) and the Postsparkasse (Post Office Savings Bank), are truly pioneering achievements. With the Secession (► 126), the exhibition hall of the new artists' association, Joseph Maria Olbrich created another Viennese emblem which also gave its name to the

bove: Otto Wagner's urban railway stations have been renovated

ight: Generous nd functional: ne Post Office avings Bank

If the whole city seems to you like one giant accumulation of museums then you've got the right impression. Vienna has almost twice as many museums as, for example, Munich. And more keep opening every year. The amazing thing is that each new museum is even more spectacular than the last.

Until a few years ago the city of Vienna was proud of having almost 100 museums with exhibits from every era. But recent developments put the past in the shade. Since the mid-Palais Liechtenstein. This "place of baroque joie de vivre" presents life and art as a great, sumptuous artistic unity, with music, literature and dance forming the framework to the exhibitions

MQ became an exciting place for urban encounters

1990s Vienna has caught what can only be described as museum-fever, with one gigantic museum boasting vast exhibition areas following another.

The construction of the Museumsquartier (Museum District) had already given Vienna more exhibition space than any other city, but this was followed by the Albertina and in spring 2004 by the of the Princes' collections – which were brought from Vaduz, the capital of Liechtenstein, to Vienna to be spectacularly displayed.

The museum boom has altered the city as greatly as the construction of the Ringstrasse 150 years ago. This time the city has created an urban district devoted to art and palaces refurbished to a high standard with no

Above left: The Kunsthistorisches Museum is a gigantic treasure chest

Above right: In the MQ you can also eat, drink and listen to jazz

The most exciting museums

...xpense spared, making the ...ntire cultural district ...cessible to everyone.

New Life in the ...useums

...owever, just showing ...aluable pictures in galleries ...r exhibiting some precious, ...teresting or unusual ...bjects in glass cases is no ...nger considered enough. ...oreover, visitors are no ...nger to be enticed into a ...uick visit, taking in works ...art at the double, "ticking ...f" the latest trend as they ...o. Instead they are invited ...o surrender to a completely ...ew cultural attitude. "Life ...d enjoyment" is the motto ...r Vienna's cultural area. ...nd that's not overstating it. ...In the new temples of art ...sitors leisurely stroll around ...pleasant surroundings, they ...eet their friends here, eat ...d drink, chat and linger.

The atmosphere suits the visitors' urban lifestyle in the early 21st century. Its charm lies for the most part in the highly successful combination of old and new, the symbiosis of valuable historic masonry with modern architecture.

However, although neither the visitors to the city nor the Viennese themselves can spend their whole time in museums, more and better exhibitions are staged to woo visitors. The competition for custom is immense – enlivening each visit as well as the spirit and hopefully also boosting trade.

The Albertina is the latest highlight in the Viennese museum landscape

Die aufregendsten Museen

- Museumsquartier (➤ 103)
- Albertina (➤ 82)
- Liechtenstein Museum (Wien 9, Fürstengasse 1, tel: 01/319 57 67-0, Wed–Mon 9–8, Tram D, Bus 40A Bauernfeldplatz, admission: expensive, www.liechtensteinmuseum.at)

The journalist Alfred Polgar thought the Viennese coffee-house was a place for people who want to be alone but needed company to feel alone. It has long fulfilled this function. This delicate blend of myth and "Schmäh" goes back to the year 1685, when the Polish commercial traveller Kolschitzky obtained a licence to serve to the public "kahve, the Turkish Drink".

The Viennese Coffee House

Legend has it that for a long time the Viennese did not know what to do with the contents of the sacks which the Turkish invaders had left behind when they withdrew. The riddle was only solved when they hit upon the idea of roasting the green beans – and got a new elixir of life.

Intellectual Flights of Fancy in the Coffee-house

Around the end of the 19th century and in the interwar

Above: Café Griensteidl has always been a cultural hotspot

Left: Taking a break with a *Melange* at the Central café

What to drink in the coffee-house:

- **Melange:** coffee with a lot of milk and perhaps a topping of whipped cream
- **Schwarzer (gross/klein):** mocha without milk or cream (double/single)
- **Brauner:** mocha with milk
- **Cappuccino:** a double brauner with a topping of foamed milk
- **Einspänner:** mocha served in a glass with whipped cream

Reading the papers in Café Sperl: that's Vienna!

Background: The Einspänner, one of many sorts of coffee in Vienna

years the Viennese "public living-room" was in its heyday as the focus of intellectual life. In the Herrenhof, at Griensteidl's and in the Central, the marble tables and shabby plush benches witnessed intellectual flights of fancy. Whether literature or politics, music, architecture or psychology – all went hand in hand with a large *Brauner* and a glass of water, served on a silver tray.

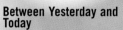

The Coffee-house as Information Exchange

In the 1980s and 90s many coffee-houses became the victims of development mania, suffering the cruel fate of being transformed into banks or even car showrooms. Others were "restored" to death or up-graded into stylized theme cafés. Even so, the cafés have largely retained their essential function, serving politicians, journalists and business people as a place to see and to be seen, to meet and exchange information and to do deals. More politics happens at Sluka's (► 111) and Landtmann's (► 111) than in the Rathaus or the Parlament.

Café Central is in the elegant Palais Ferstel

Between Yesterday and Today

All the same, many of the 500 or so coffee-houses have kept their original character. Lovers go to the romantic Sperl's, antiques dealers and fans of the writer Thomas Bernhard congregate at the Bräunerhof.

At least the human element of the coffee-house has been preserved from the old days: the waiter with his black tail-coat and bow-tie, his wallet on his hip, traditionally also with a pair of exemplary flat feet. He knows his regular guests' tastes, greets them with "Küss' die Hand, Gnä' Frau" (May I kiss your hand, ma'am) and "Habe die Ehre, Herr Hofrat" (An honour for us, sir), and expects about 10 per cent tip.

Who wrote where?
- **Peter Altenberg, Josef Roth:** Café Central (► 66)
- **Thomas Bernhard:** Café Bräunerhof (► 89)
- **Felix Salten, Karl Kraus, Anton Kuh:** Griensteidl (► 90)
- **Hugo v. Hofmannsthal, Franz Werfel, Sigmund Freud:** Herrenhof (Wien 1, Herrengasse 10)

Of Nymphs and Fauns

Turn on the tap and you'll be amazed: what gushes out is the purest, freshest spring water. It really is! The quality and flavour of Vienna's water is legendary – water flows direct from sources in unpolluted mountain areas into the city. And wherever it flows out of the artistically formed figures of the city's many fountains it also refreshes the

Vienna is indeed privileged. While other cities find it hard to keep up with the ever-increasing demand for water, in Vienna every tap is a small mountain spring. Two conduits, constructed under

A world of fountains

This unpolluted spring water also supplies a series of beautiful old fountains. These are a world of their own. Symbolic figures crowd around the bowls and basins, vessels and jugs, beings from the realm of fantasy united in complete – or almost complete – harmony. It wouldn't be Vienna after all, if there hadn't been an element of disruption, although caused by something as harmless as the fountains.

Above: The main figure on the Donner-Brunnen

Far left: Pallas Athene in front of the Parlament

Left: The figure of Austria on the Freyung

Emperor Franz Joseph, bring the pure spring water to the city from the high limestone ranges of Rax, Schneeberg and Hochschwab, situated some 100km (62 miles) from the city.

The Austria Fountain

The magnificent fountain in front of the Parliament building, for example, was to have a statue of Austria as its central figure. But to spare the feelings of the other

Background: Water-jets in the Hochstrahlbrunnen

countries of the empire, Austria had to give way to Pallas Athene, the Greek goddess of wisdom. Admittedly a politically correct solution but ill-considered all the same. If you look closely you'll see that the goddess now has no specific link with the allegorical images of the four main rivers at her feet. Still, it gave the Viennese something to mock: "Wisdom stands outside Parliament, with her back to it!"

On the **Freyung** square, on the other hand, it is the figure of **Austria** who is surrounded by the monarchy's four main rivers: the Danube, Po, Elbe and Vistula. Goethe's granddaughter Alma stood model for Austria, but few now remember that.

The Citizens' Fountain

In 1739, the citizens of Vienna had a fountain erected on the Neuer Markt. It was the first time that a civic commission had been carried out unaccompanied by a loyal address to the emperor. Originally called Providentia-Brunnen, it is now known as the **Donner-Brunnen**, after its sculptor, the 24-year-old Georg Raphael Donner. The talk of the time was the strong resemblance of the central figure in the fountain, the scantily clad Providentia, to the wife of Donner's landlord.

Hours and Days on a Fountain

The **Hochstrahlbrunnen** on Schwarzenbergplatz (➤ 130) is more astronomical than anatomical. The 365 little jets round the edge of the basin stand for the days of the year, while the island and its six fountains represent the days of the week. Twelve high jets symbolize the months, 24 smaller ones the hours and the 30 jets on the central island mark the days of the month.

The Donner-Brunnen risked removal for being "a chronic traffic obstruction"

The Hochstrahlbrunnen marked the opening of the first mountain spring conduit

Paradoxically, virtually none of the dishes generally associated with Vienna actually come from here. Everything that is simmered, steamed and braised in the pots and pans of the former metropolis on the Danube was inherited from other parts of the empire. Goulash comes from Hungary, dumplings from Bohemia and the ubiquitous Wiener Schnitzel from Milan. What does that prove? That Vienna has always known how to select the very best from everywhere.

To experience the flavours of the imperial era you only need to go to a genuine

One of the cornerstones of traditional Viennese cuisine is beef. It's served as Tafelspitz (boiled) with accompaniments such as roast potatoes, spinach or dill

The Wiener Schnitzel is the undisputed number one

Viennese inn. There the empire is everywhere. Emperor Franz Joseph is represented by his favourite dish, the creamy Kaiserschmarren (sweet pancakes with raisins), the Hungarian aristocracy by the Esterházy-Rostbraten (roast beef), which gets its characteristic flavour from a rich sauce of root vegetables and sour cream, and the most famous of field-marshals by the Radetzky-Torte (cake).

Schnitzel, Pancakes & Co

Above: The city's culinary visiting-card: the original Sacher-Torte

Far left: Palat-schinken (stuffed pan-cakes) are a real temptation

Left: The crowning touch on the Kaiser-schmarren: a light dusting of icing sugar

sauce, as roast beef or as beef goulash. The latter is unthink-able without Kaisersemmel (crisp emperor's bread-rolls) and a cold beer.

In the "Beisl ums Eck" (pub around the corner), a typically simple and very cosy inn, good plain cooking is on the menu – which is often chalked up on a black-board at the entrance. Soups are standard fare, with leber-knödel or griessnockerl (liver or semolina dumplings) or "Fritatten" (pancakes cut into strips). And for a main course there's roast pork

with dumplings, Szegedin pork and cabbage or Wiener Schnitzel with potato salad.

As well as Kaisers-chmarren, the exquisite desserts include Palatschin-ken and Buchteln (jam turn-overs), strudel and poppy-seed noodles, Powidltascherl (plum-filled potato pockets) and Topfenknödel (sweet dumplings). The uncrowned queen of all desserts, however, is the Sacher-Torte – the rich chocolate cake with a layer of apricot jam, whose original recipe has been claimed for years by both Demel and Sacher cafés.

Wiener Würstl (Viennese sausage)

The Wiener Würstel is an institution. Its repertoire includes the traditional boiled sausage served hot, then Bratwurst (fried or grilled/broiled), Leberkäs (meat loaf) and Käsekrainer (fried and filled with cheese), all served with mild or sharp mustard and pickled chillies in oil. In the small hours the sausage stall becomes the centre of Viennese gossip. Elegantly dressed visitors after a night at the ballroom or opera stand eating their sausages next to cabbies and refuse collectors before their morning shift. Among the best known sausage stalls are the ones Am Hof and by the Staatsoper (Albertinarampe).

Did You Know ...

• ...that Vienna is the only capital city in the world with a large vineyard area? In the Middle Ages the yield was already so great that by imperial decree sour wine had to be used to mix the mortar for the Stephansdom. Today about 400 vintner families produce around 20,000hl (450,000 gallons) of wine from 690ha (1,700 acres) of vineyard.

• ...that the first woman to travel alone around the world came from Vienna. On her journeys, **Ida Pfeiffer** (1797–1858, ► 179) reached South America, Sumatra with its "cannibals" and Madagascar. Her diaries became bestsellers.

• ...that the famous "Kaiserschmarren" was originally called "Kaiserinschmarren". It was dedicated to Kaiserin Elisabeth in 1854, on the occasion of her marriage to Franz Joseph. As the emperor liked the dessert better than the figure-conscious empress did, it was renamed.

• ...that the Viennese have always played a large role in Hollywood? **Fred Zinnemann** (1907–97) directed *High Noon, From Here to Eternity* and *A Man for all Seasons*. The producer of *The Silence of the Lambs* and *Dancing with Wolves*, **Eric Pleskow** (born 1924), was also Viennese. **Billy Wilder** (1906–2002), the incomparable director of *Some Like it Hot* and *The Apartment*, is often put down as Viennese; in fact, he was born in Sucha near Krakow (now Poland), but he spent his childhood and youth in Vienna.

Finding Your Feet

First Two Hours

Vienna is a city of manageable size. Whether you arrive by plane, train or car, the journey into the centre won't take long.

Wien-Schwechat Airport (VIE)

Vienna International Airport, situated about 15km (10 miles) southeast of the city, is Austria's most important airport. There is an information desk in the arrivals hall, and the airport's information hotline is available around the clock on (01) 70 07-222 33.

Airport Transfers

CAT, S-Bahn and bus lines operate from 5 am to midnight, running once every 30 minutes.

- The **CAT** (City Airport Train) is the fastest airport transfer – you'll be in the city in just 16 minutes (U-Bahn station Landstrasse/Wien Mitte). A single ticket is 9 euros, a return 15 euros. The tickets are not valid on the rest of the Vienna public transport network. An interesting option for your return flight: some airlines allow you to check in your luggage in advance at the terminal Wien Mitte. You can do so the evening before and up to 75 minutes before departure.
- The least expensive option is the **Schnellbahn** or **S-Bahn** (express train): S7 takes you to Landstrasse/Wien Mitte in 32 minutes, stopping at a number of other stations. The 3-euro ticket entitles you to continue your journey by any other means of public transport in Vienna.
- A ticket for the **buses** operated by the **Vienna Airport Line** costs 6 euros, but does not permit you to change to other forms of transport. The journey from the airport to Schwedenplatz takes only 20 minutes, but it may take longer during the rush hours. Another route runs from the airport to Südbahnhof and Westbahnhof stations.
- There is a **taxi** rank north of the arrivals hall. A taxi journey into the centre will take about 20 minutes and costs 35 euros. A cheaper option is to go to the centre by public transport, then take a taxi to your hotel.

Railway Stations

- **Westbahnhof** was built in 1950s style. Leaving the platforms you will arrive in a two-floor hall with ticket offices and shops. Like in most other stations, there is a mixed crowd milling about, so keep an eye on your luggage. The station is situated at the top end of the shopping street Mariahilfer Strasse. There is a U-Bahn station in the railway station.
- **Südbahnhof**, where the trains from the south, mainly Italy or Slovenia, arrive, is about to undergo a general overhaul. The station is situated outside the city centre, close to Schloss Belvedere. From here, S-Bahn or tram is the best way to get into the centre.

Tourist Information

The Tourist-Info Wien provides free tips and information on Vienna and current events, and helps you find hotel accommodation. The Tourist-Info **Zentrum** in Wien 1, Albertinaplatz, is open daily from 9 am to 7 pm. The Tourist-Info **Flughafen Wien** is situated in the arrivals hall opposite the baggage hall. It is open from 8:30 am to 9 pm.

Getting Around

Finding your Way

Vienna is divided into 23 districts which circle around its central district Wien 1. Between Ringstrasse and Gürtel are the urban districts 2 to 9, which are home to many old buildings and the embassies. The outer districts vary significantly from each other: Wien 10, 11 and 16 are typical workers' districts, while Wien 13 and 19 are considered elegant residential areas. Districts 21 and 22, on the opposite bank of the Danube, are being developed as new suburbs with modern high-rises.

Vienna's Streets

Vienna's most important streets are:

- **Kärntner Strasse, Graben, Kohlmarkt** – elegant shopping streets in the centre
- **Ringstrasse** – the road that encircles the inner city
- **Mariahilfer Strasse** – the most popular shopping street
- **Gürtel** – despite the heavy traffic many pubs and trendy bars are now based in the historic S-Bahn arches

Public Transport

Public transport can take you anywhere in Vienna; the U-Bahn is the fastest but trams are the most interesting way to travel.

U-Bahn

- Officially, the Viennese U-Bahn was **opened in 1976**, but some routes run on tram tracks that are over 100 years old. The U-Bahn network is constantly being extended.
- The U-Bahn runs **every day from about 5 am**. The last trains depart from the centre at about 12:30 am. Trains run at 5-minute intervals (every 2–4 minutes during the rush hours and every 7–8 minutes after 8:30 pm).
- There are **five colour-coded** U-Bahn lines (U1 – red, U2 – violet, U3 – orange, U4 – green, U6 – brown).
- On the platforms, an **electronic board** indicates the destination of the next train and the approximate waiting time before its arrival.
- Next to the station name you'll find signs in white writing indicating **the exits** (often far apart!) and **interchanges with other lines**.

Trams, S-Bahn and Buses

- **Trams** (Strassenbahn) are identified by numbers or letters (eg. 1, 10 or D), **buses** by a combination of number and letter (eg. 1A, 10A or 156B), and the **S-Bahn** (Schnellbahn) is recognizable from the S (eg. S45, S7).
- Bus routes **1A**, **2A** and **3A** or short-distance inner-city hoppers.
- Not all the routes operate from 5 am to midnight every day. Consult the timetables in the stations for **detailed information**. Timetables and routes can also be checked on the internet at www.wienplan.com or www.vor.at.
- A good network of **night buses** operates every night from about 12:45 am to 5 am. The normal tickets are valid on these lines. The stops are marked with a blue N.

Tickets

- Within the Vienna city limits, the **same ticket** can be used on all means of transport, including changes.

- There are frequent **ticket controls**, and if you don't have a valid ticket, you may have to pay a fine of 60 euros.
- **You can buy tickets** from the machines in U-Bahn stations and at newsagents, advance ticket sales points, or directly on the tram or bus (keep some coins ready).
- It is worth buying a **Wien-Card**. For a around 17 euros this ticket grants you unlimited travel around the city for 72 hours and also gives reductions on the admission price to some sights and discounts in shops, restaurants or wine taverns. Tickets are available from the Tourist-Info and at many hotels.
- You can also buy a 24-hour ticket costing about 5 euros, a 72-hour ticket for about 12 euros, an 8-day ticket for about 24 euros which can be used by several passengers at the same time or single tickets at around 1.50 euros. Please note: most tickets need to be **validated before the start of the journey!**
- **Children** up to the age of six travel free at all times, children up to age 15 travel free on Sundays and public holidays, as well as during the Viennese school holidays.

Taxis
There are taxi ranks at nearly every busy corner of Vienna, at traffic hubs and in front of the main hotels. You can also hail a taxi that's available (with a lit-up yellow sign) or book one by phone (eg.: 01/601 60, 401 00, 01/313 00 or 01/814 00). There is a small surcharge for night journeys and on Sundays and public holidays.

Cars
- Vienna's district 1 is a **short-term parking zone** operating on a **pay-and-display** basis on weekdays between 9 am and 7 pm; parking in districts 2–9 and 20 is chargeable from 9 am to 8 pm. To avoid being fined, place a valid parking ticket behind your windscreen. You can obtain free ten-minute parking tickets (which cannot be combined with other tickets), as well as tickets for 30 minutes, 1 hour or 1½ hours from tobacconists/newsagents.
- The **maximum parking time** is 1½ hours. Days of validity and maximum parking periods may vary in busy shopping streets. Check the signs.
- On the outskirts of the city you'll find **park-and-ride car parks** with U-Bahn connections, in the central districts **pay car parks**.
- Detailed information is available on the internet: **www.parkeninwien.at**

Sightseeing by Bus
Bus sightseeing tours are popular and convenient. The hop-on-hop-off buses stop at all major sights. Depending on your ticket type you can get on and off these buses whenever you like. There are other bus companies offering fixed sightseeing tours (www.viennasightseeingtours.com, tel: 01/712 46 83; www.cityrama.at, tel: 01/534 13-0).

Sightseeing by Horse-Drawn Carriage
Take a *fiaker* (horse-drawn carriage) to see the city, as they did in imperial times. The carriages stand at Stephansplatz, Heldenplatz and in front of the Albertina. A tour of the Old Town costs between 40 euros (for 20 minutes) and 95 euros (for 1 hour).

Cycling
Around 300 bicycles are available to rent at about 40 terminals, next to U-Bahn, bus and tram stops. To use a bicycle, just log in with your ATM

ank card. When you are finished with it, return the bicycle. For the first
our the use of the bicycle is free, after that it costs 2 euros.

Admission Charges
The cost of admission to museums and places of interest mentioned
in this guide is indicated by three categories:
inexpensive: under 3 euros
moderate: 3–7.50 euros
expensive: over 7.50 euros

Accommodation

n Vienna you can find accommodation in stylish designer rooms or in
esplendent suites. Hotels and guesthouses can be found all over the city –
he most luxurious and expensive ones are in the centre, the less expensive
nes in the suburbs. Whether you are after the ultimate in luxury, require
i-tech equipment or seek an inexpensive private room, Vienna is bound to
he right accommodation for every taste and every wallet.

Reservations

o ensure that you find exactly what you are looking for it's worth booking
n advance. The website www.info.wien.at allows you to book a room
nline in one of 260 hotels, guesthouses and apartments. Or book by
honing the hotline daily 9–7 on tel: (01) 245 55. If you have not booked
room before your arrival, the Tourist-Info (➤ 36) will help you.

Hotels and Guesthouses

ienna has some elegant **luxury hotels**, which are truly superb but not
asily affordable for everyone. However, you can still enjoy the luxury of
he surroundings by just having a drink or a cup of coffee in the hotel bar.
uesthouses are smaller and often less expensive than hotels. The
eception may not be on the ground floor because many guesthouse
ccupy only part of the building. The room prices generally include
reakfast, usually a breakfast buffet. Local and other taxes are also
sually included.

Apartments

or a longer stay, consider renting an apartment with cooking facilities
nd regular cleaning service. Prices may vary considerably depending on
ocation and furnishings. The **Schlossquadrat** apartments (Wien 5, Margare-
enstrasse 77, tel: 01/545 14 71, www.schlossquadr.at) are very pleasant.

Youth Hostels and Seasonal Hotels

ienna has some inexpensive youth hostels, but it's worth reserving in
dvance because they are always busy. **Jugendherberge Myrthengasse** (Wien
, Myrthengasse 7/Neustiftgasse, tel: 01/523 63 16, fax: 01/523 58 49)
s right in the centre and offers great views over Vienna. A little farther out
s the **Schlossherberge am Wilhelminenberg** (Wien 16, Savoyenstrasse 2, tel:
1/485 85 03-700, fax: 01/485 85 03-702). **Seasonal Hotels** are student
ostels that can be rented during the holidays. They may have no great
omforts or atmosphere but they're inexpensive; try for example the Hotel

Atlas near the Museumsquartier (Wien 7, Lerchenfelderstrasse 1–3, tel: 01/401 76 55, fax: 01/401 76 20, www.academia-hotels.co.at).

Hotels

Accommodation Prices
Prices for an ensuite double room with breakfast:
€€€€ over 180 euros
€€€ 120–180 euros
€€ 80–120 euros
€ under 80 euros

Altstadt Vienna €€€
This stylish hotel is centrally located near the Mariahilfer Strasse shopping street. It has a specially welcoming atmosphere, and the rooms are very tastefully appointed. To start the day, help yourself from the wide selection of foods on the breakfast buffet. You'll feel well looked after in this hotel, its almost like staying with friends.
🔢 192, west of A2   ✉ Wien 7, Kirchengasse 41
☎ (01) 526 33 99-0, fax 523 49 01
🚇 Volkstheater
❓ www.altstadt.at

Anatol €€€
A modern city hotel very close to Mariahilfer Strasse and Westbahnhof, the Anatol has only recently been renovated. The rooms are furnished in a neutral modern and tasteful style, offering all the facilities and hi-tech equipment you might wish for (including WiFi internet hot spots). There are frequently special packages on offer, which make your stay particularly good value.
🔢 192, west of A1   ✉ Wien 6, Webgasse 26   ☎ (01) 599 96-0, fax 599 96-55   🚇 Zieglergasse
❓ www.austria-trend.at/anw

Arcotel Wimberger €€
One of the greatest attractions of this hotel is its central location: it's only 5 minutes walk from here to Westbahnhof and the U-Bahn station. The concert halls and many other venues, including the Raimundtheater, are also in easy walking distance from the hotel. The rooms are inexpensive, the staff friendly and helpful, and on Sundays there's a popular brunch with live music.
🔢 198, east of C4   ✉ Wien 7, Neubaugürtel 34–36
☎ (01) 521 65-0, fax 521 65-81(
🚇 Westbahnhof
❓ www.arcotel.at

Art Hotel €
A young hotel in every respect, with low prices and lots of colour, although the name "Art Hotel" promises more art and design than actually can be found here. But the staff are enthusiastic, the hotel is close to the Naschmarkt and the rooms acceptable, making this hotel a perfect choice. An internet area is available to guests.
🔢 194, southwest of A1
✉ Wien 5, Brandmayergasse 7–9
☎ (01) 544 51 08,
fax 544 51 08-10
🚇 Pilgramgasse
❓ www.thearthotelvienna.at

Austria Trend Hotel Beim Theresianum €
A family hotel close to the centre, in the immediate vicinity of many historic sights including Schloss Belvedere. The rooms are well appointed, the staff very friendly, and one of the highpoints is the sunny terrace. In the afternoon,

guests can help themselves to free coffee and a selection of cakes and pastries from the buffet.

➕ 194, south of C1 ✉ Wien 4, Favoritenstrasse 52
☎ (01) 505 16 06, fax 505 16 09
Ⓜ Südtirolerplatz
❓ www.austria-trend.at/thw

Bristol €€€€

This impressive imperial building, between Staatsoper and the Kärntner Strasse shopping area, has been a byword for elegant hospitality since 1892. A classic luxury hotel with beautiful rooms and elegant suites, uniformed porters, outstanding service and everything else you might expect. The in-house Korso restaurant is considered to be one of the best eateries in the city; the bar is a traditional piano bar.

➕ 193 D2 ✉ Wien 1, Kärntner Ring 1 ☎ (01) 515 16-0, fax 515 16-550 Ⓜ Karlsplatz
❓ www.westin.com/bristol

Coburg €€€€

Vienna's newest luxury hotel is in a 19th-century palace right in the middle of the city. Recently restored with great attention to detail, it opened in 2004 to great acclaim. All the suites have stylish marble baths, some even have their own gardens. The amenities are to the highest specifications and the spa is the best place to be pampered. The Coburg restaurant has probably the most exciting food in Vienna; make sure you reserve a table.

➕ 193 E2/3 ✉ Wien 1, Coburgbastei 4 ☎ (01) 518 18-0, fax 518 18-1 Ⓜ Stubentor
❓ www.coburg.at

Das Triest €€€€

This designer hotel, based in the former stables of the Vienna-Trieste post coaches, is considered one of the most attractive in the city. Modern design is tastefully incorporated into the old rooms. The room prices include the breakfast buffet, and the use of gym and

sauna. The hotel-restaurant Collio is excellent and the Silverbar legendary. This is where Robbie Williams and David Bowie have stayed when they visited Vienna.

➕ 194 B1 ✉ Wien 4, Wiedner Hauptstrasse 12 ☎ (01) 589 18-0, fax 589 18-18 Ⓜ Karlsplatz
❓ www.dastriest.at

Domizil €€€

True grandeur and genuine Viennese charm are the plus-points in this pleasant hotel-guesthouse. All 40 rooms have been lovingly and individually styled. One of the main attractions is the central location: the Stephansdom is only 50m (55 yards) away, and the Figaro-Haus is just around the corner. Thus the Domizil is the ideal starting point for exploring the Old Town. The extensive breakfast buffet makes for a great start to the day – enjoy it with a glass of sparkling wine!

➕ 193 E3 ✉ Wien 1, Schuler-strasse 14 ☎ (01) 513 31 99, fax 512 34 84 Ⓜ Stephansplatz
❓ www.hoteldomizil.at

Donauwalzer €

Close to the centre, tasteful and popular with families, this city hotel also has rooms at impressively low prices, including special weekend packages and other special offers, as well as bicycles for rent. Nearby you'll find, among others, the *heurigen* wine taverns in Ottakring and the Volksoper. The only disadvantage: the hotel's location on the Gürtel, one of Vienna's busiest thoroughfares.

➕ 194, west of A4 ✉ Wien 17, Ottakringer Strasse 5
☎ (01) 405 76 45-0, fax 40 57 64 59 99 Ⓜ Alserstrasse
❓ www.donauwalzer.at

Dorint Biedermeier €€

In the midst of the romantic Biedermeier complex in the Sünnhof is this well appointed and friendly hotel, which advertises its "rooms for wellbeing". Close to the centre and the City-Airport-Train terminus, a stay here is especially festive over Advent, when there's a Christmas market in the Sünnhof.

➕ 195 E3 ✉ Wien 3, Landstrasser Hauptstrasse 28 ☎ (01) 716 71-0, fax 716 71-503 🚇 Landstrasse/Wien Mitte, Rochusgasse ❓ www.dorint.com/wien

Hilton Vienna €€€€

The 1970s building has been completely overhauled and renovated. Brighter, modernised and attractive, the Hilton Vienna is now Austria's largest conference hotel, located right next to Stadtpark and Ringstrasse, not far from the centre. With almost 600 luxurious rooms and suites, a fantastic restaurant and the Birdland jazz club, the Hilton is an excellent choice. Particularly convenient is its direct link to the airport: the City-Airport-Train terminus is opposite the hotel.

➕ 195 E3 ✉ Wien 3, Am Stadtpark ☎ (01) 717 00-0, fax 713 06 91 🚇 Landstrasse/Wien Mitte ❓ www.hilton.de/wien

Ibis Wien Mariahilf €

A giant hotel building, yet with pleasant rooms. The hotel is close to Westbahnhof (and the U-Bahn network) and not far from the Raimundtheater. Unless you expect luxury toiletries and palatial rooms, you'll be happy here thanks to the reasonable prices.

➕ 198, east of C4 ✉ Wien 6, Mariahilfer Gürtel 22–24 ☎ (01) 599 98, fax 597 90 90 🚇 Westbahnhof ❓ www.ibishotel.com

Imperial €€€€

The exceptionally beautiful Ringstrassenpalais was converted into a hotel on the occasion of the World Exhibition of 1873, since when it has been one of the best hotels in the city. Guests of state enjoy the aristocratically elegant hospitality, as do actors and popstars. A show-case hotel, right on the Ringstrasse with a butler service unique in the German-speaking world, pressed newspapers and every imaginable kind of comfort. By the way, you can always just try the home-made *Imperial-Torte* in the pleasantly quiet hotel-café.

➕ 193 D1/2 ✉ Wien 1, Kärntner Ring 16 ☎ (01) 501 10-0, fax 501 10-410 🚇 Karlsplatz ❓ www.luxurycollection.com/ imperial

König von Ungarn €€€€

If you'd like to experience imperial Vienna, then this is the place for you. This hotel, in the heart of the Old Town, immediately behind the Stephansdom, accurately conveys the atmosphere of traditional Viennese hospitality. Part of the hotel is based in Mozart's former residence, the Figaro-Haus. The roofed inner courtyard is a particularly pleasant place to relax after sightseeing, shopping or strolling through the city.

➕ 193 D3 ✉ Wien 1, Schulerstrasse 10 ☎ (01) 515 84-0, fax 515 84-8 🚇 Stephansplatz ❓ www.kvu.at

Landhaus Fuhrgasslhuber €€

This rustic-romantic hotel is the ideal place for all those who wish to be in the middle of the city and at the same time in the middle of the country. The country house, situated in the *heurigen* village Neustift am Walde, is surrounded by picturesque green vineyards. If you like a rural atmosphere, country walks and evenings with a glass of new-vintage wine, you'll enjoy your stay at this hospitable guesthouse. There's an excellent breakfast buffet and the service is very attentive – perfect relaxation is guaranteed.

➕ 194, northwest of A5 ✉ Wien 19, Rathstrasse 24 ☎ (01) 440 30 33, fax 440 27 1 🚌 Bus 35A Neustift am Walde ❓ www.fuhrgassl-huber.at

Le Meridien €€€€
This hotel is a good example of modern hotel design, with trendy furnishings and stylish fittings. The elegant restaurant, glamourous bar and extensive spa area with gym have ensured that this establishment, opened in 2004 as part of a chain of luxury hotels, lives up to its luxury tag. Its location between the opera house, Hofburg and MuseumsQuartier is superb.

➕ 192 C2 ✉ Wien 1, Opernring 13–15 ☎ (01) 588 90-0, fax 588 90 90 90 🚇 Karlsplatz ❓ www.tiscover.at/lemeridien-vienna

Neuer Markt €€
A guesthouse on the 2nd and 3rd floors of a late 19th-century building, located close to Neuer Markt, and only a few minutes from Stephansdom and Kärntner Strasse. The rooms in this family-run establishment, although not modern, are clean and pleasant, staff are friendly, and the prices are low for so central a location.

➕ 193 D3 ✉ Wien 1, Seilergasse 9 ☎ (01) 512 23 16, fax 513 91 05 🚇 Stephansplatz ❓ www.hotelpension.at

Palais Schwarzenberg €€€€
The accommodation in the hotel in the Palais Schwarzenberg is princely indeed. In the centre of Vienna, many of the 44 rooms overlook the palace's private park. The 38 rooms in the main building have period furniture and paintings in the appropriate period style. The six Designer Park Rooms in a side wing were styled by the Italian . They feature South African timber for the parquet flooring, marmorino walls, Venetian lamps and Wittmann furniture, as well as original works of art.

➕ 195 D2 ✉ Wien 3, Schwarzenbergplatz 9 ☎ (01) 798 45 15, fax 798 47 14 🚇 Karlsplatz 🚃 Tram D Gusshausstrasse ❓ www.palais-schwarzenberg.com

Sacher €€€€
Probably the most charming of the large hotels with numerous stars – rich in tradition, world-famous and still owned by the same family. The hotel is in a historical building, with much style – and home to the legendary Sacher-Torte. A first-class luxury establishment with a personal touch, the Sacher is centrally located, just behind the opera house, between Kärntner Strasse and Albertinaplatz. Even if your money won't stretch to one of the superb rooms, furnished with antiques, a visit to the Sacher-Eck' near Kärntner Strasse for a slice of Sacher-Torte is a must for every visitor to Vienna!

➕ 192/193 C/D2 ✉ Wien 1, Philharmonikerstrasse 4 ☎ (01) 514 56-0, fax 514 56-810 🚇 Oper ❓ www.sacher.com

Viennart €€€
A well-appointed fluxury hotel, featuring functional and modern, tasteful and bright design. But what's special about the Viennart is its excellent location: in the immediate vicinity you'll find Volkstheater, Museumsquartier, Spittelberg, Ringstrasse, Mariahilfer Strasse and numerous restaurants, bars and pubs.

➕ 192 A2 ✉ Wien 7, Breite Gasse 9 ☎ (01) 523 13 45-0, fax 523 13 45-111 🚇 Volkstheater ❓ www.austrotel.at

Zur Schwalbe €€
A charming family-run hotel in the 16th district, a little farther from the centre. A 12-minute journey on the U-Bahn will take you from this hotel to Stephansplatz, and if you wish to relax among nature, a 5-minute walk takes you right into the Vienna Woods. Friendly rooms, warm-hearted service and moderate prices make this suburban hotel an attractive choice.

➕ 194, west of A4 ✉ Wien 16, Degengasse 45 ☎ (01) 486 11 81 🚇 Ottakring

Food and Drink

If you'd like to find out all about Viennese cooking, there are plenty of opportunities for trying out the local dishes in one of Vienna's numerous restaurants, taverns, snackbars and coffee-houses.

Traditional Food

Typically Viennese cuisine has always been "fusion" food – it's rooted in Bohemian, Austrian, Hungarian and Balkan traditions. These are still honoured today, but often they are brought up-to-date in combination with surprising additions from around the world.

Snacks and Small Dishes

- Traditionally, the **Viennese breakfast** consists of a bread roll or a vanilla croissant with butter and jam, plus a cup of coffee. However, other breakfast variations are also served, including some very extensive brunches.
- If you feel hunger pangs in between the main meals, don't forget the Viennese **Würstelstand** (sausage stall) in the face of competition from hamburgers, pizza or kebabs. The classic sausage snacks here are *Debreziner* (spicy!), *Käsekrainer* (sausage with cheese) and *Burenwurst* (farmers' sausage).
- A more elegant option are the traditional bread rolls at **Trzesniewski** (➤ 79).
- A **Wiener Beisl** is a sort of small inn where you'll be served typical local food; specials are often advertised outside the inn on a slate board. A good modern Beisl is **Immervoll** (Wien 1, Weihburggasse 17, tel: 01/513 52 88, daily noon–midnight).
- The best **vegetarian** meal can be had at **Wrenkh** (Wien 1, Bauernmarkt 10, tel: 01/533 15 26, daily 11:30–3 and 6–11).

Drinks

- **Coffee** has a century-old tradition in Vienna and is served in numerous different ways (➤ 28).
- Viennese **wine** is generally drunk young (known as *Heuriger*). You can best enjoy it at a *Heuriger* wine tavern on the outskirts (for example, in Grinzing, Neustift am Walde or Stammersdorf). In the city, **Zum Haydn** (Wien 6, Haydngasse 7, tel: 01/597 21 60, daily 4 pm–11 pm) also conveys a typical *Heuriger* atmosphere.
- There is also a tradition for **beer** in Vienna. One beautiful brewery tavern in a former abbey is the **Salm Bräu** (➤ 155).

Restaurant Tips

- To avoid disappointment, you are strongly advised to **reserve** a table if you wish to visit one of the top restaurants.
- Most restaurants **stop serving food** around 10 or 11 pm, many are closed on Sundays.
- Prices usually include a cover charge; if they don't, this has to be stated on the menu. A **tip/gratuity** of around 5 or 10 per cent is expected.

> **Prices**
> Prices given are for one person, excluding drinks.
> **€** under 12 euros **€€** 12–25 euros **€€€** over 25 euros

Shopping

Elegant boutiques, personable shops, colourful markets and functional shopping centres – Vienna makes shopping a pleasurable experience, whether you're looking for luxury goods or bargains.

Where to shop

- Vienna's main shopping street is **Mariahilfer Strasse**, between the inner city and Westbahnhof. Here you'll find all the large fashion chains and hundreds of shops with trendy gear for a young clientele. If you're after something more unusual, whether clothes, shoes or accessories, try **Neubaugasse**, a side street off Mariahilfer Strasse.
- In the inner city, **Kärtner Strasse**, **Graben** and **Kohlmarkt** with their designer shops, jewellers and perfumeries, are a paradise for shoppers with a larger wallet.
- Trendy department stores such as **Steffl** (Wien 1, Kärntner Strasse 19) and **Gerngross** (Wien 7, Mariahilfer Strasse 38–48), as well as the **Ringstrassengalerien** (Wien 1, Kärntner Ring 5–7), have extensive shopping areas for you to explore come rain or shine.
- The edge-of-town shopping centres are typically interchangeable and soulless shopping malls. The **Gasometer** shopping centre, in a former gas-container-making factory, at least has some the interesting architecture.

The Best Markets

- **Naschmarkt** (➤ 135) is Vienna's largest and most atmospheric market. On Saturdays, after the market, a famous **fleamarket** opens up.
- **Brunnenmarkt** (Wien 16, Brunnengasse) is a multicultural market in an area with many immigrant workers.
- **Rathausplatz** and **Spittelberg** have charming Advent markets in the pre Christmas period, and on **Freyung** (➤ 58) farmers' markets take place, as well as Easter and Advent crafts markets.

Shopping Tips

Stylish souvenirs and traditional gifts from Vienna are known as **Wien Products**. Tourist-Info has an information sheet on these products, from Manner Schnitten (wafers) and modern jewellery to elegant furniture fabrics, listing all the quality outlets (www.wienproducts.at).

Opening Hours

The markets set up stall as early as 6 am. Supermarkets are usually open Monday to Thursday 8 am–7 pm, Friday until 7:30 pm and Saturday until 5 pm. Shops in Vienna's main shopping streets and shopping centres are generally open Monday to Friday 9 am–6:30 pm and Saturday 9 am–6 pm; many open late on Thursdays, until 9 pm.

Tax

Visitors from non-EU countries are entitled to reclaim VAT (20 per cent), which is included in the purchase price, on any purchases over 75 euros. Ask the sales assistant for a Global Refund Cheque, and get this stamped at the toll booth when you leave the country. It entitles you to money back from one of 600 refund outlets. After the deduction of a handling charge, this will amount to approximately 13 per cent of the sale price.

Entertainment

From opera to disco, from jazz to DJ music – there's always something going on in Vienna. Whatever your particular style of fun and entertainment, you're certain to find what you're after.

Information

The city listings magazine *Falter* is indispensable. It is published every Wednesday and lists the events of the coming week, including exhibitions, cinema screenings, guided tours, concerts, fleamarkets and special events (www.falter.at). *Falter*, like Vienna's second listings magazine, *City,* is available from newsagents. You'll also find listings on the internet under www.hauptstadt.at.

Booking in Advance

Check out www.ticketline.cc for what's on and book tickets in advance, before you leave home. Telephone bookings can be made on 880 88. You can also purchase a ticket at the venue, in your hotel and from ticket offices in the centre.

Opera, Theatre, Musical and Jazz

- **Staatsoper** (➤ 98) and **Volksoper** (Wien 9, Währingerstrasse 78, tel: 01/ 514 44-30, www.volksoper.at) are famous for performances and productions of world renown. The concerts at the **Musikverein** (➤ 131) and at the **Konzerthaus** (➤ 136) also promise classical pleasures.
- The **Burgtheater** (➤ 102) and its outpost, **Akademietheater**, are the most highly regarded theatres in Vienna. The **Theater in der Josefstadt** and **Kammerspiele** (www.josefstadt.org) stage traditional productions, while the **Volkstheater** (www.volkstheater.at) and the **Schauspielhaus** (www.schauspielhaus.at) tend to showcase modern drama.
- The hits of world-famous musicals can be enjoyed at the **Raimundtheater** (Wien 6, Wallgasse 18, tel: 01/599 77-0, www.musicalvienna.at).
- Vienna's top jazz club is the **Porgy & Bess** (➤ 68), and the most elegant club is Joe Zawinul's **Birdland** (➤ 158).
- The highpoint of the ball season are the Viennese **Opernball** during Carnival, which is attended each year by celebrities from around the world; the **Life Ball**, an HIV charity event in May; and the **Kaiserball** in the Hofburg, where people waltz on New Year's Eve into the New Year. It's important to book tickets well in advance for these balls!

Live Music, Bars and Clubs

- While long stretches of the Gürtel are known as red-light district, a lively scene has established itself underneath the **Stadtbahnbögen** (S-Bahn arches). Among the most popular are **rhiz** (Bogen 37, tel: 01/409 25 05, Mon–Sat 6 pm–4 am, Sun until 2 am), **Buddha Club** (Bogen 172, tel: 01/479 88 49, daily 6 pm–4 am) and **babu** (Bogen 181, tel: 01/ 479 48 49, Mon–Thu 7 am–2 am, Fri until 4 am, Sat 9 am–4 am, Sun until 2 am).
- In the **"Bermuda-Dreieck"** (Bermuda Triangle, ➤ 68), near Schwedenplatz, there's one bar after another, the guests are young and enjoy their drinks; a great party mood is almost inevitable.
- One of the hippest clubs in Vienna is the **Flex** on the Danube Canal (Exit Augartenbrücke, tel: 01/533 75 25, from 10 pm). The **Volksgarten** (➤ 112) is the oldest disco in the city, and the **U4** (Wien 12, Schönbrunner Strasse 222, tel: 01/815 83 07, daily 10 pm–5 am) the most fabled club.

Medieval
Vienna

Getting Your Bearings

In the historic centre of Vienna every stone tells a story. The alleyways round the towering Stephansdom are very romantic, but that's not all. Vibrant new life has grown up between the ancient walls of churches, convents, institutions and historic palaces.

A walk through the oldest part of Vienna is like a journey into the past. In many of these picturesque lanes time seems to have stood still. They are still paved with old cobblestones, and in numerous inner courtyards ivy and roses clamber up the walls.

There's much to discover in these nostalgic surroundings. Places of interest range from the foundations of the Roman Vindobona through the oldest city churches to the former Jewish

Schottenstift

Schotten-kirche

13 Freyung

Palais Ferstel

12 Am

Herrengasse

GASSE

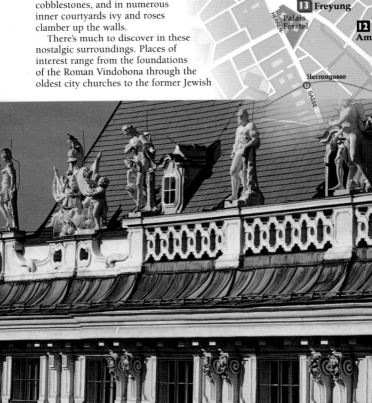

In the narrow lanes you'll find beautiful things at every turn

Ruprechts-kirche **9**

MORZIN-PLATZ

FRANZ-

Donaukanal

Schwedenplatz

SCHWEDEN-PLATZ

JOSEFS-KAI

JULIUS-RAAB-PLATZ

Fleisch-markt **7**

Griechen-beisl **8**

G.-COGH-PLATZ

Hoher Markt **10**
Ankeruhr

Heiligen-kreuzerhof **6**

BAUERN-

ROTENTURM-

LUG-ECK BÄCKER

SONNENFELS-

Erzbischöfliches **2**
Palais

STEPHANS-PLATZ
hans-

STR.

Jesuiten-kirche **5**

DR.-IGNAZ-SEIPEL-PLATZ

STUBEN-

RING

Stephans-dom **1**

ZEILE

Figaro-Haus **4**

DOMGASSE

WOLLZEILE

OCK-IM-
SEN-PL.

SINGERSTRASSE

RIEMERG.

Stubentor

Franziskaner-platz **3**

Franziskaner-kirche

Page 47: The view from the north tower of Stephansdom

Baroque splendour: Kinsky Palace on Freyung

quarter and the beautifully renovated palaces on the oddly shaped Freyung. Today, smart shops and chic bars have found homes in the old lanes, interspersed with refreshing fountains. At night, too, there's a whole lot going on, for this is the centre of Vienna's lively clubbing scene where bars stay open half the night.

★ Don't Miss

In the shadow of the Stephansdom, one of Vienna's main emblems, a maze of narrow alleyways takes you back into the Middle Ages. Enjoy the atmosphere of the thick, ancient masonry and the entrancing mysticism of the churches, before returning to modern life, with all its diversions, on the broad squares.

Medieval Vienna in a Day

9:00 am

The day begins with a visit to the **1** **Stephansdom** (► 52). Walk round the cathedral, then take the lift up the north tower, marvel at the mighty bell called "Pummerin", Austria's largest and heaviest, and enjoy the wonderful views of the city. Have a coffee in Aida (► 66) on Stephansplatz then walk down Singerstrasse to **3** **Franziskanerplatz** (► 60).

11:00 am

The **4** **Figaro-Haus** (► 60) where Mozart lived, is in the sleepy Domgasse. Then continue to the **5** **Jesuitenkirche** (left; ► 61) – you should pause on Dr-Ignaz-Seidel-Platz and take time to admire the beautiful early-baroque façade. Stroll down the romantic alleyways Sonnenfelsgasse and Schönlaterngasse to the idyllic, peaceful **6** **Heiligenkreuzerhof** (► 61). Then continue your tour on to the **7** **Fleischmarkt** (► 62) with its numerous shops.

12:30 pm

If you lunch in the **8** **Griechenbeisl** (► 62), which is probably the oldest inn in Vienna, you certainly won't be alone, as it's a real magnet for visitors from around the world. It's well worth putting up with a bit of hubbub for the sake of the atmosphere and the delicious traditional food.

2:00 pm

Stroll up into the narrow, romantic lanes of the so-called "Bermuda Triangle" (➤ 68). This is a very lively entertainment quarter, which – naturally – doesn't become really interesting until evening. In the centre of the area is the ivy-clad **9 Ruprechtskirche** (left; ➤ 62). Walk on across the **10 Hoher Markt** (➤ 63), one of Vienna's oldest and most historic squares, to **11 Judenplatz** (➤ 56). On no account fail to visit the Misrachi House, before going on to **12 Am Hof** (➤ 63).

4:30 pm

On **13 Freyung** (right; ➤ 58) it's pretty well compulsory to go down the Palais Ferstel passage and have a coffee in Central Café. Then do a tour of Freyung, taking in the magnificently renovated palaces; feel free to go into any of the pretty courtyards – you'll like the atmosphere. The Schottenstift and the Schottenkirche are of course also worth a visit, but now it's time for the Kunstforum (Art Gallery); if you have the time and inclination you should definitely go to the current exhibition, which is certain to be first-class. Or would you rather do a bit of shopping? There's no lack of attractive shops on Freyung – and you could always restrict yourself to window-shopping…

7:00 pm

If you feel like some jazz, then Porgy & Bess (left; ➤ 68) with its varied programme of international music will be just the thing for this evening. And you can relax afterwards with a glass of champagne in the Eden Bar (➤ 68), a Viennese institution.

❶ The Stephansdom

The "Steffl", as the Viennese call their beloved and revered Stephansdom, the Cathedral of St Stephen, is the undisputed central feature and the soul of the city. It is a high point of Viennese Gothic architecture, a masterpiece of the stonemason's art. More than that: the towering edifice is also the national emblem of Austria.

The technical data of the Stephansdom alone are impressive. The mighty cathedral is made of 20,000cu m (26,000 cubic yards) of sandstone, it's 108m (118 yards) long and 39m (42 yards) wide, and the tip of the south tower stretches 137m (450 feet) into the sky.

The Gothic pulpit, the artistic jewel of Stephansdom

The history of the church's construction goes back to the 12th century, to the time when the new rulers, the Babenbergs, needed a prestigious place of worship. They began to build a basilica dedicated to Saint Stephen, which was burnt down twice. Around 1260 King Ottokar II of Bohemia had a Romanesque church built. Its remains now form the main entrance, the great portal and the west façade. Not until a generation later, under Duke Albrecht II, was any further building done. In 1359 the founder of the present cathedral, the Habsburg Duke Rudolf IV, gave the order to rebuild in the contemporary Gothic style. The choir, the nave with its massive saddle roof faced with colourful glazed tiles and the south tower were then constructed.

Steadfast Against Many Foes

At the start of the 16th century, when the Turks posed an imminent danger to Vienna, building work had to be stopped – it was more important to build fortifications for the city, and consequently the north tower was never finished. In 1579 it was capped with a helm, under which swings the Viennese' favourite bell, the "**Pummerin**", cast from the metal from Turkish cannons. Weighing a solid 21 tonnes, it is Austria's

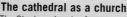

heavily bell, and said to be the second largest in the world. Even though two Turkish cannon-balls are still lodged in the facade of the south tower, the "Steffl" came through the Turkish sieges relatively unscathed. Later, the French too failed to harm it. In the last days of

The cathedral as a church

The Stephansdom is of course not only of cultural importance, it is also a working church. On weekdays seven services are held and on Sundays ten. Especially on high feast-days like Easter, Whitsun and Christmas numerous worshippers attend mass. Special services are often broadcast live on television. On high feast-days and at New Year the "Pummerin" bell is rung.

World War II, though, it suffered severe damage. In April 1945 a fire reduced large parts of the nave to rubble and ash. The fire also consumed the wooden roof trusses, a brilliant example of Gothic craftsmanship. Reconstruction of the cathedral was started in 1948 and, because the whole of Austria supported the work, it was so far advanced after only seven years that services could again be held there. Thus the "Steffl" became a symbol of solidarity after the horrors of the Hitler dictatorship.

It's worth pausing in front of the entrance to the Stephansdom, with its **Riesentor** (the Giants' Doorway) flanked by the two Towers of the Heathens, to have a good look at the Romanesque statues. Dragons, lions and serpents symbolize demonic powers, the struggle between good and evil. As the square in front of the cathedral long served as a market place, the so-called Viennese measures are still to be seen embedded in the masonry next to the portal: a loaf of bread and two measures of length, the (shorter) Bohemian and the (longer) Viennese ell.

The Most Spiritual Church Interior in the World

The Jugendstil architect Alfred Loos (1870–1933) called the Stephansdom "the most spiritual church interior in the world". As soon as you enter you'll see that he was right. The soaring pillars, the high ribbed vaulting and the dim light give the triple aisles of the nave a feeling of rapture, of timelessness. But pleasant though it is to just stand and gaze, there's plenty more to see in this mighty church.

The most famous artistic treasure of the Stephansdom is the **Gothic pulpit**. The filigree masonry, made in 1514 from seven sandstone blocks, presents four not particularly flattering portraits of princes of the church, and on the plinth the image (affectionately known as *fenstergucker*, meaning "Peeping Tom") of the master-mason Anton Pilgram. Stone toads and lizards, symbols

of evil, crawl up the staircase balustrade. These are held at bay by a dog, a symbol of good.

Other highlights include Master Pilgram's base for the **gigantic organ** comprising 10,000 pipes. In the left side-chapel the **Wiener Neustädter Altar** from 1447 has 72 images of saints painted on its inner and outer wings. And the right side-chapel contains the red marble **tomb of Emperor Friedrich II**. The noble simplicity of the 650-year-old *Dienstbotenmadonna* (Serving-girl Madonna) is particularly moving. Legend has it that the innocence of a serving-girl accused of theft was proved after she appealed to this Madonna for help. The statue of Mary, which she had implored, was relocated in Stephansdom and later much-visited by servants in need.

TAKING A BREAK

Left: Old and
new – the glass
façade of the
Haas House
and Stephans-
dom's Towers
of the Heathens

Have a drink and a snack in the **Dachcafé des Haas-Hauses** on Stephansplatz. From this roof café, the Stephansdom is so close you could almost touch it. And on the way there you can admire the interior of the Haas Haus, Hans Hollein's modern temple of consumerism, whose architectural boldness provoked much discussion.

🕂 193 D3 ✉ Wien 1, Stephansplatz ⏰ Interior Mon–Sat 6–10, Sun 7–10; Guided tours Mon–Sat 10:30 am, 3 pm, Sun only 3 pm; Lift up Nordturm Apr–Jun, Sep–Oct daily 8:30–5:30, Jul–Aug 8:30–6, Nov–Mar 8:30–5 🚇 Stephansplatz 🚌 Bus 1A, 2A, 3A Stephansplatz 💶 Führungen moderate; Lift up Nordturm moderate ❓ www.stephansdom.at

STEPHANSDOM: INSIDE INFO

Top tips If you're fit enough, climb the 343 steps up to the **Türmerstube im Südturm** (Watchman's Room in the South Tower, daily 9–5:30, admission: moderate). The view from the four windows is magnificent and it will make you forget all your troubles.
• You can only go down into the **Gruftanlagen** (crypt) on a guided tour (daily 10–11:30 am/1:30–4:30 pm, admission: moderate). The crypt contains the tombs, urns for viscera and sarcophagi of the Habsburg rulers and a number of bishops, together with skeletons from the city cemetery, which was laid out round the cathedral in the 18th century.
• In fine weather from June to September **evening tours with a roof visit** are on offer every Saturday at 7 pm. Meet at the south tower.

Hidden gem Visit the Stephansdom in the **early morning or late evening**. The quietness really enhances the atmosphere.

⑪ The Judenplatz

From the Roman barracks through the medieval Jewish quarter to a moving place of remembrance – very few other squares reflect the long and varied history of the city in the same way as the Judenplatz.

For a long time the square was quite unremarkable. It wasn't until 1995–98 that its long history came to light with the excavations made for the construction of the memorial proposed by Simon Wiesenthal in 1994. This part of the city was first settled by the Romans, who in the first century AD built legionaries' barracks here for a large camp. In the 12th century the square became the centre of the Jewish quarter for which it is named (Jewish Square) today.

One of the Largest Medieval Jewish Quarters
The ghetto had 70 houses, built so as to form a continuous wall. In the centre stood the school- or prayer-house, first mentioned in 1205; it was one of the largest synagogues in Europe. The Viennese Jewish community then formed some 5 per cent of the population of the city. Most families were not rich, but the ghetto developed into a famous centre of Jewish scholarship. In 1421, 210 Jews were burnt at the stake, the rest were expelled and the synagogue was destroyed. More than five centuries later archaeologists discovered the remains of the synagogue: the foundations, parts of the tiled floor and the hexagonal *bima*, where the Torah was read.

The Holocaust Memorial
Today the Judenplatz with its memorial, excavations and museum is a place of remembrance. The square is dominated by the memorial by the British sculptress Rachel Whiteread.

Rachel Whiteread's memorial on Judenplatz

The white reinforced concrete cube, measuring 10m by 7m and 3.8m high (32.8 ft by 23 ft and 12.5 ft high), was unveiled in 2000. With its powerful symbolism it portrays a library of 7,000 books turned inside out. The doors are locked, the book-spines are turned inwards.

The Misrachi House, an annexe of the Jewish Museum

The exhibition in the lower ground floor of the Misrachi House

The inaccessible interior and the no-longer-readable books stand for the irreparable loss of the lives of 65,000 Austrian Jews, who were victims of the Nazi regime. On flagstones around the memorial are inscribed the names of all places where they were put to death.

TAKING A BREAK

With its Viennese and Bohemian cuisine, the **Gustl Bauer** restaurant in the narrow alleyway leading to Am Hof square provides a nutritious and relaxing break. Don't be surprised if you overhear some lively political discussions. This is the favourite restaurant of the former mayor Dr Helmut Zilk and of many Viennese city politicians.

🕂 192 C4 🚇 Herrengasse 🚌 Bus 1A Heidenschuss/Am Hof

JUDENPLATZ: INSIDE INFO

Top tips The excavations can be viewed on the ground floor and in the cellars of the **Misrachi-Haus** (Wien 1, Judenplatz 8, Sun–Thu 10–6, Fri until 2 pm, admission: moderate), and in an outreach of the Jewish Museum in the Palais Eskeles (11 Dorotheergasse, Vienna 1, tel: 01/535 04 31, Sun-Fri 10–6, Sat 10–8; U-bahn station: Stephansplatz; admission: free. www.jmw.at). Audio-visual equipment in three modern exhibition rooms gives information on the daily life, commercial and religious activites of the medieval community. A computer animation reconstructs the ghetto of around 1400 and lets you take a virtual tour of the alleyways and the synagogue. In addition, numerous excavated objects are displayed in showcases.

13 Freyung

Freyung is one of Vienna's most elegant and visited squares. Lined with magnificent, lavishly restored palaces, it has developed into an urban centre with a special ambience, where art lovers will always find spectacular, ever-changing exhibitions. The attractive passages and courtyards of the palaces, with their pretty shops and inviting bars, also contribute to the metropolitan feel.

In the Middle Ages the virtually triangular square had the dubious privilege of serving as the city's rubbish dump. If the mounds of rubbish were not too high, travelling entertainers and minstrels performed here, and in an emergency, gallows for traitors were swiftly erected. There is now no trace of the square's sombre past.

A temple of art
On the site of the former oratory of the Schottenkirche there now stands the **Kunstforum** of Bank Austria. Its regular exhibitions of modern art are always worth visiting. (Wien 1, Freyung 8, tel: 01/537 33; Sat–Thu 10–7, Fri 10–9; admission: expensive; www.kunstforumwien.at)

Plenty of Palaces...

The Schottenkirche on Freyung

One side of the square is formed by Lukas von Hildebrandt's **Palais Daun Kinsky**, a masterpiece of baroque architecture. Festive banquets are held in its princely rooms. Since 1994 the staterooms of the equally baroque **Palais Harrach** have been used by the Kunsthistorisches Museum (Museum of Art History) for top-flight exhibitions, lectures and concerts. The adjoining **Palais Ferstel** was built in the Italianate style in 1856–60 by Heinrich Ferstel for the Österreichisch-Ungarische Bank. Until 1877 it was the home of the Wiener Börse (Vienna Stock Exchange). Later the building deteriorated, until in 1975 it was restored, together with the Café Central (► 28, 66). Today the staterooms on the first floor are let out for conferences and banquets.

Café Central, once a meeting point for Vienna's literati

...and Plenty More

On the north side of Freyung stands the **Schottenstift** (Scottish Foundation). Founded in 1155 by the Babenberg Duke Heinrich II Jasomirgott, it actually has nothing to do with Scotland – the Duke brought monks to Vienna from Ireland, which at that time was called *Scotia maior*. The monks had the right to shelter asylum-seekers, who could not be prosecuted by the courts while they were in the foundation – hence the name of the square, *freyung*, meaning "freeing". Heinrich II Jasomirgott is buried in the Schottenstift's church. On the corner of the traffic-calmed square and Renngasse stands the grand **Austria-Brunnen** (➤ 30), the Austria Fountain designed in 1846 by Ludwig Schwanthaler. Its female bronze figures symbolize the rivers Elbe, Danube, Weichsel and Po, the principal rivers of the empire. The fountain is crowned by the figure of Austria.

TAKING A BREAK

Go down the passage in the Palais Ferstel into Herrengasse. The **Café Central's** (➤ 66) cake shop has delicious pastries and sweetmeats, set out in a lofty, airy room.

🞦 192 B/C4 🚇 Herrengasse, Schottentor 🚋 Tram 1, 2, D Schottentor, Bus 2A, 3A Herrengasse

FREYUNG: INSIDE INFO

Top tips In the **Museum** of the Schottenstift important works of art, mainly paintings, from the 17th, 18th and 19th centuries are displayed (Thu–Sat 10–5, Sun 11–5; admission: moderate). The highlight is the late-Gothic altar by the "Wiener Schottenmeister" (1469–80) whose The *Flight into Egypt* detail shows the earliest topographically accurate view of Vienna.

At Your Leisure

🄫 Erzbischöfliches Palais

The baroque Archbishops' Palace was built in 1632–41 to the design of Giovanni Coccapani. The extensive building has façades on Stephansplatz, Rotenturmstrasse and Wolfzeile. The palace was, and still is, the seat of the bishops and archbishops of Vienna. It houses the Dom- und Diözesanmuseum (Cathedral and Diocesan Museum), which has sacred art from the Gothic, Renaissance and baroque periods. At the core of the collection are objects from the cathedral treasury, including some very valuable vestments from the Stephansdom.

🚹 193 D3 🖂 Wien 1, Stephansplatz 6 ☎ (01) 515 52-35 60 ⏱ Tue–Sat 10–5 pm 🚇 Stephansplatz 🚌 Bus 1A, 2A, 3A Stephansplatz 🅿 Moderate ❓ www.dommuseum.at

🄫 Franziskanerplatz

In this square, shut off from traffic by a row of large stone balls, you feel yourself at once in a medieval town in Italy. This feeling is conveyed by the **Franziskanerkirche**, Vienna's only ecclesiastical building in the Renaissance style, whose gable looms over the narrow façade. The high altar was created by Andrea Pozzo, the Italian master of *trompe-l'oeil* architecture. Of particular interest is

The idyllic courtyard of the Erzbischöfliches Palais

the miracle-working statue *Madonna with the Axe* from the 15th century. Its name originates in the story that the Protestants tried to destroy it but failed to do so either by fire or with an axe, for the axe is still there, sticking into Mary's left shoulder.

🚹 193 D3 🚇 Stephansplatz 🚌 Bus 1A, 2A, 3A Stephansplatz

🄫 Figaro-Haus

In the narrow, picturesque Domgasse you can retrace Mozart's steps. The composer moved house 11 times in Vienna, but the only place still standing is the apartment where he lived from September 1784 to April

The indestructible *Madonna with the Axe*

1797, on the first floor of the so-called Camesina-Haus, at Domgasse 5. According to his biographer, Mozart spent the happiest years of his life in this house, together with his wife Constanze and his son Karl. He composed numerous works here, including the opera *The Marriage of Figaro*. Nowadays the apartment is set up as a memorial.

🚩 193 D3 ✉ Wien 1, Domgasse 5
☎ (01) 513 62 94 🕐 Tue–Sun 9–6
🚇 Stephansplatz 🚌 Bus 1A, 2A, 3A Stephansplatz 💰 Moderate, Sun free

5 Jesuitenkirche

The Jesuit Church, the former university church, was built in the mid-18th century as the dining hall for the Alte Universität (Old University).

north, so Pozzo had to contend with particularly poor lighting. He therefore integrated the altarpiece, which shows the Assumption of the Virgin into Heaven, into the architecture. He set the painting into a shallow bay and created two sources of natural light by opening up narrow windows between the picture and its frame. In the chapels at the back on the right, where an adjoining high building shuts out the light, Pozzo's solution is even more interesting: he diverted the light by replacing the narrow side windows with mirrors. He included himself in the piece at the bottom left, as the Apostle Andreas.

🚩 193 E3 ✉ Wien 1, Dr-Ignaz-Seipel-Platz 🚇 Stubentor 🚋 Tram 1, 2, D Stubentor, Bus 1A Riemergasse

Together with the Alte Universität and the Akademie der Wissenschaften (Academy of Sciences), it encloses Dr-Ignaz-Seipel-Platz. The charm of this square is particularly marked in the evening, when floodlights bathe the perfectly harmonious early-baroque edifice in an unreal light. Built in 1623–31, the church was founded by Emperor Ferdinand II, when he entrusted the university to the Jesuits. Of particular interest is the *trompe-l'oeil* painting by Andrea Pozzo in the main aisle. The church faces

"Historyworld" really brings history to life

6 Heiligenkreuzerhof

Between Köllnerhofgasse and Schön-laterngasse lies a large, particularly idyllic courtyard, which belongs to the Cistercians of the Holy Cross Abbey. The residences round the

The towers of the Greek Church soar above Fleischmarkt

courtyard are let as private apartments (the famous cabaret artist Helmut Qualtinger lived here for a while). The vaults, which date in part from the Middle Ages, are now given over to the "History-world", a sort of Viennese waxworks. Some 100 life-size figures narrate the history of Austria. Scenes of medieval torture sit next to tableaux from Mozart's time; famous paintings, including Leonardo da Vinci's *Last Supper*, are shown in 3D models. Empress Maria Theresa and Emperor Franz Joseph are also represented.

🔒 193 E4 ✉ Wien 1, Schönlatern-gasse 5 ☎ (01) 513 78 78
🕐 Daily 9–7 pm 🚇 Stephansplatz
🚌 Bus 1A, 2A, 3A Stephansplatz
💶 Expensive, Sun free
❓ www.historyworld.co.at

7 Fleischmarkt

At the start of the 18th century, with the Turks defeated and no other danger threatening, Vienna grew into a key centre for trade with the East. Turkish, Levantine and Greek merchants settled in the area of Fleischmarkt (Meat Market) and developed this trade with the Orient. The Byzantine look of the Greek Non-United Church is a reminder of this time.

🔒 193 E4 🚇 Schwedenplatz 🚋 Tram 1, 2, 21, N, Bus 2A Schwedenplatz

8 Griechenbeisl

In the city's records there is an entry for 1447 about the sale of a house, which shows the Griechenbeisl (Greek Snackbar) to be the oldest pub in Vienna. Its origins go still further back: the foundations are Roman. It was here, in the mid-17th century during the plague years, that the minstrel Augustin composed and sang the famous song *Oh du lieber Augustin, alles ist hin* (➤ 20) (Dear Augustin, everything is over). The statue of Augustin, peering out of a barred-off room in the cellar, is a reminder of it. The Griechen-beisl has had many prominent customers: Beethoven and Mozart, Einstein and Gina Lollobrigida – all immortalized themselves on the ceiling of one of the restaurant's vaults.

🔒 193 E4 ✉ Wien 1, Fleischmarkt 11
☎ (01) 533 19 77 🕐 Daily 11 am–1 am (hot food 11:30–11:30)
🚇 Schwedenplatz 🚋 Tram 1, 2, 21, N, Bus 2A Schwedenplatz
❓ www.griechenbeisl.at

9 Ruprechtskirche

This small, ivy-hung church is Vienna's oldest. Rising above today's turbulent "Bermuda Triangle", it stands on a mound overlooking the Danube Canal, where (➤ 68) in the Middle Ages already steps led down to the landing-stage for the salt-trading ships. The Ruprechtskirche

Maître Leherb
Have a look at the house at No 6 Franziskanerplatz. Until his death in 1997, it was the home of the Viennese surrealist artist Maître Leherb. He also created the pretty dove-fountain in front of the house.

is said to have been founded as early as 740. The plain 12th-century hall church was remodelled in the Gothic style in the 13th century. It still has stained glass windows from the 1200s and a "Black Madonna", who was invoked in times of plague or the Turkish attacks.

✚ 193 D4 ✉ Wien 1, Ruprechtsplatz 🚇 Schwedenplatz 🚋 Tram 1, 2, 21, N, Bus 2A Schwedenplatz

🔟 Hoher Markt and Ankeruhr

Beneath the paving of Ruprechtskirche, archaeologists found Roman remains. In the Middle Ages it was the site of the law courts known as Schranne, the pillory and the gallows for carrying out sentence and the "idiots' cells", where lunatics were locked up. For a long time the square was also a fish-market, and Vienna's first water-conduit ended here. The Vermählungsbrunnen (Wedding Fountain) in the middle was built first in wood by Joseph Emanuel Fischer von Erlach, then rebuilt in marble by his son, in 1792.

The glory of the square, in its eastern corner, is the **Ankeruhr** (Anchor Clock). It was created in

The baroque splendour of the church "To the nine choirs of angels"

Roman remains
Be sure to take the path down from the Café Salut im Garten (Hoher Markt 3) to the Roman excavations. These show the remains of the Roman camp at Vindobona and the foundations of the palace where the Roman Emperor Marcus Aurelius probably once stayed. (Tue–Sun 9–12:15 and 1–4:30, admission: inexpensive)

1911 by the Jugendstil painter Franz von Matsch as a decoration for the arch between the headquarters of the Anchor Insurance Company and the house next-door. The clock's special feature is a parade of statues. Each day on the stroke of twelve, doors open and twelve over-life-size figures

The "Anchor Clock" at Hoher Markt is a famous Jugendstil work

appear, illustrating the history of the city, among them Marcus Aurelius, Charlemagne and Rudolf I.

✚ 193 D4 🚇 Stephansplatz 🚌 Bus 1A, 2A, 3A Hoher Markt

🔟 Am Hof

In 1155 the Babenberger Heinrich II Jasomirgott had a conqueror's palace built on Am Hof, a wide square. This developed into a centre of chivalric culture, where poets such as Walther von der Vogelweide appeared. Even today Am Hof has a lordly feel about it, not least thanks to the church Zu den neun Chören der Engel (To the Nine Choirs of the Angels), Collalto Palace, where the six-year-old Mozart had his concert debut, and the giant Mariensäule (Mary Column), which commemorates the menace of the Swedes in the Thirty Years War.

✚ 192 C4 🚇 Herrengasse 🚌 Bus 1A Am Hof

Where to...
Eat and Drink

Prices

Prices given are for one person, excluding drinks.
€ under 12 euros €€ 12–25 euros €€€ over 25 euros

Restaurants

Cantinetta Antinori €€

The restaurant nearest to the Stephansdom belongs to the renowned aristocratic Antinori family from Florence, which has been making wine now for 26 generations. All the wines served at the restaurant were made by the Antorinis. The furnishings of the restaurant are tasteful, with a simple elegance. The food, based on delicious specialities from Tuscany, can be pretty substantial.

🚹 193 D3 ⊠ Wien 1, Jasomirgott-strasse 3/5 ☎ (01) 533 77 22 🕙 Daily 11:30 am–midnight (hot food until 11 pm) Ⓤ Stephansplatz 🚌 Bus 1A, 2A, 3A Stephansplatz

Fabios €€€

Fabios restaurant, bar and lounge is reputed to have the finest design of any restaurant in the city, an architectural jewel. The glass doors open onto the arbour are opened wide in summer, making the whole place into a terrace. The cuisine is creative Mediterranean, light and delicate; specialities include warm braised octopus and fillets of turbot. The ambience is chic – and the place is very popular.

🚹 192 C4 ⊠ Wien 1, Tuchlauben 6 ☎ (010) 532 22 22 🕙 Mon–Sat 10 am–1 am (hot food noon–23:30 pm) Ⓤ Stephansplatz 🚌 Bus 1A, 2A, 3A Petersplatz

Figlmüller €

This cosy restaurant and wine bar is in the narrow alleyway between Wollzeile and Lugeck. It serves the biggest Wiener Schnitzel in Vienna, traditionally accompanied by a mixed salad and a *gspritzer* (a spritzer). The wine is from the restaurant's own vineyards. The atmosphere at Figlmüller is always free and easy.

🚹 193 D3 ⊠ Wien 1, Wollzeile 5 ☎ (01) 512 61 77 🕙 Daily 11 am–10.30 pm Ⓤ Stephansplatz 🚌 Bus 1A, 2A, 3A Stephansplatz

Gösser Bierklinik €

Even after renovation the furnishings have remained the same, traditional and very cosy, with a medieval ambience. In the Gösser Bierklinik everything revolves round Gösser beer, reputed to be the best in the city. To accompany the amber nectar there's good Viennese food on the ground floor, while on the floor above the chef serves ever-changing dishes of the day. Prepare to be surprised!

🚹 192 C4 ⊠ Wien 1, Steindlgasse 4 ☎ (01) 533 75 98 12 🕙 Mon–Sat 10 am–11:30 pm Ⓤ Stephansplatz 🚌 Bus 1A, 2A, 3A Petersplatz

Haas & Haas €€

Behind the Stephansdom lies hidden one of the most agreeable restaurants in the city. To the right of the Haas & Haas café, an unobtrusive door leads to the restaurant of the same name. In summer it has one of the finest gardens, shut off from the hubbub of the city by thick walls. There you can enjoy modern, light cooking, for example roast beef with mixed-leaf salad.

🚹 193 D3 ⊠ Wien 1, Stephansplatz 4 ☎ (01) 512 26 66 🕙 Mon–Fri 8 am–8 pm, Sat until 6.30 pm Ⓤ Stephansplatz 🚌 Bus 1A, 2A, 3A Stephansplatz

Indochine 21 €€€

Far-Eastern food is all the rage in Vienna, and the culinary culture of Vietnam, Laos and Cambodia combined with the spirit of 21st-century Europe, are the thinking behind this trendy eatery. Its charm lies not only in the authentic Asian cuisine but also in the colonial-inspired ambience. The wickerware furniture and the stylish combined restaurant-bar-lounge, serving some of the best cocktails in town, make it quite special.

✚ 193 F3 ☒ Wien 1, Stubenring 18 ☎ (01) 513 76 60 ⊙ Daily noon–midnight (hot food noon–3, 6–midnight, barfood 6 pm–midnight) Ⓜ Stubentor 🚋 Tram 1, 2, Bus 1A, 74A Stubentor

Martinelli €€

In the wonderfully Italianate courtyard of the Palais Harrach the trattoria Martinelli adds a touch more Italian atmosphere. The decor is elegant, with a southern feel, and the cooking is inspired by the Tuscan hills. On the menu are favourites, such as veal, beef and rabbit fried with olives or braised in red wine. In this special ambience, a simple evening meal feels like a short break in Italy.

✚ 192 C4 ☒ Wien 1, Freyung 3 ☎ (01) 533 67 21 ⊙ Daily noon–3, 6–midnight Ⓜ Herrengasse, Schottentor 🚋 Tram 1, 2, D Schottentor, Bus 2A, 3A Herrengasse

Neu Wien €€

At Neu Wien, the possibilities are manifold. They include just an *achterl* (⅛-litre of wine) at the bar, agreeable company, a meal at the neatly laid tables or spending your evening in KIK (*Kultur im Keller*, culture in the cellar). The tavern has the pleasant atmosphere of a private living-room, the cooking is good and not over-the-top trendy. With styling to match, it is a sophisticated rendezvous for artists.

✚ 193 E3 ☒ Wien 1, Bäckerstr. 5 ☎ (010) 512 09 99 ⊙ Mon–Sat 6 pm–1 am Ⓜ Stubentor 🚋 Bus 1A Riemergasse

Ofenloch €€

The owner of this 300-year-old restaurant in a baroque house is a collector. For years he has been gathering in whatever takes his fancy, from every possible source. The rooms are decorated with equal care – in pride of place is a substantial collection of corks. The food and wine combines the traditional and contemporary, and the menu is laid out in the form of an old newspaper, *Ofenloch's Locablatt*.

✚ 192 C4 ☒ Wien 1, Kurrentgasse 8 ☎ (01) 533 88 44 ⊙ Mon–Sat 10 am–midnight (hot food noon–10:45 pm) Ⓜ Stephansplatz 🚋 Bus 1A, 2A, 3A Petersplatz

Oliver's Restaurant €

This small, cosy restaurant opposite the entrance to Heiligenkreuzerhof specializes in fresh fish and pasta. At lunch and in the evening there's a good set menu at very reasonable prices. It is also an artist's haunt with frequent exhibitions.

✚ 193 E4 ☒ Wien 1, Schönlaterngasse 4 ☎ (01) 512 71 68 ⊙ Mon–Sat 11 am–2:30, 5:30–midnight Ⓜ Stephansplatz 🚋 Bus 1A, 2A, 3A Stephansplatz

Oswald & Kalb €

This mixture of fashionable bar and restaurant has been a favourite meeting place for two decades. The dimly-lit rooms are rustic and comfortable, the food is traditional Styrian and delicate. Many well-known personalities and artists meet here for dinner, especially at the regulars' tables at the back of the vaulted room.

✚ 193 E3 ☒ Wien 1, Bäckerstrasse 14 ☎ (01) 512 13 71 ⊙ Daily 6 pm–2 am Ⓜ Stubentor 🚋 Bus 1A Riemergasse

Zu den 3 Hacken €

This restaurant, once the favourite haunt of Franz Schubert and his friends, is still an absolutely typical inn. In the little garden in front of the house you sit at simple tables with green-and-white chequered tablecloths. The cooking is very traditional, ranging from the classical *tafelspitz* (boiled beef) to offal dishes like braised heart, accompanied by a fine selection of wines from Austria and Italy.

🕂 193 E3 🖂 Wien 1, Singerstrasse 28 ☎ (01) 512 15 19 🕓 Mon–Sat 11:30 am–midnight 🚇 Stephansplatz 🚌 Bus 1A, 2A, 3A Stephansplatz

Zum Scherer €

This "stand up or sit down pub with flair", as it calls itself, has panelled walls and comfortable, traditional furniture. The young proprietors have taken care to retain the atmosphere of an old-fashioned tavern and yet to give it a contemporary touch. The menu has predominantly old-Austrian dishes such as fried liver or onion-roast. In summer most people sit outside, in the garden in front of the restaurant.

🕂 192 C4 🖂 Wien 1, Judenplatz 7 ☎ (01) 533 51 64 🕓 Mon–Sat 10 am–midnight 🚇 Herrengasse 🚌 Bus 1A Heidenschuss/Am Hof

Cafés

Aida

To date, there are 27 red-and-white painted Aida cafés in various parts of Vienna. They're a favourite place to meet friends for a quick espresso or a slice of delicious gateau from the Aida patisserie. The cakes can also be bought from the shop.

🕂 193 D3 🖂 Wien 1, Stock-im-Eisen-Platz 2 ☎ (01) 512 79 25 🕓 Mon–Sat 7 am–8 pm, Sun 9 am–8 pm 🚇 Stephansplatz 🚌 Bus 1A, 2A, 3A Stephansplatz

Central

The Café Central in Palais Ferstel is legendary. For generations it has been the chosen meeting place of writers and intellectuals, including in the past Lenin, Trotsky and the psychologist Adler. The latest round of renovations has removed its rather sleepy patina, but a lifesize figure of the writer Peter Altenberg, sitting at one of the marble tables, is a reminder of the intellectual glories of the past. You eat well in Café Central; the Viennese dishes and the pastries are first class.

🕂 192 C4 🖂 Wien 1, Herrengasse 14 ☎ (01) 533 37 63 26 🕓 Mon–Sat 8 am–8 pm, Sun 10 am–6 pm, Jul–Aug closed on Sun 🚇 Herrengasse, Schottentor 🚌 Tram 1, 2, D Schottentor, Bus 2A, 3A Herrengasse

Das Kleine Café

Designed in the mid-1970s by the architect Hermann Czech, Das Kleine Café (The Little Café) lives up to its name. It has just five marble tables, a few Thonet chairs and leather-covered benches. The favourite haunt of the Viennese actor Hanno Pöschl, it has a distinctive feel and is a popular meeting-place for artists. In fine weather the café can take extra guests – they put a few more tables outside.

🕂 193 D3 🖂 Wien 1, Franziskaner-platz 3 🖀 No telephone 🕓 Mon–Sat 10 am–2 am, Sun 1 pm–2 am (food served after midnight) 🚇 Stephansplatz 🚌 Bus 1A, 2A, 3A Stephansplatz

Delia's

Chic and stylish, with a pretty bar, Delia's is the modern alternative to Korb café (see overleaf). The menu is limited; you can have savoury or sweet snacks with your *caffè forte e più*. The garden adjoins Korb.

🕂 193 D4 🖂 Wien 1, Tuchlauben 8 ☎ (01) 533 04 26 🕓 Mon–Sat 8 am–midnight, Sun 10 am–midnight 🚇 Stephansplatz 🚌 Bus 1A, 2A, 3A Stephansplatz

Diglas

The tasteful, roomy corner café in Wollzeile keeps up the old Viennese coffee-house traditions. It is splendidly furnished, with marble floors, wall-panelling and cut-glass doors. There is an extensive range of hot foods, from breakfast to lunch, with a set menu, and afternoon pastries from their own shop. In the evening, discreet piano music provides a relaxing ambience for diners who enjoy a delicious meal and fine wines. The coffee-house is always crowded and it is often hard to get a table, even in the garden in front of the house.

🏠 193 E3 🖂 Wien 1, Wollzeile 10
☎ (01) 512 57 65 🕐 Daily 7 am–midnight 🚇 Stephansplatz, Stubentor
🚌 Bus 1A Riemergasse

Korb

This café is not distinguished for its modern furnishings – on the contrary, everything looks pretty shabby. All the same, or perhaps even because of its agreeable patina, "the Basket" is a legendary Viennese institution. The café provides more hot dishes than many pubs and boasts of having the best *apfelstrudel* in town. The Korb is a favourite meeting place for business people and artists. In the summer, guests fill the garden. The cellar also has a particular attraction: there's an old-fashioned skittle-alley.

🏠 193 D4 🖂 Wien 1, Brandstätte 7–9
☎ (01) 533 72 15
🕐 Mon–Sat 8 am–midnight, Sun 11–11
🚇 Stephansplatz
🚌 Bus 1A, 2A, 3A, Stephansplatz

Where to... Shop

The narrow alleyways in the old city centre are not just well suited to strolling and gazing round, they are also good for shopping. There are numerous boutiques, antique and book shops, and a mass of interesting stores with specialized, often original offerings. There is something for most tastes, at least for browsing and window-shopping. Many of the shops have remained true Viennese in style, but others have a modern feel.

Behind the Stephansdom

Vinothek St Stephan (Stephansplatz 6) has a vast range of international wines, rare and old vintages and single-malt whiskies, as well as olive oil and balsamic vinegar. The **Galerie Ambiente** (Lugeck 1A) specializes in traditional bentwood furniture; of especial interest is the new Design Marlowe furniture, which is made in the old style, and the teddy-bear museum, whose exhibits, however, are not for sale. The small but elegant **Schatzecke** (Treasure Trove, Wollzeile 5, Passage) has antique ornaments at all price levels, even for the smallest purse. The **Geschenks-Gewölbe** (Fleischmarkt 16) has antique and new bears and dolls, as well as pretty little antiques and gift articles. The shoe boutique **Le Petit Chou** (Kühfussgasse 2/Petersplatz 9) specializes in small sizes, with particularly cute children's shoes and accessories.

Freyung

Following the traffic-calming in the square and the renovation of the palaces, a row of fine shops has opened on Freyung. In the passage leading from Freyung to the Palais Ferstel arcades, two small shops merit special attention. **Katze & Kater** (Cat & Tomcat, Freyung 2) has delightful model tigers, in painted wood or porcelain and in all colours and sizes. The **Xocolat** (Freyung 2) describes itself as a pleasure ground for explorers and conquerors, and with some justification, as they have every possible sort of chocolate. **Tomas Lisa Interiors** (Herrengasse 14) on the other side of Palais Ferstel, has a selection of pretty things for the home such as lamps, accessories and small lifestyle items and gifts such as note-blocks. **Klosterladen im Schottenstift** (Freyung 6), the Abbey Shop, sells religious artefacts. A specialist shop for monastic products, which existed in the 18th century, it stocks brandies, herbal liqueurs and wine as well as groceries of its own cultivation (fruit, sausages, poppy oil). As might be expected, they also do a good line in devotional books and religious objects.

Where to be... Entertained

At night the oldest part of Vienna is where the action is. In the narrow lanes and alleyways round the Stephansdom life really gets going after nightfall. This is where the Viennese do their *beisltouren* (pub crawls), going from one trendy bar to the next.

Bermuda Triangle

In the early 1970s, a vibrant entertainment area, known as the "Bermuda Triangle", grew up around the Ruprechtskirche, in Rabensteig, Seitenstettengasse and Ruprechtsplatz. Suddenly a series of lively pubs and bars appeared. You could eat, drink, listen to music and then simply move on. Many of the original venues are still there,

and they are still very much the "in" places to go to even now.

Zum Kuchldragoner (Seitenstettengasse 3, tel: 01/533 83 71, Sun–Thu 11 am–2 am, Fri–Sat until 4 am) opened in 1973; it offers good Viennese cooking and a warm, uncomplicated ambience. **Ma Pitom** (Seitenstettengasse 5, tel: 01/535 43 13, Sun–Thu 5 pm–3 am, Fri–Sat until 4 am) is an up-beat beer house with an especially fine beer garden by the Ruprechtskirche. **Krah Krah** (Rabensteig 8, tel: 01/533 81 93, Mon–Sat 11 am–2 am, Sun until 1 am) specializes in beer – it has varieties from all over the world. **Salzamt** (Ruprechtsplatz 1, tel: 01/533 53 32, Mon–Fri noon–2 am, Sat–Sun 5 pm–2 am) is a popular gastropub. **Der Rote Engel** (Rabensteig 5, tel: 01/535 41 05, Sun–Tue 4 pm–2 am, Wed–Thu until 3 am, Fri–Sat until 4 am) is the place for live music: in recent years 700 groups have played rock, pop, funk and jazz here. But no-one seems to be tired of it.

MUSIC

Already in the mid-19th century there was a theatre in the cellars of No 11 Riemergasse. Later cabaret, revue and cinema moved in. The present occupants, **Porgy & Bess** (Riemergasse 11, tel: 01/512 88 11, Mon–Sat from 7 pm, Sun from 8 pm) have modern, lavishly furnished rooms. Anyone interested in jazz comes here – the programme is varied and interesting.

At **Jazzland** (Franz-Josefs-Kai 29, tel: 01/533 25 75, Mon–Sat from 7 pm, music from 9 pm) time seems to have stood still. The place is as dimly lit and smoky as you'd expect from a true jazz club, and the mood is often really great. The music varies from swing, blues and dixie to modern jazz.

BARS

For some 20 years the small but elegant **Broadway Piano-Bar** (Bauernmarkt 21, tel: 01/533 28 49,

Mon–Sat from 9 pm) with its old Austro-Hungarian aura has been a rendezvous for artists and epicures. The programme includes drama and chanson evenings, and there's live music nightly, when the landlord Béla Koreny himself plays the piano – every evening is a wonderful, unforgettable experience.

The legendary **Eden Bar** (Liliengasse 2, tel: 01/512 74 50, Mon–Sat 9 pm–4 am) has lost none of its charm over the years. All the Viennese celebrities come here, from industrial tycoons to leading politicians, for *reden in der Eden* (a chat at the Eden bar). Every evening there's live music. The landlord Heinz Schimanko, Vienna's "king of the night", insists on strict etiquette. Gentlemen without ties are not admitted – though in emergencies the cloakroom can help out. On the noticeboards outside you can see photos of the bar's illustrious former customers. They are a real draw in Liliengasse, as is the well-stocked bar.

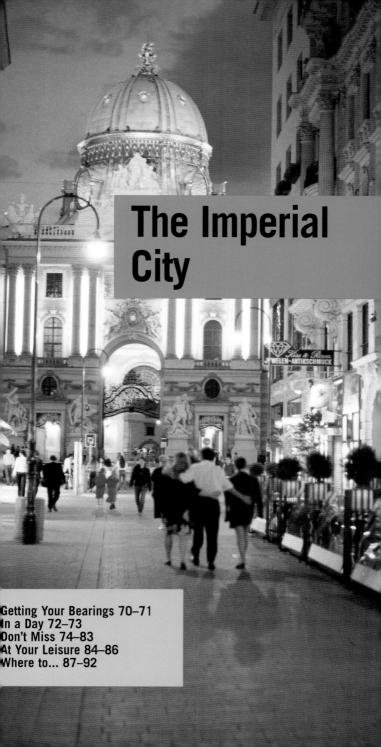

The Imperial City

Getting Your Bearings

More than any other, this part of Vienna bears witness to the splendour of the imperial era. The Hofburg, the Albertina and the busy streets reflect the power and elegance of the former city on the Danube. There are still shops here with a pleasingly dusty imperial feel, but there are also great pubs and real temples of consumerism with an international reputation.

The heart of the old imperial city beats with an almost youthful vigour. This is particularly evident in the Kohlmarkt and Graben areas, which have seen many changes in the past few years. The old has given way to the new, and everything has been updated in tasteful metropolitan style. A new, urbane lifestyle is apparent, not least by of the numerous and elegant pubs and bars. In the past few years the tourist attractions have also been refurbished, at great expense. From the Hofburg with its great museums through the Hofreitschule (Riding School) to the Albertina, everything is resplendent after their renovation.

**Above:
The Hofburg
attracts crowds
of people**

**Left: Rest your
feet in Graben**

**Right:
Swarovski's
gleaming
paradise**

**Page 69:
The Kohlmarkt
leads to the
Michaelertor**

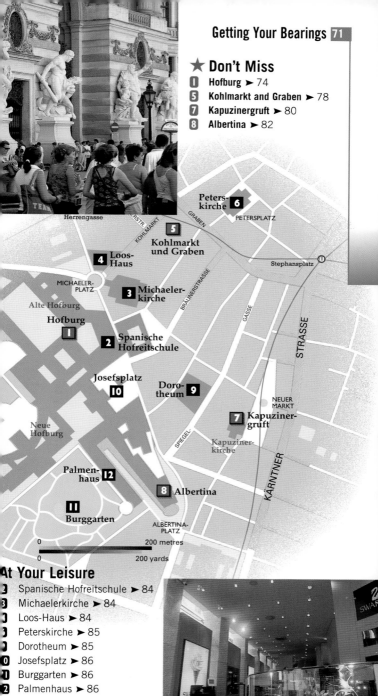

★ Don't Miss

Peters-kirche 6
PETERSPLATZ
Herrengasse
KOHLMARKT
GRABEN
5 Kohlmarkt und Graben
4 Loos-Haus
Stephansplatz
MICHAELER-PLATZ
Alte Hofburg
3 Michaeler-kirche
BRÄUNERSTRASSE
Hofburg 1
2 Spanische Hofreitschule
GASSE
STRASSE
Josefsplatz 10
Doro-theum 9
Neue Hofburg
SPIEGEL-
7 Kapuziner-gruft
NEUER MARKT
Kapuziner-kirche
Palmen-haus 12
KÄRNTNER
11 Burggarten
8 Albertina
ALBERTINA-PLATZ
0   200 metres
0   200 yards

At Your Leisure

The Hofburg and Albertina are the high points at the heart of the imperial city, and you can experience the atmosphere just by strolling through the streets that formed Vienna's reputation for elegance and splendour.

The Heart of the Imperial City in a Day

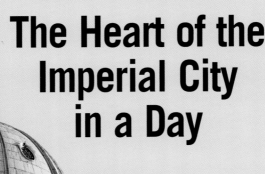

9:00 am

Start the day by exploring a royal residence with a visit to the ❶ **Hofburg** (left; ➤ 74). Don't just gaze at the so-called "Habsburgs' labyrinth" from the outside. The imperial apartments, the Sisi-Museum, the Silberkammer (Silver Chamber) and the Schatzkammer (Treasury) have plenty to offer – both the exhibits and a special atmosphere that is unique. The celebrated ❷ **Spanische Reitschule** (Spanish Riding School, ➤ 84) adjoining the Hofburg, is also special.

Noon

Recharge yourself in the Café Hofburg (➤ 90) and then stroll across ❺ **Kohlmarkt** (➤ 78). Admire the elegant contemporary jewellery at Schullin's (➤ 91) and the antique jewellery at Siedler's (➤ 91) Look at Demel's (➤ 90), which always has imaginative window-dressing, and buy some candied violets here (Sisi's favourite nibble), then stroll past the stylish displays at Chanel, Gucci and Louis Vuitton to ❺ **Graben** (➤ 78).

1:00 pm

Vienna's leading coffee-roaster, Meinl am Graben (right; ➤ 88) serves a choice, light lunch. Afterwards you could enjoy the window displays at the Schwäbische Jungfrau (Suabian Virgin, above right; ➤ 91), which specializes in fine linen, and then at Rasper's opposite, a furnishing

store which has everything to make a home chic and up to date. The displays at Heldwein's and Haban's jeweller's shops (►91) sparkle with life, but after this things get rather serious – steel yourself for a visit to the **7** **Kapuzinergruft** (►80) where you'll experience the Habsburgs' unique take on death.

3:00 pm

The bold modern architecture of the stairway and the lavishly restored rooms of the **8** **Albertina** (►82) art gallery will soon elevate your spirits after your visit to the Kapuzinergruft. Visit the current exhibition and then stroll around to your heart's content.

5:00 pm

The ancient, narrow side-streets off Graben invite all who love beautiful old things to rummage. Here large and small antiques shops stand side by side, selling exclusive objects as well as little ornaments at more reasonable prices. Don't fail to walk round the **9** **Dorotheum** (►85) auction house. You'll be charmed by the mixture of art and kitsch in the beautiful palace atmosphere.

7:00 pm

Finally, take a gentle stroll through the **11** **Burggarten** (►86), where you'll find the **12** **Palmenhaus** (Palm House, right; ►86) with its butterfly house as well as great brasserie. No better place for supper. And after that? Why not try your luck at the casino (►92)…

❶ Hofburg

The "Habsburgs' labyrinth" is how the Hofburg is often described, and with some justification. The Hofburg was the Habsburg dynasty's residence for six centuries, almost without interruption. During this time the rulers added one wing after another, creating a gigantic, and slightly confusing, complex.

The Sisi-Museum brings the imperial era to life

Nowadays the Hofburg feels like a separate city within the city. The palace is spread over an area of 240,000sq m (287,000 square yards), and comprises 18 wings and 19 courtyards with a total of 2,600 rooms. Some 5,000 people work in the Hofburg palace.

The Origins

It all began with the **Schweizerhof** (Swiss Court) named after the Swiss Guard who were stationed here during the reign of Maria Theresa. It is not known when this, the oldest wing, was built, but it is first mentioned in records in 1279. The ***castro wiennensi***, a proper fortress with four corner turrets, a moat and a drawbridge, was used as a residence by the Habsburg ruler Rudolf I. The central part of this fortress is still standing, as is the **Burgkapelle** (Castle Chapel), although altered at a later date.

The **Schweizertor** (Swiss Gate), with its striking red, black and gold paintwork, is also later – it was constructed in 1552 by Pietro Ferabsco. The **Schatzkammer** (Treasury) is in this wing; here, along with many other precious secular and religious objects, you can see the insignia of the Holy Roman Empire, including the 1,000-year-old imperial crown, the orb, the sword, the cross and the fabled 15th-century Burgundian treasure.

Other buildings

The second-oldest part of the Hofburg, the **Stallburg** (the Stables), lies outside the main complex, and is separated by the Reitschulgasse. This Renaissance palace was built in 1558–65 by Emperor Ferdinand I for his son Maximilian, on the latter's return from

Incredible but true

In Empress Maria Theresa's time, lavish banquets were held, which the populace could watch, in order to demonstrate the power and the wealth of the rulers. Each of these meals cost as much as the construction of the Karlskirche.

The Schweizertor is one of the oldest parts of the Hofburg

Spain. Since the 18th century, this building with its three-storey arcaded courtyard has been the home of the Lipizzaner, the horses from the **Spanische Reitschule** (Spanish Riding School, ► 84).

The **Amalienburg**, which dates from the 16th century, was originally a free-standing building opposite the Schweizertrakt. Later, Empress Elisabeth lived there. On 24 April, 2004, to mark the 150th anniversary of the wedding of Elisabeth and Emperor Franz Joseph, the **Sisi-Museum** was opened here. It's not a museum in the usual sense but rather a celebration of the fascinating personality of the Empress. The main exhibits are Sisi's poems, portraits of the Empress, her clothes and her jewellery (reproduced by the firm of Swarovski).

In the Hofburg's inner courtyard stands the monument of Emperor Franz I

In 1668–80 Emperor Leopold I had the Schweizertrakt linked to the Amalienburg. Later Maria Theresa and Joseph II lived in this **Leopoldinischer Trakt** (Leopold Wing). The magnificent main rooms have been used since 1946 as the official residence of the Austrian president, and so this part of the Hofburg cannot be visited.

A Spectacular Baroque Makeover

Probably the most spectacular alteration to the Hofburg was made when Emperor Karl VI commissioned Johann Fischer von Erlach to design extensions. In 1723–35 the **National-bibliothek** (National Library) was built – its main room is one of the finest in the world. Then he built the **Winterreitschule** (Winter Riding School, ▶ 84), 57m (62 yards) by 19m (21 yards), and the **Redoutensäle** (Ballrooms) adjoining it on the Josefsplatz side. The Winterreitschule has a suspended roof and a circular gallery supported by 46 columns.

In 1725–30 Fischer von Erlach and Johann Lukas von Hildebrandt built the **Reichskanzeltrakt** (Chancellery Wing), Emperor Franz Joseph's residence from the mid-19th century. The Kaiser-tor leads to the **Kaiserappartements** (Emperor's Apartments), where the original furnishings give an authentic insight into his living and working quarters. In the neighbouring **Silberkammer** (Silver Chamber) are displays of valuable table-settings, the silver, bronze, glass and porcelain which was in use both daily and on state occasions.

In the early 19th century the **Zeremoniensaal** was added next to the Leopoldinischer Trakt. Many balls are still held in this Ceremonial Hall designed by Louis de Montoyer.

The Completion of the Complex

Emperor Franz Joseph carried out the last big addition to the Hofburg. He commissioned Ferdinand Kirschner to build the **Michaelertrakt**. In 1913, just one year before World War I, the building was completed; its 50-m (165-feet) high copper

The Neuer Hofburg forms one side of Heldenplatz

For Kids

Children can learn about Empress Elisabeth and life in the Hofburg on a **Family Tour** through the Sisi-Museum. At the end of the tour, the greatest attraction for children is trying on clothes from the imperial era, which allows them to transform themselves into miniature royalty. (Sat–Sun and public holidays 10:30 am and 2:30 pm, tours last one hour, to book tel: 01/533 75 70-15, admission: moderate).

The eagle and crown on the Neue Hofburg are symbols of imperial power

roof looks especially elegant seen from Kohlmarkt. Emperor Franz Joseph was also responsible for the **Neue Hofburg** (New Hofburg).

Since the end of World War I, the Hofburg has no longer needed to house an emperor and his 1,000-strong corps of servants. The various wings now contain government and commercial offices, private apartments and conference rooms – and the Lipizzaners' stables. The Hofburg lives on.

TAKING A BREAK

From the **Café Spanische Reitschule** (Michaeler-kuppel entrance) you can watch the Lipizzaner going to the morning's work.

➕ 192 C3 🚇 Herrengasse
🚋 Tram 1, 2, D, J Burgring, Bus 2A, 3A Hofburg
❓ www.hofburg-wien.at

Kaiserappartements, Silberkammer, Sisi-Museum
☎ (01) 533 75 70 🕐 Daily 9–5; Jul–Aug 9–5:30 💶 Expensive

Schatzkammer
☎ (01) 525 24-0 🕐 Wed–Mon 10–6 💶 Expensive

Burgkapelle
☎ (010) 533 99 27 🕐 Mon–Thu 11–3, Fri until 1 💶 Inexpensive

Prunksaal Nationalbibliothek
✉ Wien 1, Josefsplatz 1, 1st floor ☎ (01) 534 10-0 🕐 May–Oct daily 10–4, Thu until 7; Nov–Apr daily 10–2, Thu until 7 💶 Moderate
❓ www.onb.ac.at

HOFBURG: INSIDE INFO

Top tips From mid-September to the end of June you can hear the world-famous **Wiener Sängerknaben** (Vienna Boys' Choir) sing at Sunday Mass in the Burgkapelle, accompanied by members of the Staatsoper choir and orchestra. Reservations are essential (fax 01/533 99 27-75), but unsold tickets can also be bought on Friday at the Burgkapelle box office.

5 Kohlmarkt and Graben

Kohlmarkt and Graben are, together with Kärntner Strasse, the most elegant streets in Vienna, well worth a gentle stroll. The ever-changing face of the the city is also evident here: in recent years many stylish and sophisticated stores have been replaced by multinational chains – and the exquisite outlets of famous luxury brands.

Graben

Graben (which means "ditch") is not just an expensive strip, it also has historical associations. Indeed, the Romans built a broad defensive ditch here, which the Babenberger rulers filled in around 1200 during their expansions of the city. English soldiers from the imprisoned King Richard the Lionheart' entourage are said to have been brought in to help with the work – but this may just be a historic myth.

Graben was already a shopping street in the Middle Ages. They didn't sell expensive jewellery then, as they do now, but bread, meat and vegetables. Since 1993 the centre of activity has been the **Dreifaltigkeitssäule** (Trinity Column) which still dominates Graben. During the plague of 1679 some 100,000 Viennese died, and Emperor Leopold I recommended

A lively scene round the Dreifaltigkeitssäule on Graben

the construction of a memorial column. Lodovico Burnacini created the splendid column, on which the Holy Trinity surmounts a mountain of clouds.

In the baroque era Graben became an urban centre; palaces were built and coffee-houses opened. The only survivor from that time is the **Palais Bartolotti-Partenfeld** (Graben 11), built by Johann Lukas von Hildebrandt in 1720 as an early apartment block.

The buildings which you see now down both sides of Graben mostly date from the 19th and 20th centuries. Otto Wagner's **Ankerhaus** (Graben 10) is especially worth a look. The upper floor with the glass roof extension was the home of Friedensreich Hundertwasser (1928–2000), the Austrian artist known for his bold, revolutionary architecture.

Graben
seduces with
its stylish
shops

Kohlmarkt

The history of Kohlmarkt also extends back to the Romans. It was on the trade route which crossed Limessstrasse at Michaelerplatz. In the Middle Ages the Viennese could get their supplies of wood and charcoal here, hence the name, meaning "coal market". The large Michaelerhaus (Kohlmarkt 11), where the young Joseph Haydn had a garret room, dates from the baroque era.

Today the pedestrianized Kohlmarkt is Vienna's showcase of absolute luxury. Here all the famous designer brands have their flagship stores, for example Armani (Kohlmarkt 3), Gucci (Kohlmarkt 4), Chanel (Kohlmarkt 5) and Louis Vuitton (Kohlmarkt 6), the coffee-roaster and delicatessen Meinl am Graben (➤ 88) and the legendary patisserie Demel (➤ 90) with its unforgettable gâteaux and pastries.

Trzeniewski's
snacks are
legendary,
and not just
with ladies
who lunch

TAKING A BREAK

Trzeniewski (Dorotheergasse 1) has the best fillings for sandwiches in town. In summer you can eat a light snack (including bacon and egg!) at a table outside.

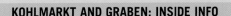

✚ 192/193 C/D3 🚇 Stephansplatz 🚌 Bus 2A, 3A Habsburgergasse

KOHLMARKT AND GRABEN: INSIDE INFO

Top tips In the narrow passage between Michaelerplatz and Habsburgergasse you'll come across an unexpected relic from medieval Vienna: a 1494 **limestone relief of the Mount of Olives** and a 1430 **Man of Sorrows**.

Hidden gem Whether you need to or not, make sure you go down into the public toilets in Graben. Wilhelm Beetz's 1904 walnut wood and Venetian glass interior is a real stunner!

⑦ Kapuzinergruft

The Viennese Imperial Crypt under the Kapuzinerkirche is a striking testimonial of the passing of the Habsburg dynasty. Buried here are 146 members of this aristocratic family and more than three centuries of Austrian history.

A steep flight of steps leads down to the imperial vaults; written above the entrance is the word "Silentium". This request for silence is a reminder that the last resting place of the Habsburgs is consecrated ground. In 1617 Empress Anna ordered that a Capuchin monastery and a burial-place for her and her husband, Emperor Matthias, be built within the city walls. In 1633 the mortal remains of the founders were buried in the Imperial Crypt. Since then a further 144 perople have found here their last resting-place, conscientiously watched over by the Capuchin brothers. The dead include 12 emperor and 19 empresses and queens.

Emperor Karl VI's tomb

The Changing Cult of the Dead

The individual rooms reflect their time – as is evident from the bare "Founders' Crypt", the baroque, theatrical "Maria Theresa Crypt" and the simple "New Crypt", started in 1960. Particularly impressive in the mausoleum is the **Prunksarkophag von Maria Theresia und Franz Stephan** (Sumptuous Sarcophagus of Maria Theresa and Franz Stefan), adorned with bas-reliefs and designee by the imperial couple themselves. Only one non-Habsburg is buried here: Countess Caroline Fuchs-Mollardt, the Empress's tutor.

The unadorned copper coffin of Maria Theresa's son and successor, Joseph II, illustrates clearly the changing attitudes from baroque era to the Enlightenment.

The Kapuzinergruft has been frequently extended. In 1908 Emperor Franz Joseph had a suitable mausoleum built in the monastery's cellars for himself, his spouse Elisabeth and Crown Prince Rudolf. The most recent burial here was of Empress Zita, the wife of the last Austrian emperor, Karl I.

Habsburg Hearts

For three centuries the Habsburgs have been laid to rest in accordance with their own particular ritual. The corpses were opened up, the hearts were placed in silver goblets kept in th

Herzgruft (Hearts Crypt) in Augustinerkirche, their innards were stored in the Herzogsgruft (Dukes' Crypt) deep under the Stephansdom, and only their embalmed bodies were laid to rest in the Kapuzinergruft.

TAKING A BREAK

Just a few steps from the Kapuzinergruft is **Culinarium Österreich Haus** (Neuer Markt 10–11) which serves many Austrian specialities.

➕ 193 D3 ✉ Wien 1, Tegetthoffstrasse 2 ☎ (01) 512 68 53/16 🕐 Daily 9:30–3:30
🚇 Stephansplatz 🚌 Bus 1A, 2A , 3A Stephansplatz 💶 Moderate 🔗 www.kaisergruft.at

KAPUZINERGRUFT: INSIDE INFO

Top tips Ask the Capuchin monk at the entrance whether any **groups or school classes** are currently visiting the crypt. The general level of noise is not conducive to the nature of the place; just return later and enjoy the memorials in peace and quiet.

Hidden gems Take your time while studying **Maria Theresa's sarcophagus**. The details and carvings are a unique symbol of the struggle between Death and the power of a determined ruling family set on continuance.
• Have a look at the **display case by the entrance**. The Capuchin monks have recently begun to exhibit here 12 objects from their treasury, such as reliquaries or a rock-crystal cross.

8 The Albertina

The Palais Albertina, in the historic centre of Vienna, was an unattractive sight for many decades. But the palace, which houses one of the largest collections of drawings in the world, was lavishly renovated and eventually reopened in March 2003. Since then, the Albertina has become a shining light in Vienna's new museum landscape, beating all visitor records.

The Albertina has been reborn in splendour and glory. Hans Hollein's bold wing-shaped roof, the much-debated Soravia Wing, the glass-and-steel lift which rises 11m (12 yards) from street level to the entrance, the escalator and the remodelled

The Albertina in renewed splendour

entrance: it's all very striking architecture, which continues in the interior. Visitors come first to a marble-clad anteroom, then through the foyer, dressed in Travertine limestone, into the Harriet Hartmann Court, where the ticket-counters and the entrances to the elegant restaurant and the stylishly furnished shop are situated.

Eighteen Newly Resplendent Rooms

The main stairway leads up to the showcase rooms. For the first time in 100 years, these 18 Habsburg rooms have been restored to their original glory. The smaller rooms of the **Herrenseite** (Gentlemen's Side), from the Goldkabinett (Golden Gallery) to the Billardzimmer (Billiard Room), are decorated in the style of Louis XVI. The **Damenseite** (Ladies' Side), on the other hand, with its Musensaal (Hall of the Muses) and Audienzsaal (Audience Chamber), is pure classicism.

The palace took its present form essentially at the end of the 18th and start of the 19th centuries, when Albert, Duke of Sachsen-Teschen, and his wife, Archduchess Marie Christine,

The high point of the "Ladies side" is the Hall of the Muses

the favourite daughter of Maria Theresa, had it remodelled to the designs of Louis de Montoyer. The classical parts come from the next owner, Archduke Karl, who defeated Napoleon in the Battle of Aspern (1809). He gave the commission to Joseph Kornhäusel.

Among new additions are the **White Cube** hall, erected in the bastion for exhibitions of modern art, and the **Propter-Homines-Halle** on the first floor with about ten equal-sized rooms. The **Pfeilerhalle** (Pillar Hall) attached to the portico serves as a third exhibition hall.

The exhibitions held in the renovated Albertina, above all the splendid Albrecht Dürer exhibition in 2003, have proved to be real magnets for the public. In its first nine months alone, around 800,000 visitors came. Interesting as these exhibits were, the treasures which cannot be on permanent display because of their sensitivity to light are just as valuable: 65,000 drawings and around a million prints. The architectural collections contains 25,000 plans, sketches and models, and the Albertina's photographic collection gives Austria, for the first time, a centre for historical and contemporary photography.

TAKING A BREAK

The Albertina's very elegant **restaurant** is a decent place for a light snack.

➕ 192 C2 ✉ Wien 1, Albertinaplatz 3 ☎ (01) 534 83 🕐 Daily 10–6, Wed until 9 🚇 Oper 🚊 Tram 1, 2, D, J Oper, Bus 3A Albertinaplatz 💰 Expensive 🌐 www.albertina.at

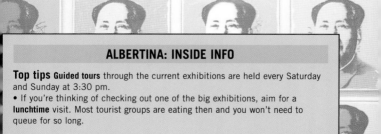

ALBERTINA: INSIDE INFO

Top tips Guided tours through the current exhibitions are held every Saturday and Sunday at 3:30 pm.
• If you're thinking of checking out one of the big exhibitions, aim for a **lunchtime** visit. Most tourist groups are eating then and you won't need to queue for so long.

At Your Leisure

🔢 Spanische Hofreitschule

If you hear the noise of hooves between the Stallburg and the Hofburg, it's bound to be the Lipizzaner horses. In 1580 the imperial stud, which bred horses for riding displays, was founded in the village of Lipica, in what is now Slovenia. Today the Lipizzaner are the oldest breed of show horses in Europe, characterized by perfect physique, intelligence and graceful strength. In the magnificent Winter Riding School visitors can watch as 64 stallions are trained every morning.

🚩 192 C3 ✉ Wien 1, Michaelerplatz 1
☎ (01) 533 90 31 🅖 Visitor Centre
(entrance Michaelerkuppel) Tue–Sat
9–4: tickets and programme for
morning training with music (Tue–Sat
10–noon) and other performances
🅖 Herrengasse 🚌 Bus 2A Michaelerplatz 💰 Expensive 📶 www.srs.at

🔢 Michaelerkirche

This church, where Mozart's *Requiem* had its first performance shortly after his death, combines Romanesque, Gothic and baroque elements. Large parts of the triple-aisled, columned basilica date from the 13th century, as does the lower part of the slender tower, which points like a finger into the sky. The last big alterations to the church came in the 18th century. The imposing stucco relief *The Fall of the Angels*, created by Karl Georg Merville in 1782, is particularly impressive. Between 1631 and 1784, around 4,000 people were buried in the catacombs. Today, a macabre display of hundreds of painted coffins and mummified corpses can be seen there, some clad in baroque frock coats and wigs.

🚩 192 C3 ✉ Wien 1, Michaelerplatz
☎ (01) 533 80 00 🅖 Guided Crypt Tours
Mon–Thu 11 am, 3 pm, Fri 11 am, 1 pm
🅖 Herrengasse
🚌 Bus 2A Michaelerplatz

🔢 Loos-Haus

Hardly any building in Vienna has provoked such heated debate as the Loos-Haus on Michaelerplatz. For this office and residential block, built in 1910–11 for the gentlemen's tailors Goldmann & Salaatsch, Adolf Loos designed it without decoration and

The performances of the Lipizzaner are a great tourist attraction

Angels feature prominently inside and outside of the Michaelerkirche

ornament. The Viennese called the building, whose windows don't even have a frame, the "house with no eyebrows". Emperor Franz Joseph hated the Loos-Haus, which for him stood for a new, sober age that he no longer understood. As often as possible he avoided leaving the Hofburg by the Michaelerplatz exit so he would not have to see this eyesore. In 1989 the Loos-Haus was renovated for the Raiffeisenbank.

🔢 192 C3 ✉ Wien 1, Michaelerplatz 3 🚇 Herrengasse 🚌 Bus 2A Michaelerplatz

6 Peterskirche

What is probably Vienna's finest baroque church stands on the site of an earlier, 4th-century church, which might have been the city's first. It had been constructed from parts of a barracks for the Roman camp. The present Peterskirche, designed by Gabriele Montani, was begun in 1703 on the orders of Emperor Leopold I and completed in 1733 by Johann Lukas von Hildebrandt. Seen from Graben, the church with its great green dome and two corner towers looks especially striking. The most impressive parts of the interior are Michael Rotmayr's frescoes on the dome ceiling and Matthias Steindl's richly decorated pulpit.

🔢 193 D3 ✉ Wien 1, Petersplatz 🚇 Stephansplatz 🚌 Bus 1A, 2A, 3A Petersplatz

9 Dorotheum

The Dorotheum, affectionately known as *pfandl* (Deposit) to the locals, is a Viennese curiosity. Founded as a Pfandamt (official pawnbroker) in 1707 to protect the people from usurers, it moved in 1788 to the abandoned Dorotheer convent. About 100 years ago it was given its own magnificent palace in Dorotheergasse. Today it is the largest auction house in the German-speaking world, hosting some 600 auctions each year. In a suite of display rooms collectors can find whatever their heart desires. You can buy the goods direct or at auction. "Aunt Dorothy" has long been seen as a good opportunity to turn silver spoons or an inherited worn-out Persian rug into cash. Minor auctions, catering for all tastes and wallet sizes, are held every Sunday.

🚩 192 C3 ✉ Wien 1, Dorotheergasse 17 ☎ (01) 515 60 🕐 Mon–Fri
10–6, Sat 9–5 🚇 Stephansplatz
🚌 Bus 3A Plankengasse
❓ www.doro
theum.com

🔟 Josefsplatz

Because of its
severe beauty and
unity of style,
this square is
often described
as one of the
finest in Europe.
Its qualities
can be fully
appreciated now
that it is free of
traffic. In the middle of
the square stands the equestrian
statue of the reforming Emperor
Joseph II, created in 1795–1807 by
the Tyrolese sculptor Franz Anton
Zauner. On the plinth are reliefs
showing the Emperor with Europa
and Mercury, symbols of travel and
trade. The backdrop to the square is
formed by the gorgeous baroque
façade of the Nationalbibliothek
(National Library), adjoined right
and left by the side wings and the
ballrooms.

🚩 192 C3 🚇 Stephansplatz
🚌 Bus 3A Plankengasse

🔟 Burggarten

This park, originally called the
Kaisergarten, was reserved for the
emperor's family and not opened to
the public until 1919. Laid out in

**In the Dorotheum many a collector's item
goes under the hammer**

front of the Neue Hofburg and the
Palmenhaus, it is a good example of
garden landscaping as well
as a splendid green oasis
in the middle of the
city. You can relax by
the great lake with its
ducks, enjoy the
open space and
admire the lead,
marble and bronze
statues of Mozart and
the emperors Franz I
and Franz Joseph I.
As in all of Vienna's
public parks, though,
dogs are not allowed!

🚩 192 C2 ✉ Wien 1, Burgring
🚇 Oper 🚋 Tram 1, 2, D, J, Bus 57A
Opernring

🔟 Palmenhaus

"A swan-song of Habsburg greatness"
is how the Palm House in the Burggarten is often described. In fact, it
is the last large orangery in Europe.
The court architect Friedrich
Ohmann built it in 1901, a time
when it was fashionable to replace
nature with "urban greenery". The
bold construction of steel and glass
was restored a few years ago. Now
it houses one of the city's most
attractive restaurants (▶ 89) and
the Schmetterlingshaus (Butterfly
House), where, with hundreds of
butterflies, you can experience the
magic of a tropical rainforest.

🚩 192 C2 ✉ Wien 1, Burggarten
☎ (010) 533 85 70 🕐 Apr–Oct
Mon–Fri 10–4:45, Sat–Sun, public
holidays until 6:15 pm; Nov–Mar daily
10–3:45 🚇 Oper 🚋 Tram 1, 2, D, J,
Bus 57A Opernring 💶 Moderate

Where to...
Eat and Drink

Prices

Prices are given for one person, excluding drinks.
€ under 12 euros **€€** 12–25 euros **€€€** over 25 euros

Restaurants

Barbaro €€

This fine Italian place with three floors on Neuer Markt has that "city feeling". The cantina is in the cellar, the bistro on the ground floor, and the spacious bar and sophisticated restaurant on the first floor. The food is Mediterranean-Italian, and one of its signature dishes is lamb with beans.

🚹 193 D3 🖂 Wien 1, Neuer Markt 8
🕾 (01) 955 25 25 🕙 Bistro daily 8 am–midnight, Cantina daily 6 pm–midnight, Bar-Restaurant daily 11:30 am–4 am
🚇 Stephansplatz 🚌 Bus 1A, 2A, 3A Stephansplatz

Do&Co Albertina €€

Two principal materials were used for this restaurant's furnishings: dark jacaranda wood hewn from a single tree and East Anatolian red Levantine marble. Their warm colours give the place an agreeable atmosphere. The marble bar is also unusual – customers sit facing each other. The food is refined Viennese cuisine and international dishes – you can watch it being prepared in the open kitchen. In summer, the large terrace looking towards the Burggarten is particularly beautiful.

🚹 192 C2 🖂 Wien 1, Albertinaplatz 1
🕾 (01) 532 96 69 🕙 Daily 10 am–midnight, hot food served all day
🚇 Oper 🚋 Tram 1, 2, D, J Oper, Bus 3A Albertinaplatz

Do&Co Stephansplatz €€€

This exclusive restaurant high up on the seventh floor in the Haas Haus is already a classic. The food – refined Viennese and international cuisine and fish as at the Albertina branch – is delicious. But again the best part is the really unique view of the Stephansdom from the terrace. There's a tapas bar on the third floor.

🚹 193 D3 🖂 Wien 1, Stephansplatz 12
🕾 (01) 535 39 69 🕙 Daily noon–3, 6–midnight 🚇 Stephansplatz 🚌 Bus 1A, 2A, 3A Stephansplatz

Ephesus €€

This fine Turkish restaurant, very close to Graben, has a wide range of Levantine and Turkish specialities, including sea bass, lamb and *huslama*.

The delicately cooked food tastes even better in the garden.

🚹 192 C3 🖂 Wien 1, Bräunerstrasse 8
🕾 (01) 533 90 91 🕙 Mon–Sat 11 am–midnight 🚇 Stephansplatz 🚌 Bus 1A, 2A, 3A Stephansplatz

Esterhàzykeller €

Steep stairs lead down into subterranean Vienna. During the Turkish siege, the defenders of Vienna took comfort in wine in this cellar with its earthy atmosphere. Good plain cooking, including roasts and dumplings, and outstanding wines from the cellars of the Esterházy castle in Eisenstadt.

🚹 192 C4 🖂 Wien 1, Haarhof 1
🕾 (01) 533 34 82 🕙 Mon–Fri 11 am–11 pm, Sat–Sun 4 pm–11 pm (hot food until 10 pm) 🚌 Herrengasse
🚌 Bus 2A, 3A Herrengasse

Göttweiger Stiftskeller €

This pub is one of the few remnants of Old Vienna. There's not a trace of design or fashion, and that's its attraction. It has a long bar-counter, a function room and in summer even a few tables outside. The Mayrwöger family welcome guests with generous helpings, and because of the rapid turnover the food is always fresh. The good plain Austrian fare is accompanied, as is appropriate for a Stiftskeller, by fine wines.

⊞ 193 D3 ⊠ Wien 1, Spiegelgasse 9 ☎ 512 78 17 ⏰ Mon–Fri 8 am–11 pm (hot food until 10 pm), Sat until 4 pm Ⓤ Stephansplatz Ⓑ Bus 1A, 2A, 3A Stephansplatz

Ilona Stüberl €

This small local tavern is ideally situated close to Stephansplatz but in a quiet side street. Visitors who look forward to superb Hungarian specialities, including hearty stuffed cabbage, various sorts of goulash and chicken paprika. There's a small garden for summer.

⊞ 192 C3 ⊠ Wien 1, Bräunerstrasse 2 ☎ (01) 533 90 29 ⏰ Daily noon–11 pm (hot food until 10 pm) Ⓤ Stephansplatz Ⓑ Bus 1A, 2A, 3A Stephansplatz

Levante €

The high quality of the food at this large Turkish restaurant means that it is usually crammed full. Turkish specialities, including delicate hors d'oeuvres, lamb kebabs and large vegetable salads, are always fresh and smell delicious. They also do a take-away service.

There's a counter with Viennese pastries and gâteaux.

⊞ 193 D2 ⊠ Wien 1, Maysedergasse 2 ☎ (01) 512 34 58 ⏰ Daily 10:30 am–11 pm Ⓤ Oper Ⓑ Tram 1, 2, D, J, Bus 3A Oper

Meinl am Graben €€€

This restaurant, based inside Vienna's best delicatessen, is an absolute must for gourmets. It has an enormous selection, and the standard of the food and drink is first-rate. But what makes it so pleasant is the relaxed atmosphere.

⊞ 192 C3 ⊠ Wien 1, Graben 19 ☎ (01) 532 33 34–35 ⏰ Mon–Fri 8 am–midnight, Sat 8:30 am–midnight (hot food until midnight) Ⓤ Herrengasse Ⓑ Bus 3A Bognergasse

Mörwald im Ambassador €€€

This stylish modern restaurant in the Ambassador hotel is a gourmet's delight and a favourite place for sophisticated business lunches. The cooking is imaginative and the selection of wines extensive.

Marktrestaurant Rosenberger €

You can eat well and inexpensively in this massive restaurant's two lower ground floors. The centre is set out like a marketplace, where you can select your meal yourself. Or you can choose at your table from a selection including "Vienna coffee-house", "summer house" or "Grandma's cooking". The menu lists Austrian favourites, Hungarian goulash, American steaks and Italian pasta dishes, and there's a

separate counter with Viennese pastries and gâteaux.

⊞ 193 D3 ⊠ Wien 1, Neuer Markt 5 ☎ (01) 96 16 11 61 ⏰ Mon–Sat noon–11 pm (hot food noon–3, 6–11 pm) Ⓤ Stephansplatz Ⓑ Bus 1A, 2A, 3A Stephansplatz

Novelli €€€

This high-class Italian restaurant is opposite the Café Bräunerhof in an old palace. The interior is stylish and the menu impressive, especially the fine pasta and fish specialities. The Novelli has even published a book of its most popular recipes. The large garden brings a touch of Florence to the city centre.

⊞ 192 C3 ⊠ Wien 1, Bräunerstrasse 11 ☎ (01) 513 42 00–0 ⏰ Mon–Sat 11 am–1 am (hot food noon–2, 6–11 pm) Ⓤ Stephansplatz Ⓑ Bus 2A, 3A Habsburgergasse

Orpheus €€

This Greek restaurant is almost a Viennese institution. The lamb and fish specialities from Crete are invariably of good quality and served in pleasant surroundings.

It's particularly pleasant sitting in the garden in front of the house, and in the evening the mood in the cellar vaults is convivial. They have a popular Sunday brunch and great children's entertainments.

➕ 193 D3 ⌖ Wien 1, Spiegelgasse 10 ☏ (01) 512 38 88 ⏰ Mon–Thu, Sun 11:30 am–midnight, Fri–Sat noon–midnight (hot food until 11 pm) Ⓤ Stephansplatz 🚌 Bus 1A, 2A, 3A Stephansplatz

Palmenhaus im Burggarten €€€

The light-flooded Jugendstil ambience of this restaurant makes it one of the most beautiful in the city, and the menus in café, brasserie and bar are in no way inferior to the elegant setting. The choice includes fine Viennese and Mediterranean dishes and a well-selected wine-list, chiefly from France and Austria, which changes each month.

➕ 192 C2 ⌖ Wien 1, Burggarten, entrance behind the Albertina ☏ (01) 533 10 33 ⏰ Daily 10 am–2 am (hot food noon until midnight); Nov–Mar Mon, Thu closed Ⓤ Oper 🚃 Tram 1, 2, D, J Oper, Bus 3A Albertinaplatz

Sky-Restaurant €€

This stylish modern restaurant on the top floor of Steffl's department store has Viennese classics such as *tafelspitz* (boiled beef) and international food, influenced by Asian and Mediterranean cuisine. From the broad terrace there's a superb view over the roofs of the city centre towards the Stephansdom.

➕ 193 D3 ⌖ Wien 1, Kärntnerstrasse 19 ☏ (01) 513 17 12 ⏰ Mon–Sat noon–3, 6–1 am (hot food until 11 pm) Ⓤ Stephansplatz 🚌 Bus 1A, 2A, 3A Stephansplatz

Yugetsu €€€

"Japan in Vienna" extends over two floors. The ground floor has the largest selection of sushi in Vienna, on the first floor is the gastronomic experience of *teppanyaki* cuisine. On weekends and public holidays there's a self-service sushi bar. The food is interesting and delicate.

➕ 192 C2 ⌖ Wien 1, Führichgasse 10 ☏ (01) 512 27 20 ⏰ Daily noon–3, 6–midnight (hot food noon–2:30, 6–11 pm) Ⓤ Oper 🚃 Tram 1, 2, D, J, Bus 3A Oper

Zum Schwarzen Kameel €€

The consistent quality of its food has made this smart restaurant, which dates back to 1618, a favourite. In the front rooms there's a delicatessen and somewhere to enjoy snacks, such as the tasty filled rolls, and drink a glass of excellent wine from their own wine-merchant. The dining room has preserved its tasteful art deco style, with copper chandeliers, panelling and ceramic tiles.

➕ 192 C4 ⌖ Wien 1, Bognergasse 5 ☏ (01) 533 81 25 ⏰ Mon–Sat 8:30–midnight (hot food noon–2:30, 6–10:30) Ⓤ Herrengasse 🚌 Bus 3A Bognergasse

Cafés

Bräunerhof

In this legendary café, which was the favourite of Austrian writer Thomas Bernhard (1931–89), the style and atmosphere of the old Viennese coffee-house culture has survived. Antiques dealers from the neighbourhood come here for lunch, and it's a favourite spot for business meetings or a date. At weekends Trio Schelz plays live music.

➕ 192 C3 ⌖ Wien 1, Stallburggasse 2 ☏ (01) 512 38 93 ⏰ Mon–Fri 8 am–9 pm, Sat until 7 pm, Sun 10 am–7 pm Ⓤ Stephansplatz 🚌 Bus 2A, 3A Habsburgergasse

Café de l'Europe

This café, from which you have a front-row view of life on Graben, has a fresh and chic stylishness. It's a great place to sit and people-watch while you have a snack and a drink. The tea-room on the first floor is especially pleasant.

➕ 193 D3 ⌖ Wien 1, Graben 31 ☏ (01) 532 14 69 ⏰ Mon–Fri 7 am–midnight, Sat 7:30 am–midnight, Sun 9 am–midnight (food until 11 pm) Ⓤ Stephansplatz 🚌 Bus 1A, 2A, 3A Stephansplatz

Demel

This former confectioner to the imperial court, founded in 1786, creates the ultimate in Viennese *torten*. Demel has a varied history: recently it was taken over by Do&Co. A show bakery was built in the winter garden, and the Marzipan Museum in the basement displays examples of the confectioner's art, including elegant bonbon boxes from yesteryear. In the rooms on the side street Demel's sells its delicious sweetmeats – chocolates, sweets and candied violets.

📍 192 C3 ⬛ Wien 1, Kohlmarkt 14
📞 (01) 535 17 17 ⏰ Daily 10 am–7 pm
🚇 Herrengasse 🚌 Bus 2A, 3A Herrengasse

Griensteidl

This legendary literatis' café opposite the entrance to the Hofburg is now an elegant coffee-house with Thonet chairs of black wood, upholstered in red. It has an impressive selection of foods and international newspapers.

📍 192 C3 ⬛ Wien 1, Michaelerplatz 2
📞 (01) 535 26 92 17 ⏰ Daily 8 am–11:30 pm (hot food until 11 pm)
🚇 Herrengasse
🚌 Bus 2A, 3A Herrengasse

Hawelka

After 60 years, the legendary café lives on. Admittedly, where once artists and writers whiled away their nights, the shabby benches are now mainly occupied by tourists, but the atmosphere remains sensational and fresh jam dumplings are still served at 10 every night.

📍 192 C3 ⬛ Wien 1, Dorotheergasse 6
📞 (01) 512 82 30 ⏰ Mon, Wed–Sat 8 am–2 am, Sun 4 pm–2 am
🚇 Stephansplatz
🚌 Bus 1A, 2A, 3A Stephansplatz

Hofburg

This pretty café with its large terrace is in the Innerer Burghof, by the entrances to the imperial apartments, the Silberkammer and the Sisi-Museum. It has taken its culinary style from the emperor's taste – the *kaiserschmarren* (raisin pancakes) are excellent. For a snack, try a "Habs-Burger", if only for the name.

📍 192 C3 ⬛ Wien 1, Innerer Burghof 1
📞 (01) 241 00-0 ⏰ Daily 9 am–8 pm
🚇 Herrengasse 🚋 Tram 1, 2, D, J Burgring, Bus 2A, 3A Hofburg

Konditorei Lehmann

Situated in the middle of Graben, this traditional Viennese café is an ideal meeting-place for people with a sweet tooth. The house *torten* and pastries are first class, but smaller, more delicate snacks are also on offer. The garden is a great place to watch the busy life on Graben.

📍 192 C3 ⬛ Wien 1, Graben 12
📞 (01) 512 18 15 ⏰ Mon–Sat 8:30 am–7 pm 🚇 Stephansplatz
🚌 Bus 2A, 3A Graben-Petersplatz

Mozart

This coffee-house has a very long tradition, stretching back to 1794. In the Biedermeierzeit (early 19th century) it was pretty lively, as it was a favourite rendezvous for artists. One of Graham Greene's favourite haunts, it also features in *The Third Man*. Nowadays, because of its proximity to the Albertina and the Hofburg, it's an ideal place for visitors to take a break and imbibe the typical Viennese atmosphere.

📍 192 C2 ⬛ Wien 1, Albertinaplatz 2
📞 (01) 241 00–210 ⏰ Daily 9 am–midnight 🚇 Oper 🚋 Tram 1, 2, D, J Oper, Bus 3A Albertinaplatz

Yohm

It took a long time, but finally Yohm managed to defeat the bureaucrats and open a garden on Graben. Screened by glass, elegantly styled and protected from rain and sun by enormous awnings, this is a favourite place for the young and trendy. In addition to coffee and drinks the restaurant, a sister eatery to Indochine 21, serves Asian fusion cuisine of the highest quality.

📍 192 C3 ⬛ Wien 1, Graben
📞 (01) 533 29 00 ⏰ Daily 8 am–midnight 🚇 Stephansplatz
🚌 Bus 2A, 3A Graben-Petersplatz

Where to... Shop

Graben, Kohlmarkt and Kärntnerstrasse are the heart of the inner city, and there is plenty on offer for visitors who want to take a small piece of Vienna home with them. There are masses of opportunities to do this, ranging from the precious, glittering trinkets which, Marilyn Monroe told us, are "a girl's best friend", through retro-chic clothing or hippy design, to little mouth-watering chocolate sensations.

The shopping streets around the Stefansdom are ideal for buying small but elegant gift boxes, which could hold, bedded in velvet, an emerald ring from the jeweller's **Haban** (Graben 12 and Kärntner Strasse 2) or from **Heldwein** (Graben 13) or a Viennese Jugendstil brooch from **Siedler** (Kohlmarkt 3) or a

contemporary piece of jewellery from **Schullin** (Kohlmarkt 7) or **Skrein** (Spiegelgasse 5).

Somewhat larger gifts, but still typically Viennese treasures which would grace any home, can also be found here: delicate coffee-cups and complete dinner services decorated with roses from the porcelain-manufacturer **Augarten** (Stock-im-Eisen-Platz 3), wafer-thin glasses from **Lobmayr** (Kärntner Strasse 26), sparkling crystal glass items from **Swarovski** (Kärntner Strasse 8), exquisite household goods from **Rasper & Söhne** (Graben 15) and the finest table- or bed-linen from **Schwäbische Jungfrau** (Graben 26).

In recent years international luxury has also established itself in Kohlmarkt. Top designers and well-loved brands, such as **Cartier** (Kohlmarkt 1), **Armani** (Kohlmarkt 3), **Chanel** and **Gucci** (Kohlmarkt 5), **Louis Vuitton** (Kohlmarkt 16), **Ferragamo** (Kohlmarkt 7) and **Chopard** (Kohlmarkt 16), have all opened outlets here.

Knize (Graben 13) is a byword for gentlemen's outfitting. From the entrance on, the elegant shop is persuasively understated. The narrow door, designed by Alfred Loos, gives no hint that, on the first floor, suites of rooms await you, with creaking parquet floors, wardrobes, display cases and courteous, obliging staff. You certainly don't go to Knize to hunt around for a new sports jacket. You go to be fitted out with everything that a man of the world needs: made-to-measure suits, hand-made shirts, cashmere pullovers and accessories. Ladies are served in their shop next door.

But the epitome of ladies' fashion in Vienna is **Adlmüller** (Kärntner Strasse 41). The firm's reputation goes back to the time when the international fashion designer and couturier Fred Adlmüller would personally drape famous singers from the Staatsoper and society ladies in flowing evening dresses. Youthful, stylish fashion is also well represented in Vienna. The

most interesting shops include **Neumann** (Seilergasse 3) with fashions from Prada and many other international names, **Helmut Lang** (Seilergasse 6) and **Firis** (Bauernmarkt 9), who stock items from Belgian and Italian designers. Fans of elegant Italian handbags should head from the main Stephansdom door towards the Peterskirche: they will be in paradise with **Pitti's** trendy bags and numerous accessories (Gold-schmiedgasse 5). Shoes to match are sold close by, at **d'Ambrosio** (Jasomirgottstrasse 6). **Robert Horn** (Bräunerstrasse 7) is famous for leather goods. The internationally celebrated designer creates bags and purses in the classic aesthetic tradition of Alfred Loos.

The side streets off Graben have a timeless beauty and elegance. In the Dorotheergasse, Stallburggasse, Bräunerstrasse and Spiegelgasse one antiques shop follows another, their offerings ranging from baroque cabinets and Renaissance chests to superb carpets, pictures, lamps, porcelain – and above all magnificent antique jewellery. Elisabeth **Reichel** and Johann **Kilianowitsch's** shop (Dorotheergasse 14) is a hidden gem, selling exquisite Jugendstil and art deco Bakelite ornaments at reasonable prices.

Doblinger (Dorotheergasse 10), the antiques section of the Musikhaus, has first editions of Strauss, Lanner and Fahrbach, of the Wiener Schule and the Wiener Klassik. They also sell sacred and choral music.

The candied violets from **Demel** (Kohlmarkt 14), made famous by the unhappy empress Sisi, are an ideal souvenir – it doesn't get more elegant than that, or not much more, for the smallest-ever handmade sweets from **Altmann & Kühne** (Graben 30), in their little boxes with motifs from Viennese workshops, take a bit of beating. Confectionary is still traditionally crafted by hand here, according to century-old recipes.

Where to be... Entertained

In the daytime the main shopping streets of the inner city are very busy, but in the evening too there's a lot going on here. In a series of attractive bars, to the sounds of pleasant music, you can enjoy a cocktail or other elegant drink with a light snack.

Bars

The most famous bar is the tiny **Loos Bar** (Kärntner Durchgang 10, tel: 01/512 32 83, in summer daily noon–4 am, in winter Sun–Wed noon–4 am, Thu–Sat 11 am–5 am). Adolf Loos built this the "mother" of all American bars, in 1907, using mirrors to enlarge the small space optically. For a long time it was the symbol of the Viennese avant-garde in art and architecture. After a

varied, not always glorious, history it has regained its former splendour. They've even enlarged it with a little stand-up table out front.

The luxurious, sleek **Onyx Bar** (Stephansplatz 12, tel: 01/535 39 69, Mon–Sat 9 am–2 am) in the Haas Haus is one of Vienna's hippest hang-outs for arty types and real or would-be celebrities. It should also get points for its spectacular views of the beautifully illuminated Stephansdom. With your drinks you can enjoy tasty snacks and dishes from the Far East.

The **Reiss-Bar** (Marco-d'Aviano-Gasse 1, tel: 01/512 71 98, Sun–Thu 11 am–2 am, Fri–Sat 10 am–3 am), with its acclaimed architecture, is the city's "champagne spot". Here people come to "see and be seen". Whet your appetite with tasty morsels such as *tramezzini* (sandwiches), caviar and oysters.

One of the trendiest places at the moment is the **Sky-Bar** (Kärntner Strasse 19, tel: 01/513 17 12, Mon–Sat 11:30 am–4 am, Sun 6 pm–3 am)

on the top floor of Steffl's department store. The large, circular bar has live music on Tuesdays and Thursdays from 9 pm. The terrace, with its views of Kärntner Strasse and the Stephansdom, is a very pleasant spot. Great cocktails are served by friendly staff.

The **Europa Bar** (Neuer Markt 3, tel: 01/515 94–0, 11 am–1 am) is a great place to relax after the buzz of the city. Its modern ambience and dignified design create a metropolitan atmosphere which is ideal for a sophisticated rendezvous after nightfall.

Casino

If you want to try your luck at the tables, then the Viennese **Casino** (Kärntner Strasse 4, tel: 01/512 48 36, daily 3 pm–4 am) is the place for you. There's roulette and blackjack, stud poker and slot machines – perhaps you'll win enough cash for a shopping excursion along Kohlmarkt and Graben.

The Western Ringstrasse

Getting Your Bearings

Six kilometres (3¾ miles) long, 60m (65 yards) across and flanked by magnificent monuments, palaces and parks, the Ringstrasse is a spacious grand boulevard that encircles the heart of the inner city. The western section is the most interesting. This is the home of those temples to art, the Staatsoper and the Burgtheater, and of museums with unique treasures. And the museum district is a vibrant artistic quarter.

The Ringstrasse was built when, in the mid-19th century, Vienna began its rise to the status of a city. A work of art in itself and unique in Europe, it includes 150 public buildings, parks and 650 grand apartment blocks for the newly rich of the industrial and financial worlds. The great thing about the Ringstrasse is that it is still virtually intact, a mirror of imperial splendour.

Nowadays, though, it's no fun for pedestrians on the Ringstrasse, affectionately called "Ring". Day and night thousands of cars flow down the city's main traffic artery, jamming up especially behind *fiaker* (horse-drawn cabs). But provided you don't try to cross the Ringstrasse other than at designated pedestrian crossings, you can usually make good headway on foot along the side lanes.

Page 93: The neo-Gothic splendour of the Rathaus

A place with a past: Heldenplatz

The Burg-theater, one of the most famous German-language theatres

★ Don't Miss

1 Staatsoper ➤ 98
3 Kunst- und Naturhis-torisches Museum ➤ 100
6 Burgtheater ➤ 102
12 Museumsquartier ➤ 103

At Your Leisure

2 Akademie der bildenden Künste ➤ 106
4 Heldenplatz ➤ 106
5 Volksgarten ➤ 107
7 Mölker Bastei ➤ 107
8 Universität ➤ 107
9 Börse ➤ 108
10 Rathaus ➤ 108
11 Parlament ➤ 108

This is a busy day and you might like to return another time to appreciate all the sights. Move from one splendid building to another, then immerse yourself in the wonderful world of Vienna's museums and the lively artists' district, Museumsquartier, a great place to stroll, shop, eat and drink.

The Western Ringstrasse in a Day

9:00 am

Start your tour of the Ringstrasse buildings in style, with the **1** **Staatsoper** (➤ 98). Walk round the magnificent opera house and pause awhile on the highest level, over a coffee in the grand Sacher Hotel (➤ 110). On your way to the **2** **Akademie der bildenden Künste** (Fine Art Academy, ➤ 106) you'll pass the Goethe and Schiller memorials. The Akademie, designed in a sumptuous style based on the Italian high Renaissance, is very striking. You might like to look at the building from the inside, even if you haven't the time to visit every room.

10:30 am

Cross the Ringstrasse to go to the **3** Kunsthistorisches Museum (Museum of Fine Arts, above; ➤ 100). Don't rush from one room to the

next, but first take in the glamour and splendour of the building itself. And when you've visited the Brueghels on the first floor, pause for a snack in the Kuppelsaal (domed hall). In the **3** **Naturhistorisches Museum** (Natural History Museum) (➤ 101) immediately opposite the Fine Arts Museum you can revel in the wonderful atmosphere of past times. The original furnishings and the numerous display cases and exhibits are a world of their own.

12:30 pm

After visiting the two museums, cross the Ringstrasse and go through the Äusseres Burgtor to the **4** **Heldenplatz** (➤ 106). Continue into the **5** **Volksgarten** (➤ 107), and drop a curtsey to the marble "Sisi" memorial. Take a seat and breathe in the scent of the roses. How about lunch in the **6** **Burgtheater** (above; ➤ 102). The stylish surroundings of the famous theatre make eating and drinking in the Vestibül restaurant a pleasure.

2:00 pm

Stroll across Rathausplatz to the **11** **Parlament** (➤ 108) and then across Maria-Theresien-Platz to the **12** **Museumsquartier** (➤ 103). Don't let the baroque façade of the Museumsquartier put you off. The ancient walls conceal a very modern, state-of-the-art museum. Walk round the Museum Moderner Kunst (Museum of Modern Art), and then enjoy a restorative coffee in the newly reopened Glacis Beisl.

4:30 pm

If you still have sufficient energy, the paintings by Egon Schiele in the Museumsquartier (left) are well worth a visit. Otherwise, just head back to your hotel and relax before the evening's entertainments.

7:00 pm

If you haven't bought any advance tickets for a visit to the Burgtheater or Staatsoper, just ask your hotel porter. You never know, he may just "happen" to have some tickets stashed away.

❶ Staatsoper

The Vienna Staatsoper, one of the most illustrious opera houses in the world, was criticized right from the start for looking like a railway station. But it's the music that counts, and Vienna's reputation as a musical centre is founded on this "House on the Ring". It has since become a part of the Austrian national identity.

The new Imperial Court Opera was designed to be the first monumental building on the Ringstrasse. Begun in 1863, public opinion had "demolished" the neo-Romantic building, before it had even opened in May 1869. Its loggia, side arcades and metal tunnel roof provoked such devastating

criticism that the interior designer, Eduard von der Nüll (1812–68), took his own life. And the engineer responsible for the construction, August von Siccardsburg (1812–68), was so distressed that he died a few weeks later of a heart attack.

In World War II, bombing raids reduced the Staatsoper to rubble and ashes, along with all its stage sets and costumes. After seven years of restoration work, its reopening on 5 November, 1955, with a performance of Beethoven's *Fidelio*, amounted to something akin to an unofficial celebration of the restoration of Vienna's 19th century splendour.

For the Opera Ball, the Staatsoper is transformed into one vast ballroom

Art of the Highest Calibre

From the start, the Vienna Staatsoper set the very highest standards, with top international performers, producers and

You can buy tickets on the street but they'll probably cost more than at the box office

set-designers. The list of conductors has always included important musicians, for example Gustav Mahler (1897-1907), Richard Strauss (1919–24), Herbert von Karajan (1956–64) and Claudio Abbado (1986–91). Mind you, even the most celebrated conductors soon found out that there's no pleasing a Viennese audience. They all had to learn that quibbling and intriguing is one of the secret passions of music lovers here. If they revere you, however, they'll praise you to the skies – some world-class artists were lucky enough to have learnt that too.

Impressive repertoire

The Vienna Staatsoper is one of the leading opera venues in the world. Performances are given on 300 days a year. The repertoire comprises some 50 operas and 20 ballets, including works like Verdi's *Aida*, Mozart's *Magic Flute*, Wagner's *Ring* cycle and Puccini's *La Bohème*.

Once a year, on the last Thursday of Fasching (carnival), the stage and stalls of the Staatsoper are transformed into one gigantic dance floor. Then the flower-bedecked hall is the scene of the most glittering event of the season, the Opera Ball. The "night of nights" is, what's more, a night when everyone's a winner. On this evening the Staatsoper actually makes a profit.

TAKING A BREAK

Have a quick espresso in the **Aida** café opposite the opera (Opernring 7). The tiny coffee-tables will transport you back to the 1970s!

🚇 192 C2 ✉ Wien 1, Opernring 2 ☎ (01) 514 44-0 🚇 Karlsplatz
🚊 Tram 1, 2, D, J, 62, 65 Karlsplatz 🌐 www.staatsoper.at

STAATSOPER: INSIDE INFO

Top tips You can only see the interior of the Staatsoper on a **40-minute guided tour** (admission: moderate). The starting times depend on whether rehearsals are currently being held; they are advertised on a board at the entrance. In July and August there are six tours a day. (Booking tel: 01/514 44-26 06, fax: 01/514 44-26 26)

3 Kunst- and Natur-historisches Museum

On the outside the Museum of Art History (KHM) and the Natural History Museum (NHM) are identical twins. Each structure has four floors, two courtyards, a large octagonal domed tower and four smaller turrets. But inside the two buildings are totally different.

Both imposing museums were built by Karl von Hasenauer and Gottfried Semper in Renaissance style. They are identical – with one minor exception: whereas the Fine Arts Museum is surmounted by a statue of Pallas Athene, the Greek patron goddess of art and science, the Natural History Museum has the figure of the Greek sun god Helios.

Maria Theresa and her retinue are enthroned between the two large museums

Fine Arts

The entrance itself is an experience. The stairway and the domed marble hall with the cafeteria are of unsurpassed grandeur and elegance. Antonio Canova's Theseus group in marble, Hans Makart's paintings in the ceiling lunettes and Ernst and Gustav Klimt's in the spandrels provide a foretaste of the treasures to come – though one treasure is missing: in May 2003 the *saliera*, the saltcellar by Benvenuto Cellini, was stolen. With a value of 50 million euros, it is now one of the world's "most wanted" works of art.

Most of the KHM's treasures came about thanks to the Habsburgs' passion for collecting. The Egyptian-Oriental collection has fascinating exhibits from the ancient Nile

ulture; the antiques collection
with its miniatures and cameos is
one of the most important in the
world; the Münzkabinett
(Cabinet of Coins) comprises
some 700,000 specimens from
three millennia, which provide an overview of the
history and development of money; and the Kunstkammer
(Art Cabinet) has a mass of larger and smaller sculptures,
scientific instruments, automata and clocks.

The picture
gallery boasts
superb Rubens
paintings

The first floor houses the museum's absolute pinnacle,
the Gemäldegallerie (Picture Gallery), which is the fourth
largest anywhere. In the East Wing, in Room X, you'll find the
world's largest collection of Brueghels (*The Tower of Babel, The
Peasant Wedding, Room X*), as well as numerous works by
Dutch and Flemish painters, including paintings by Rubens
which are particularly impressive for their sensuality (*The Fur*
in Room XIII shows that cellulitis on the thighs wasn't always
considered a blemish). The West Wing's exhibits are virtually
a cross-section through the history of European painting.

Natural History

While in recent years the KHM has
developed into a major attraction,
through events and special exhibitions,
the Natural History Museum has been
more of a Sleeping Beauty. And that
despite the fact that it possesses one of
Europe's greatest scientific collections.
There are countless exhibits in its
39 vast exhibition halls, including
some stupendous treasures, such as
the first-ever model of a sabre-tooth
tiger and the *Venus of Willendorf*, the oldest
known statuette of the human figure. There's also a
transmission of images from live webcams, located in the
USA, Australia and Spain and aimed at the sun.

Young visitors
love the NHM's
dinosaurs

TAKING A BREAK

Beneath the domes of both museums are **cafés** with a very
special atmosphere (► 109).

192 B2 ⊠ KHM: Wien 1, Burgring 5; NHM: Wien 1, Burgring 7 ☎ KHM:
(01) 525 24-0; NHM: (01) 521 77 🕐 KHM: Tue–Sun 10–6, Thu until 9 (Gemälde-
galerie); NHM: Wed–Mon 9–6:30, Wed until 7 🚇 Volkstheater 🚋 Tram 1, 2,
D, Bus 2A, 57A Burgring 💰 Expensive 🌐 www.khm.at; www.nhm-wien.ac.at

6 Burgtheater

The Burgtheater was one of the last large structures to be built in Ringstrasse, but it was the first to install electric lighting. From the start it has been regarded as one of the best German-language theatres, even if at times it takes an avant-garde approach not appreciated by the audience.

The Burgtheater was built in 1874–88 to the designs of Karl Hasenauer and Gottfried Semper. Just as with the Staatsoper, the reaction of the Viennese public was initially hostile. But this is long forgotten today. The auditorium proudly displays its past as the "imperial court theatre" – the the boxes and circles are all clad in red velvet.

The glittering interior of the Burgtheater

Over the years countless renowned actors have delighted the Burgtheater's public, and appearing on its stage still represents the peak of an actor's career. Violent disputes on the nature of art are frequent. When Claus Peymann put on *Die Burg* (The Fortress) in 1986–99, he was accused of "deconsecrating" the house, and storms still rage under the current director, Klaus Bachler. For many, dramatic art stops with Schiller, and new, progressive or unusual productions take a lot of getting used to. And there are many such productions!

TAKING A BREAK
The **Vestibül** (► 111) is the best place for a break.

🗺 192 B4 ✉ Wien 1, Dr-Karl-Lueger-Ring 2
☎ (01) 514 44-41 40 🕐 Box office daily 8–6 and
1 hour before performances; guided tours Mon–Fri
3 pm, Sat–Sun 11 am and 3 pm 🚇 Rathaus,
Herrengasse 🚋 Tram 1, 2, D Burgtheater
💰 Moderate ❓ www.burgtheater.at

BURGTHEATER: INSIDE INFO

Top tips The bookshop **Leporello** stocks works on drama and literature (daily 5–10 pm, except on days when there are no performances).

Hidden gem Have a look at the **frescoes** on the grand staircase. Some are by Ernst and Gustav Klimt.

12 Museumsquartier

Seen from the Maria-Theresien-Platz, the Museumsquartier has a long baroque façade with two vast cubes towering up behind it, one white and the other black. But as you enter the enormous courtyard, it becomes clear that something entirely new and exciting has been created here: an urban habitat for the arts, spacious – covering an area of 60,000sq m (72,000 square yards) – and forward-looking.

For 300 years the area of the present MQ (Museums' Quarter) bore the stigma of incomplete grandeur. It started when, in 1713, Emperor Karl VI commissioned the baroque architect Johann Fischer von Erlach to build imperial stables on the glacis, the open slopes outside the city walls. The plan was never completely realized, but the emperor's horses never-theless were

The dark basalt hulk of the "Mumok"

happily housed behind Vienna's longest baroque façade.

In the early 20th century, times were changing. The monarchy was abolished, the invention of the automobile put the horses out of their jobs, and the gigantic stable and carriage building was no longer needed. From 1921 the former luxury quarters of the imperial horses found a new use, as a site for exhibitions and trade fairs.

Controversial New Ideas

By the end of the 20th century, the complex could no longer be described as a "palace". The façade was indeed still standing, but many of the buildings on the vast area were slowly deteriorating – until in 1980 a completely different way of using the complex was proposed. Then the arguments began.

The Leopold Museum, in gleaming white limestone

For a start, the idea of a "museum quarter" was discussed for six years, from 1980 to 1986. Several commissions put forward proposals. In 1990 the Viennese office of Ortner &

Ortner won an architectural competition. That really did it. Protests rained down, and a citizens' initiative even managed to have the planned "reading tower" taken out of the scheme.

Despite all the disputes, building started in 1998, and the biggest cultural project of the Second Republic was underway. At the opening in 2001 the mood was quite different, now people were jubilant. It turned out that Ortner & Ortner had carried out their basic architectural concept to perfection: the mutual integration of historical and modern architecture, a spectacular blend of the old and the new, of art and relaxation.

The Leopold Café, an urban communications centre

Great Variety

The Museumsquartier has developed into an exciting cultural district and a place of great diversity. Fine arts and the performing arts, architecture, music, fashion, film, new media, culture for children and small cultural projects are just as much at home here as museums and exhibition halls.

Three large buildings give the courtyard of the complex its character: the Leopold Museum with its cladding of white limestone, the Museum Moderner Kunst Stiftung Ludwig Wien Ludwig ("Mumok", the Ludwig Foundation's Museum of Modern Art in Vienna), clad in dark basalt, its roof curving down low on the edges, and the brick-built Kunsthalle Wien (Vienna Art Gallery). The latter is

For Kids

The **Zoom Kindermuseum** aims to introduce children to the world of museums. In the multimedia **Zoomlab**, children from the age of seven can move between the real and the virtual world, acting as producers, sound technicians, writers and actors. The **Zoom Ocean** takes children under six on a jourey through a magic underwater world, and the **Zoom Workshop** gives budding young artists the chance to be creative.

In the evening, the MQ turns into a strolling district

hidden behind the E+G hall, the former Winter Riding School, which now houses Vienna's dance-halls.

The **Leopold Museum** contains Rudolf Leopold's extensive, originally private collection. Works by Austrian artists are displayed on five floors, with the emphasis on 19th and 20th century painting. Vienna around 1900 is well represented with works by Gustav Klimt, Richard Gerstl, Koloman Moser and Oscar Kokoschka. The museum's highlight is on the lower ground floor: the great Egon Schiele collection, whose numerous drawings are outstanding even by international standards.

The **Mumok** is the largest Austrian museum of modern and contemporary art. The emphasis of the collection is on Classic Modernism, Pop Art, Photo-realism, Fluxus, Nouveau Réalisme and Viennese Actionism.

Visitor numbers show that the MQ is a tremendous tourist attraction from which Vienna has profited greatly: in the first year around two million came. Just over half of these came to visit exhibitions or special events, including festivals. But the other half just came to experience the unique atmosphere of the cultural district, and to enjoy its advantages as a local

The baroque architecture has been retained at the entrance to the MQ

entertainment centre, where it is possible to meet friends, relax, sit and chat, eat and drink, stroll and shop.

TAKING A BREAK

The **Kantine** has a small but tasty selection of hot meals of the day, and a comfortable lounge area.

➕ 192 A2 ✉ Wien 7, Museumsplatz 1 ☎ (01) 523 58 81, Infoline 0820 600 600 (only within Austria) 🕐 Leopold Museum Wed–Mon 10–7, Thu until 9; Mumok Tue–Sun 10–6, Thu until 9 🚇 Museumsquartier 🚋 Tram 49, Bus 48A Volkstheater, Bus 2A Museumsquartier 💷 Expensive 🔗 www.mqw.at

---

MUSEUMSQUARTIER: INSIDE INFO

Top tip Walk a short way up Mariahilfer Strasse to Leiner's furnishing store (Wien 7, Mariahilfer Strasse 18). They have a cafeteria where you could stop for a coffee on the **roof terrace** – it has the best overview of the entire Musemsquartier area.

At Your Leisure

2 Akademie der bildenden Künste

The frescoes and the terracotta figures in the niches between the bow windows make a striking façade for Theophil Hansen's Academy of Fine Arts. Inside, the atrium with Anselm Feuerbach's ceiling painting is even more spectacular. This world-renowned picture gallery houses works of art from five centuries, including paintings by Bosch, Cranach the Elder, Rubens and Rembrandt. Hieronymus Bosch's *Last Judgement* triptych is particularly worth seeing, with its bizarre and gruesome fantasies. The etchings room has a great range of early 19th-century pictures and old architectural plans.

➕ 192 C2 ✉ Wien 1, Schillerplatz 3
☎ (01) 588 16-0 🕐 Tue–Sun 10–6
🚇 Karlsplatz 🚊 Tram 1, 2, D, J Oper/Babenbergerstrasse, Bus 59A Oper, 57A Babenbergerstrasse 💲 Expensive
❓ www.akbild.ac.at

4 Heldenplatz

Heldenplatz is one of the most beautiful squares in the city. Seen from the main entrance to the Neue Burg it presents a panorama: in the

The Italian-inspired façade of the Akademie der bildenden Künste

foreground the equestrian statues of Archduke Karl and Prince Eugen of Savoy, to the right the Leopold Wing of the Hofburg, then the outlines of the Burgtheater, Rathaus and Parliament, and the Äussere Burgtor, with the memorial to the resistance fighters killed in 1939–45.

The Neue Burg contains incredible treasures: the splendid reading rooms of the Nationalbibliothek (National Library), the Ephesos Museum, the Papyrus Museum with the largest collection of papyruses in the world, and a little farther on, towards the Ringstrasse, the Völkerkundemuseum (Museum of Ethnography).

Heldenplatz became a fateful place in 1938, when, from the balcony over the main entrance to the Neue Burg, Hitler announced the "Anschluss" (Annexation) of Austria to the Third Reich. Today this large square is a starting point for a leisurely tour of the city by horse and carriage.

➕ 192 B3 🚇 Volkstheater
🚊 Tram 1, 2, D, J, Bus 2A Burgring

5 Volksgarten

The Volksgarten is a paradise for rose-lovers, with thousands of roses of every conceivable colour. The plant labels give information about whom each rose is named after. The Theseus temple, erected in 1822, is a historic gem. The romantic memorial to Empress Elisabeth is a pilgrimage site for Sisi fans. And the cheekiest sparrows in the city flit about in the small dairy café. They alight without a by-your-leave on the edge of your plate and help themselves to some of your *apfelstrudel*.

🔶 192 B3 🚇 Herrengasse
🚋 Tram 1, 2, D, J Dr-Karl-Renner-Ring

7 Mölker Bastei

The Mölker Bastei is one of the few remaining parts of the city fortifications. In the Pasqualati House two rooms are set up as memorials to Beethoven, who composed *Fidelio*, amongst other works, in this house (Tue–Sun 10-12:15, 1-4:30). Round the corner in the Schreyvogelgasse is the "Dreimäderlhaus". It became known through the operetta of the same name based on Franz Schubert's romance with the "three lasses" who lived here. The romance is invented, but the pretty house with the early 19th-century façade is very real.

🔶 192 B4 🚇 Schottentor
🚋 Tram 1, 2, D Schottentor

Devastated by fire

Diagonally opposite the Vienna Stock Exchange (Börse, ➤ 108), in a plain new building, you can now see the headquarters of the Vienna police. Once the Ringtheater stood on this site. In 1881 the theatre was destroyed by a fire which killed 400 people. The fire at the Ringtheater is one of the legendary catastrophes in Vienna's history.

8 Universität

The construction of the university was started in 1870. Heinrich Ferstel planned the central building in neo-Renaissance style. Vienna University, founded in 1365, is in fact the oldest German-language university. Reforms in the late 19th century resulted in the foundation of many new departments. The university expanded further in 1998 when the city's hospital (dating from 1693), became the university campus.

🔶 192 B4 ✉ Wien 1, Dr-Karl-Lueger-Ring 1 🚇 Schottentor 🚋 Tram 1, 2, D Schottentor

When the roses are in bloom the Volksgarten is a scented paradise

9 Börse

A brick-red façade identifies the Börse (Stock Exchange), on the right-hand side of the otherwise uninteresting Schottenring. In 1877, after numerous moves, it finally took possession of this building contructed by Theophil Hansen. Founded by Maria Theresa in 1771, the late 1980s were its heyday; for a short time it was even the fastest growing financial centre in the world. Today it is also a good place for gourmets and lovers of flowers.

🚇 192 C5 ✉ Wien 1, Schottenring 16 🚇 Schottentor 🚋 Tram 1, 2, D, Bus 3A Börse

10 Rathaus

It was the liberals, with Kajetan Felder at their head, who in 1870 wrung from the emperor the permission to build a Rathaus (Town Hall). Today the Rathaus, built in 1872–83 by Friedrich Schmidt, is the administrative heart of the city. It has everything that one would expect to find in a grand neo-Gothic building: open arcades, loggias, balconies, ogive windows as well as plentiful

At the Börse you can buy stocks and shares – and delicious meals

ornamentation. The banqueting hall is the largest in Austria. The "Rathausmann", a Viennese emblem, looks out from the top of the 98-m (320-feet) high main tower. In recent years the square in front of the Rathaus has become a centre of activity. Formerly it was only used on 1 May, when the socialists gathered for the May Day parade instituted by Viktor Adler in 1889. But now there's almost always something going on here.

🚇 192 A4 ✉ Wien 1, Rathausplatz 🕐 Free guided tours Mon, Wed, Fri 1 am 🚇 Rathaus 🚋 Tram 1, 2, D Rathausplatz/Burgtheater

11 Parlament

With its harmoniously ordered façade and elegantly curving approach ramp, the Parliament counts as one of the artistically valuable buildings of the Ringstrasse era. It was built in 1873–83 to the design of Theophil Hansen. In the last decades of the monarchy it contained both houses of the then Reichstag, the elected house and the nobility – the architect's main difficulty was to fit both into one building. He solved the problem by creating an arcaded atrium with a cube-shaped chamber on each long side. Today the Nationalrat (National Council) and the Bundesrat (Federal Council), the two houses of the Austrian parliament, sit in these chambers. The conference hall, modelled on a Greek amphitheatre, is preserved in its original form. The finest adornment in front of the building, and conceived as part of the Parlament's decor, is the monumental Pallas Athene fountain (► 30).

🚇 192 A3 ✉ Wien 1, Dr-Karl-Renner-Ring 3 🕐 Guided tours Mon, Wed 10 am, 11 am, Tue, Thu 2 pm, 3 pm, Fri 11 am, 1 pm, 2 pm, 3 pm 🚇 Lerchenfelder Strasse 🚋 Tram 1, 2, D, J, 46, 49 Stadiongasse/Parlament 💰 Inexpensive

Where to...
Eat and Drink

Prices

Prices given are for one person, excluding drinks.
€ under 12 euros **€€** 12–25 euros **€€€** over 25 euros

Restaurants

Halle €

The café-restaurant of the Kunsthalle and the Wiener Festwochen (Viennese Festival Weeks) is in the former Winter Riding School. The stucco of the imperial lodge makes an interesting contrast to the modern design. The Mediterranean food is fresh and light; the breakfast menu is extensive, there's a set menu at lunchtime and sandwiches are also available. In summer you can sit outside in the courtyard.

➕ 192 A2 ⊠ Wien 7, Museumsplatz 1 ☎ (01) 523 70 01 🕐 Daily 10 am–2 am Ⓜ MuseumsQuartier 🚃 Tram 49, Bus 48A Volkstheater, Bus 2A Museums-Quartier

Hansen €€

One of Vienna's most interesting restaurants is on the lower ground floor of the Börse (Stock Exchange). It is right next to the lush greenery of the flowers and plants of the Lederleitner garden centre, and the scent wafts over. The open kitchen produces imaginative Mediterranean dishes, and the breakfast menu is also inviting.

➕ 192 C5 ⊠ Wien 1, Wipplingerstrasse 34 ☎ (01) 532 05 42 🕐 Mon–Fri 9 am–9 pm (hot food until 8 pm), Sat 9 am– 5 pm (hot food until 3 pm) Ⓜ Schottentor 🚃 Tram 1, 2, D, Bus 3A Börse

Il Museo €

This café-restaurant in the Mumok (Museum of Modern Art) has a side entrance, so it is not dependent on the museum's opening times. It serves Italian specialities and has fresh fish every day. Snacks, ices and desserts are served in the garden. The wine bar and reading-room are especially comfortable.

➕ 192 A2 ⊠ Wien 7, Museumsplatz 1 ☎ (01) 525 00-14 40 🕐 Daily 10 am– 1 am Ⓜ MuseumsQuartier 🚃 Tram 49, Bus 48A Volkstheater, Bus 2A MuseumsQuartier

KHM/NHM €€€

Recently these twin museums have added culinary delights to their other treasures. In KHM's domed atrium a delicious supper is served on Thursdays and brunch on Sundays. An expensive treat, but the surroundings makes it unforgettable. In the same area of the NHM the Café Nautilus serves a variety of fine dishes, ranging from asparagus to mussels, and a three-course seasonal menu on Wednesday evenings.

➕ 192 B2 ⊠ Wien 1, Burgring 5 bzw. 7 ☎ KHM: (01) 526 13 61; NHM: (01) 260 69–24 98 🕐 KHM: Tue–Sun 10 am–6 pm, Thu until 10 pm; NHM: Wed–Mon 9 am– 6:30 pm, Wed until 9 pm Ⓜ Volkstheater 🚃 Tram 1, 2, D, J, Bus 2A, 57A Burgring

Korso €€€

Reinhard Gerer, often seen as the most creative of Vienna's top chefs, has for years prepared food of the highest quality in this Michelin-starred gourmet temple. Haute cuisine, the fine wines and the very elegant setting make every meal here an experience. Recently a garden named Cabrio has been opened between the restaurant and the rear of the Bristol Hotel. Here, in the fresh air, you can get and students from the Akademie der bildenden Künste (Academy of Fine Arts). The menu changes daily, with seasonal specialities like asparagus, mushrooms and game. Four-legged guests have their own dogs' menu called "WUFF!".

🏠 192 C2 ⊠ Wien 1, Elisabethstrasse 8 ☎ (01) 587 13 56 ⏰ Daily 10 am–midnight (hot food until 11 pm) Ⓤ Oper 🚋 Tram 1, 2, D, J, Bus 3A Kärntnering/Oper

Una €

This restaurant in the Museums-Quartier's Architecture Centre has an interesting set-up: the French architects Anne Lacaton and Jean-Philippe Vassal clad the ceiling vaulting with Turkish tiles, creating an oriental feel. Apart from the set lunch menu they also serve Austrian, Italian and American specialities. In summer you can eat in the garden.

🏠 192 A2 ⊠ Wien 7, Museumsplatz 1 ☎ (01) 523 65 66 ⏰ Mon–Fri 9 am–midnight, Sat 10 am–midnight, Sun

---

international: nouvelle cuisine with influences from Asia, North Africa and other parts of Europe. The bar colours change three times a day: in the morning it is lit in green, at lunchtime in blue and in the evening in pink. Illuminated partitions of opaque glass form private alcoves into which you can retreat.

🏠 192 C2 ⊠ Wien 1, Robert-Stolz-Platz 1 ☎ (01) 588 90-0 ⏰ Daily 6:30 until midnight (hot food until 11 pm), bar service daily 11 am–1 am Ⓤ Oper 🚋 Tram 1, 2, D, J, Bus 3A Kärntnering/Oper

Smutny €

Smutny has fine old-world dark-green tiles and the ambience of the imperial era. The oldest city pub serving Czech Budvar beer, it is renowned for its traditional Viennese and Bohemian cooking. Regular customers include actors, singers and musicians from the nearby Staatsoper and the Theater an der Wien, as well as lecturers

---

delicious morsels, like fried quails' eggs or pike-perch fish fingers.

🏠 193 D2 ⊠ Wien 1, Mahlerstrasse 5 ☎ (01) 51 51 65 46 ⏰ Sun–Fri noon–2, 6–11 pm, Sat 6 pm–11 pm Ⓤ Oper 🚋 Tram 1, 2, D, J, Bus 3A Kärntnering/Oper

Sacher €€€

A meal or just a coffee in the legendary Sacher, a must for all visitors, guarantees you pure traditional Viennese elegance. The Anna Sacher restaurant has a collection of pictures by Anton Feistauer and the first electric candelabras in Vienna. The Red Bar has a winter garden with a view of the Staatsoper; in summer the windows are lowered and it becomes a terrace. From 7 pm the piano plays. The Sacher rule is: once in a lifetime you simply must try their world-famous *tafelspitz* (boiled beef with vegetables), followed by a genuine Sacher Torte.

🏠 192 C2 ⊠ Wien 1, Philharmonikerstrasse 4 ☎ (01) 514 56 Ⓤ Anna Sacher noon–3, 6–midnight (hot food

---

until 11:30 pm); Rote Bar daily. noon–midnight (hot food until 11:30 pm); Café Sacher daily 8 am–midnight Ⓤ Oper 🚋 Tram 1, 2, D, J, Bus 3A Kärntnering/Oper

Sacher Eck' €€

If you don't want to go for the full Sacher experience, but would rather get to know it little by little, then it's now possible to do that. The light-filled atmosphere, the tall tables with bar-stools and the elegant bar provide really stylish surroundings for a light snack and a glass of wine.

🏠 193 D2 ⊠ Wien 1, Philharmonikerstrasse 2 ☎ (01) 514 56-699 ⏰ 9 am–1 am Ⓤ Oper 🚋 Tram 1, 2, D, J, Bus 3A Kärntnering/Oper

Shambala €€

This bar and restaurant in the new Hotel Le Méridien on Opernring is innovative and stylish. Violet and mauve felt and light beige leather are the dominant furnishings, all bathed in pink light. The cooking is

10 am–7 pm ◎ MuseumsQuartier 🚋 Tram 49, Bus 48 A Volkstheater, Bus 2A MuseumsQuartier

Vestibül €€

An elegant cosmopolitan brasserie in one of the most revered places in Vienna, the Burgtheater. The rooms are marble- and stucco-clad yet modern in feel, and the atmosphere is unbeatable. The garden too is one of the finest in the city, simply for its position. The cuisine is imaginative, light Viennese, including *kalbsbeuschel* (calf's lung) and chive dumplings as well as wild duck breast and pigeon with soya beans.

➕ 192 B4 ⊠ Wien 1, Dr-Karl-Lueger-Ring 2 ☎ (01) 532 49 99 ◎ Mon–Fri 11 am–midnight, Sat from 6 pm (hot food 11–2:30, 6–11 pm) ◎ Rathaus, Herrengasse 🚋 Tram 1, 2, D Burgtheater

Cafés

Kurkonditorei Oberlaa

This café in Neuer Markt is one of the newest places for delicious

confectionery, magnificent *torten* and first-rate food. As a result, it's usually very crowded. If you can't get a seat, why not try the pub in Babenbergerstrasse opposite the Fine Arts Museum instead? The food's just as good (try the Kurbadtorte!). The confectionery also makes an ideal souvenir of Vienna!

➕ 192 B2 ⊠ Wien 1, Babenbergerstrasse 7 ☎ (01) 586 72 82 ◎ Mon–Sat 8 am–7 pm, Sun 10 am–7 pm ◎ MuseumsQuartier 🚋 Tram 1, 2, D, J, Bus 2A, 57A Burgring

Landtmann

"Vienna's most elegant coffee-house" was opened in 1873. Since then this Ringstrasse café with its broad terrace has become an institution. Customers have included Sigmund Freud, Marlene Dietrich, Romy Schneider, Burt Lancaster, Hillary Clinton and Paul McCartney. The excellent Austrian cooking, the tempting pastries and the full range of coffee specialities are enjoyed as much by the actors from the

Burgtheater opposite as by politicians from the nearby Rathaus, Parliament and the party headquarters. There is live piano music on some evenings.

➕ 192 B4 ⊠ Wien 1, Dr-Karl-Lueger-Ring 4 ☎ (01) 24 100-0 ◎ Daily 7:30 am–midnight ◎ Rathaus, Herrengasse 🚋 Tram 1, 2, D Burgtheater

Meierei Volksgarten

The Meierei in the Stadtpark might not be a gourmets' heaven or posh café, but it's a loveable piece of old-world Vienna. In its circular garden with the tiny building in the middle, it has been serving strollers with coffee, snacks and traditional Viennese dishes since 1930.

➕ 192 B3 ⊠ Wien 1, Volksgarten ☎ (01) 533 21 05 ◎ Apr–Oct depending on the weather daily 8 am–8 pm ◎ Herrengasse 🚋 Tram 1, 2, D, J, Bus 2A, 57A Burgring

Schottenring

This Ringstrasse café founded in 1879 calls itself traditional and at

the same time forward-looking. The delicate pastries and live music keep up the tradition, while the internet stations and apple strudel seminars attract younger guests. Altogether it's what a coffee-house should be: solid, unobtrusive, not "made over" and yet elegant.

➕ 192 C5 ⊠ Wien 1, Schottenring 19 ☎ (01) 315 33 43 ◎ Mon–Fri 6:30 am–11 pm, Sat–Sun 8 am–9 pm ◎ Schottentor 🚋 Tram 1, 2, D, Bus 3A Börse

Sluka

In the Rathaus arcades there's a café-cum-cakeshop which meets the highest standards. There are some delicious fish snacks on the menu as well as special meals for diabetics. Officials from the Rathaus meet here for a sweet or savoury snack or a coffee and *torte*, and it goes without saying that many a political issue is thrashed out here.

➕ 192 A4 ⊠ Wien 1, Rathausplatz 8 ☎ (01) 405 71 72 ◎ Mon–Fri 8 am–7 pm, Sat 8 am–5:30 pm ◎ Rathaus 🚋 Tram 1, 2, D Rathausplatz/Burgtheater

Where to... Shop

The western Ringstrasse is not one of the city's main shopping streets. All the same, a visit to the museum shops and one or two specialized stores could be rewarded with some pretty and original finds.

Museums shops

There are some good shopping opportunities in the **Museumsquartier**. The Architecture Centre, Kunsthalle Wien, Leopold Museum and Mumok all have their own shops, selling books, prints, T-shirts, bags and countless pretty knick-knacks. Next door to the Kunsthalle's shop, the Lomographische Gesellschaft has opened the **LomoShop**, the first anywhere to stock everything to do with these cult cameras. The little **Cheap Shop** in Quartier 21 has a large selection of sound equipment and an info-centre for web-surfing. And **MQ daily**, the health foods store by the main entrance, stocks high-quality organic products and snacks. There is also a stand-up café. In **KHM** and **NHM** you can spend ages rummaging through the art prints, ornaments, books and reproductions of exhibits, from dinosaur teeth to Klimt-style earrings.

Other shops

Sädtler Classic (Opernring 13) is a stylish florists' shop selling stunning natural plants and flowers. **Demmers Teehaus** (Molker Bastei 5) has every sort of tea, including rare varieties, and all the accompaniments that turn tea-drinking into an experience.

The **Sacher Confiserie** (Philharmonikerstrasse 4) sells the original Sacher *torten* in different sizes, packed in wooden boxes saying "a sweet gift from Vienna".

Where to be... Entertained

The Staatsoper and the Burgtheater on the western Ringstrasse are the famous homes of high art. Otherwise, this part of the city tends to be quiet in the evening. Apart from the MQ, pubs and bars are also thin on the ground. But you can always go dancing.

From early May to mid-September ballroom dancing is the attraction at the **Tanzcafé** in the **Volksgarten** (Heldenplatz, tel: 01/533 05 18, daily from 10 pm), which first opened in 1824. On Friday and Saturday there's a mixed programme of boogie woogie, rock 'n' roll and all mainstream and Latin-American dances. There are dance-floors outside and, for bad weather, inside. The whole year round it's clubbing, hip-hop, house and hits from the 1970s at the equally popular **Volksgarten Clubdiscothek**, which has the motto: "we don't make parties, we live them".

Die Passage (corner of Burgring and Babenbergerstrasse, tel: 01/561 88 00) is club culture underneath the Ringstrasse: originally, the Babenberger Passage between Hofburg and Fine Arts Museum was intended as a pedestrian subway. But it was never used, and lay empty for years. Now the events group Sunshine Enterprises has revived it as a cool club. In a futuristic decor with a flexible set-up and brilliant lighting, the programme includes club, dance and house music.

The **Café Leopold** (Museumsplatz 1, tel. 01/523 67 32, Sun-Wed 10 am-2 am, Thu-Sat 10 am-4 am) is ever more popular; it has brought a quite new urban experience to Vienna. In the evening you can have drinks at the bar or a meal after midnight, and watch videos of experimental Austrian film-makers.

Schönbrunn and Wiental

Getting Your Bearings

Schönbrunn is a powerful symbol of a bygone era.
Nothing represents the imperial age so well as this
magnificent palace and its park. The Wiental
(Wien Valley), on the other hand, is proof that
the city has always had a great liking for art and
sensual pleasures.

The palace, the unique park and the
oldest zoo in the world make Schönbrunn a marvellous advertisement
for Vienna, indeed for the whole of
Austria. The entire palace and its
grounds have long been a World
Cultural Heritage Site. Almost no other
place so well conveys the imperial family's sense of elite
beauty. Here the former glory of the Habsburg monarchy has
by no means faded.

Farther in towards the city, among the attractions in Wiental are the highly unconventional buildings of the Secession
movement, the Karlskirche, and those great, world-famous
temples of music, the Musikverein and the Konzerthaus. On
the way there, culinary delights tempt at every corner. Along
the colourful, lively Naschmarkt numerous restaurants have
opened, offering the finest foods from around the world.

Page 113:
The imperial
splendour
of Schloss
Schönbrunn

Above left:
A penguin in the
Schönbrunn zoo

Right: Vitamins
galore in the
Naschmarkt

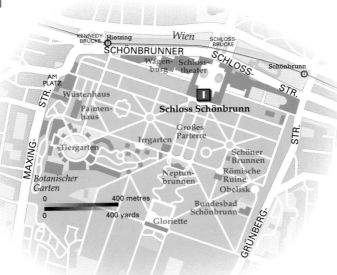

This is entirely devoted to enjoyment. First, at Schloss and Park Schönbrunn, you will see architecture and garden design of perfect beauty, followed by a culinary journey around the world in Naschmarkt. And, finally, classical music will make a perfect end to a wonderful day.

Schönbrunn and Wiental in a Day

9:00 am

Start the day at the Habsburgs' summer residence,
❶ **Schönbrunn Palace** (➤ 118). As soon as you first get sight of this palace, you'll understand at once why it is on the distinguished UNESCO World Cultural Heritage list. The effect becomes stronger as you walk through some of the splendid rooms: the Arbeitszimmer des Kaisers (Emperor's Study), the Grosse Rosa Zimmer (Large Pink Room), the adjoining Spiegelsaal (Hall of Mirrors), in which the "child prodigy" Mozart played for Maria Theresa, and the magnificent Porzellanzimmer (Porcelain Room).

11:30 am

Once outside again, take a deep breath after all that rococo splendour. It is a real pleasure to stroll through the park, all carefully trimmed and maintained according to the rules of baroque horticulture. When you arrive at the Gloriette (above), you have a view of the almost unreal beauty of the palace and Vienna. Pause here for a while, perhaps over a refreshing drink at the Café Gloriette (➤ 134).

1:30 pm

For lunch, you're spoiled for choice. On the **2 Naschmarkt** (right; ► 123), reached by U-Bahn 4, you're surrounded by wafts of a great variety of the most delicious aromas. Here the food is Turkish or Italian, Indian or Japanese, Thai or Chinese – and each dish smells and tastes even better than the last. There's nothing for it but to stroll and sample a few.

3:00 pm

At the end of the Naschmarkt another, completely different highlight of Viennese architecture awaits you, the rectilinear **3 Secession** (► 126) building, crowned with a dome of golden laurel leaves, which gave its name to an entire movement. Don't fail to see this interesting building from the inside – if only to admire Klimt's famous *Beethoven-Frieze*.

4:00 pm

After a coffee or a glass of wine in the small café behind the Secession, cross Karlsplatz and visit the **4 Karlskirche** (► 128). You'll be impressed by its bright interior, the large oval dome, which looks as though it's floating, and the magnificent baroque frescoes.

5:00 pm

Walk across the remodelled Schwarzenbergplatz to the **6 Hochstrahlbrunnen** (High-jet Fountain, below; ► 130), then take a rest. For you must be fit this evening, which belongs to classical music in the Konzerthaus (► 136) or the **9 Musikverein** (► 131). And after the inspiring notes of the Philharmonic or Symphonic Orchestras, what better than a stylish nightcap in the bar of the Schwarzenberg Palace.

① Schloss Schönbrunn

The Habsburgs' summer residence with its baroque land-scaped park and the oldest zoo in the world is one of Austria's most important cultural monuments. The imperial palace complex, which lies to the west of Vienna, was included in UNESCO's World Cultural Heritage list in 1997.

It all began when, in 1559, Emperor Maximilian II bought the manor-house in the former Katterburg, extended it to create a hunting palace and installed the first zoo for rare fish and game. "Was für ein *schöner Brunnen*!" (What a lovely fountain!) said Emperor Matthias in 1612, when he was walking through this hunting ground – and that's how the place got its name.

After it was destroyed during the Turkish siege of 1683, Leopold I commissioned Johann Bernhard Fischer von Erlach in 1696–1700 to build the imperial residence Schönbrunn Palace for his son Joseph I. The vast building project on Gloriette hill was to surpass the palace of Versailles in splendour and brilliance. However, this proved to be too expensive, so an economy version was built and painted in blue and pink – the characteristic "Schönbrunn yellow" was only applied in 1752. In 1728 Karl VI acquired the property and gave it to his daughter Maria Theresa. During her reign the court architect Nikolaus Pacassi extended Schönbrunn and remodelled it as a palatial rococo residence. It was the start of a brilliant era, when the palace became the centre of court and political life. In summer each year the whole court, with its 2,000 servants, ladies-in-waiting, gardeners and craftsmen, transferred from the Hofburg to Schönbrunn. Empress Maria Theresa oversaw the furnishing of the palace, while her husband Franz Stephan looked after the garden designs.

The view of the palace from the Neptune fountain is splendid

When Maria Theresa died, the palace, park and Gloriette were complete. In later years, Emperor Franz Joseph I and Empress Elisabeth regularly resided in in the palace. Franz Joseph was born and died here. In 1918 Emperor Karl I signed his abdication document in the Blauer Salon (Blue Salon). The palace suffered severe damage in World War II. After repairs, the public rooms re-opened to visitors in 1948.

A Tour of the Palace

The palace has 1,441 rooms, of which 40 are open to the public. These include Franz Joseph and Elisabeth's apartments in the west wing, the central section with the banqueting halls and function rooms, and the audience chamber of the imperial couple Maria Theresa and Franz Stephan in the east wing. Of particular interest are the **Arbeitszimmer des Kaisers** (Emperor's Study) with portraits of Franz Joseph and Sisi, the sumptuous **Spiegelsaal** (Hall of Mirrors)

For Kids

The palace has a museum and guided tours designed for children, in which they can hear all about the emperor's children, what they wore and how they were educated (weekends and public holidays10:30, 2:30, Jul–Aug also Mon–Fri 2:30).

in which the six-year-old Mozart gave his debut concert in front of Maria Theresa, and the **Chinesische Kabinette** (Chinese Rooms). When Napoleon occupied Vienna in 1805 and 1809, he made Schönbrunn his headquarters. He is said to have slept in what is now called the Napoleon Room. His son, the Duke of Reichstadt, grew up in Schönbrunn and died here at the early age of 21. The Habsburg emperors worked personally on the furnishing of the rooms – the designs for the decoration of the **Porzellanzimmer** (Porcelain Room) was probably drawn up by Maria Theresa's daughter-in-law Isabella of Parma, Emperor Joseph II's first wife. The 213 blue pen-and-ink drawings are by Emperor Franz I and some of his children. The west wing houses the **Schlosstheater** (Palace Theatre), where performances are still put on today. In the

Right: The young Mozart with Empress Maria Theresa, painted by Eduard Ender

former Winterreitschule you can visit the **Wagenburg**, a collection of state and everyday carriages.

The Baroque Palace Park

To the south of the palace you'll find the 185-ha (460-acre) early-baroque park, laid out in the French style in 1695. Maria Theresa had it remodelled in 1770. The **Neptunbrunnen** (Neptune Fountain, in operation 10 am–2 pm) was built at the foot of Schönbrunn hill and the **Gloriette** on the hilltop. From the roof of the pavilion, which is shaped like a three-part triumphal arch rich in ornamentation and symbols, you

The Hall of Mirrors – a perfect example of imperial splendour

have a
tremendous view
of Vienna. The mythological
figures along the **Grosses Parterre**
were also created under Maria Theresa, as were
the **Obeliskbrunnen** (Obelisque Fountain) and the
Römische Ruine (Roman Ruin) not far from the **Schöner
Brunnen** (Beautiful Fountain) which gave the palace its
name. In the western part of the park are the **Irrgarten**
(Maze), the **Tiergarten Schönbrunn** (Zoo) and the **Botani-
scher Garten** (Botanical Gardens). The monumental **Palmenhaus** (Palm House) was erected in 1882 and is renowned for
its cultivation of orchids. Nearby, the Sonnenuhrhaus (Sundial
House), the last imperial project, was built in 1904; it is now
the **Wüstenhaus** (Desert House), given over to the fauna and
flora of the desert.

The Tiergarten

There was a game park at Schönbrunn as early as 1570, but
we have Maria Theresa's husband Franz Stephan to thank for
founding the first menagerie. The centre, and still the core, of
this area is the **Frühstückspavillon des Kaisers** (Emperor's
Breakfast Pavilion), around which 13 enclosures were arranged,
some of them still extant. The first giraffe arrived in 1828,
creating an enormous sensation in Vienna:
hats, hairstyles, drinking vessels, pastries –
everything was suddenly "à la giraffe". In
1906, for the first time in any zoo, an
elephant was born here. Almost 100 years
later, the young elephants Abu and Mongu,
also born here, are great favourites with
visitors. Large enclosures and habitats
appropriate for each species are the
hallmark of this modern zoo. In the
enormous wooded enclosure wolves
howl, in the rainforest house a
tropical thunderstorm breaks out
twice daily (2:15 and 3:15 pm) and
the cheetahs hunt their prey, which
is transported through the enclosure
on a built-in ski-lift. The two
pandas eat their daily ration of

**The café in
the Gloriette
has marvellous
views**

60kg (130 pounds) of bamboo. In the Polarium penguins and seals dive, while clown fish, among other creatures, dart around in the aquarium/ terrarium houses.

TAKING A BREAK

The café in the former **Frühstückspavillon des Kaisers** in the centre of the enclosures has the greatest zoo atmosphere. The **Tirolerhof**, on the mound beyond the wolves' enclosure, is more rustic. In the park you can fortify yourself in the **Café in der Gloriette** (► 134). To the east, rather out of the way, the **Meierei** in the Kronprinzengarten exudes the charm of the 1950s – very few tourists, and the cakes are wonderful.

Tropical plants flourish under the glass and steel structure of the grand Palmenhaus

Schönbrunn Palace
➕ 198 B/C3 ✉ Wien 13, Schönbrunner Schlossstrasse
☎ (01) 81 11 32 39 🕐 Schloss Apr–Jun, Sep–Oct 8:30–5, Jul–Aug 8:30–6, Nov–Mar 8:30–4:30; Park Apr–Oct from 6 am, Nov–Mar from 6:30 am until dusk 🚇 Schönbrunn 🚋 Tram 10, 58, Bus 10A Schloss Schönbrunn
💰 Expensive ❓ www.schoenbrunn.at

Schönbrunn Zoo
➕ 198 A2 ✉ Wien 13, Maxingstrasse 13b ☎ (01) 877 92 94-0
🕐 Daily from 9 am; closing time Feb 5 pm, Mar, Oct 5:30 pm, Apr 6 pm, May–Sep 6:30 pm, Nov–Jan 4:30 pm 🚇 Hietzing 🚋 Tram 10, 58, Bus 10A, 51A, Kennedybrücke, Hietzing 💰 Expensive ❓ www.zoovienna.at

SCHÖNBRUNN PALACE: INSIDE INFO

Top tips The favourite time to visit the zoo, especially for children, is at **feeding time**. Here are the times for the most popular animals: apes 10 am and 2:30 pm; koalas 10:15 am; seals 10:30 am and 3:30 pm; king penguins 11 am; mandrils 2 pm; cheetahs Mon, Wed, Sun 3 pm; tigers and jaguars Sun–Tue, Thu, Fri 2 pm; wolves Sun–Tue, Thu, Fri 11 am; vultures Sun 11:30 am; elephants 4 pm.
• If you have plenty of time, buy a **Schönbrunn Pass Gold**. This ticket is valid for a year and entitles you to entry to all parts of the complex (once each) as well as giving certain reductions.
• Almost every day **concerts** are held in the Orangery. For information and tickets phone (01) 812 50 04.
• The **Marionettentheater** (Puppet Theatre) in the Hofratstrakt is a real experience for children. For information and tickets phone (01) 817 32 47.

Hidden gem In front of the east façade of the palace, immediately above the former kitchens, is the gorgeous **Kronprinzengarten** (Apr–Oct from 9 am). The flowerbeds in this, Schönbrunn's oldest garden, were laid out following embroidery patterns. A romantic pergola, pavilions and lemon trees make this garden fronting Crown Prince Rudolf's former apartments really worth seeing.

2 Naschmarkt and Wienzeile

The Wien river, which gave Vienna its name, is not the idyllic stream it once was; for a long time, it's been just a thin rivulet. And the grand "Kaiserboulevard", which was to lead over the Wien to Schönbrunn, never came to anything. However, where the Wien has been covered over, a very interesting district has arisen.

Fate has not dealt kindly with the Wien river. In the Middle Ages vineyards still flourished on its banks, but from then on it was all downhill. First dye-works arrived and polluted the water, to be followed by timber yards and mills and then industry. By 1900 the Wien was dead and smelly.

But since in Vienna dying is always accompanied by pomp, the Wien also became a glorious corpse. Otto Wagner was commissioned to arrange this. He straightened and deepened the Wien and built embankments from where the river could be covered over. Never was a project so appropriate to the character of a city: in the last years of the dying monarchy a grand boulevard was to be built over a dead river – the "Kaiserboulevard" (Imperial Boulevard).

On Saturdays the Naschmarkt is joined by a flea-market

The outcome of the project was also typical. It started in great style with the arching over of the river at the Stadtpark, then came the grand buildings along Wienzeile and the miserable failure of the Karlsplatz. All the rest suffered the same fate as the monarchy. The Kaiserboulevard remained a torso, a 500-m (550-yard) long tunnel from Stadtpark to the end of the flea-market (U-Bahn: Kettenbrückengasse).

Notable Buildings

Coming in from Schönbrunn, the **Kettenbrückengasse station** at the end of the tunnel immediately catches your eye. A few years ago Otto Wagner's Stadtbahn (urban railway) station was renovated true to his style. Around 100m

Theater an der Wien

Opposite the Naschmarkt is the Theater an der Wien, one of the city's theatres which is richest in tradition. It was originally built in 1798–1801, but only the Papageno gate on Millöckergasse remains of that structure. Famous works have had their premieres here, amongst them Mozart's *Magic Flute*

in 1791, Beethoven's *Fidelio* in 1805 and Johann Strauss's *Fledermaus* in 1874. From 1945 to 1955 the Theater an der Wien was the temporary home of the bombed-out Staatsoper. In the 1980s it became Vienna's leading theatre for musicals, staging hits like *Cats*. Soon it is to be turned back into an opera-house.

(110 yard) towards the city centre, in Linke Wienzeile, are two more admirable examples of the pioneering architect's work, the **Majolikahaus** (Majolica House, at No 40) and next to it the house on the **corner of Köstlergasse** (at No 38, ► 24), faced with medallions by Koloman Moser.

On Saturday mornings there is always lots going on in the grounds opposite these houses. The **flea-market** is held here, and adjoining it the farmers' market, where country produce is on sale, everything from smoked meat to organic vegetables.

The Naschmarkt

First-class fruit and vegetables are on sale at Naschmarkt

The adjoining Naschmarkt is a world in itself. It started around 1775 as a milk market, later growing into a fruit and vegetable market in the Karlsplatz area. After the Wien had been covered over, the market moved to its present location. It retains its old-world character at the end farthest from the city centre. Here the stalls are still proper wooden booths, fruit and vegetables are cheap, and haggling goes on in all the languages of this multi-ethnic former empire.

The farther you go towards the city centre, the grander the market becomes. In the middle, Turks, Iranians, Chinese, Japanese and Greeks have created a multi-cultural micro-climate. They sell fruit, vegetables, meat, cheese, olives and specialities from their own countries, and they run snack-bars and restaurants all enveloped in an aroma of kebabs.

The upper end of the Naschmarkt, towards the city, has blossomed in recent years.

Here luxury delicatessens have opened, selling delectable, gourmet

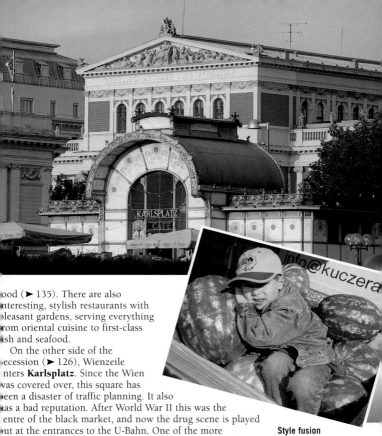

ood (► 135). There are also
interesting, stylish restaurants with
pleasant gardens, serving everything
from oriental cuisine to first-class
fish and seafood.

On the other side of the
Secession (► 126), Wienzeile
enters **Karlsplatz**. Since the Wien
was covered over, this square has
been a disaster of traffic planning. It also
has a bad reputation. After World War II this was the
centre of the black market, and now the drug scene is played
out at the entrances to the U-Bahn. One of the more
lugubrious sights on Karlsplatz is the Wien-Museum, docum-
enting the history of Vienna, from the first settlements on the
Danube right up to the present time

Style fusion
on Karlsplatz:
Musikverein
and Wagner's
Stadtbahn
station

TAKING A BREAK

All sorts of delicacies tempt you at every step. **Piccolo
Gourmet** (► 135) serves really good Italian snacks.

The fruit at the
Naschmarkt is
so good you
just have to
dive in!

🚇 192 B1 ✉ Wien 6, Naschmarkt 🕐 Stalls Mon–Fri 6 am–6:30 pm,
Sat 6–5, every 1st Sat in the month 6–6; Farmers' Market Sat 6:30–5; Flea
Market Sat 6:30–6 (including public holidays) Ⓜ Kettenbrückengasse,
Karlsplatz 🚋 Tram 62, 65 Bus 4A, 59A Karlsplatz

NASCHMARKT AND WIENZEILE: INSIDE INFO

Top tips If you don't like crowds, don't go to the Naschmarkt on Friday
afternoon or Saturday morning when it's at its busiest.

One to miss Avoid Karlsplatz and its U-Bahn entrances after dark. This is
where the drug dealers and junkies hang out.

3 Secession

Goldener Krauthappl, meaning "golden cabbage snack", is what the Viennese call the Secession, which is crowned by a large golden ball of laurel leaves. This affectionately disparaged building right next to the Naschmarkt is the most important example of Jugendstil architecture in the city.

The young, rebellious artists who formed their own group in 1897 and later became the leading proponents of Jugendstil in Vienna (▶ 24) needed their own building. And so the Secessionists, the ones who had split off from the main group, asked Joseph Maria Olbrich, who had studied under Otto Wagner, to build them an exhibition hall.

The new representative building was controversial and hotly debated from the start. Its plain, purist lines, the cubic block of the main building and the large laurel-leaf dome met with violent opposition and distaste from the start. "Ought to be torn down!", was the vociferous demand of many Viennese,

The Secession, once a scandal, now a glorious advertisement for Vienna

The Secession style is evident in the smallest details.

notwithstanding the motto over the main door: "To the age its art, to art its freedom".

A Leafy Roof for Art

All the same, Olbrich succeeded, with this temple to art, in enriching Vienna with a very interesting if unconventional building, which still today looks progressive and exciting. The "Krauthappl" with its 3,000 gilt leaves and 700 berries symbolizes the unity of art and nature – under the leafy roof art was to grow and flourish. The laurel leaf is repeated on the pilasters of the front wing and the entrance niche, as well as in the various garlands along the side elevation.

The team of lions with the Roman emperor Marcus Aurelius on one side of the Secession has much less profound origins. This was meant to be only the temporary site for the bronze group created by Arthur Strasser for the 1901 World Exhibition. It's still there – "temporary" appears to last much longer in Vienna than elsewhere.

The Secession building has remained true to its original purpose as an exhibition hall for contemporary art, still providing the stage for numerous highly regarded changing exhibitions. It still gets people worked up today: in 1988, before it was renovated for its centenary celebrations, the artist Marcel Geiger covered it in bright red – and popular anger exploded once again.

TAKING A BREAK

In a small park at the back of the building is the **Café Secession**, run by the wine experts Wein & Co opposite. Here you can relax over a snack and an excellent glass of wine (May–Sep daily 10 am–midnight).

➕ 192 C1 ✉ Wien 1, Friedrichstrasse 12 ☎ (01) 587 53 07 🕐 Tue–Sun 10–6, Thu until 8 🚇 Oper, Karlsplatz 🚋 Tram 1, 2, D, J, Bus 3A, 59A Oper, Karlsplatz 💰 Moderate ❓ www.secession.at

SECESSION: INSIDE INFO

Top tips Guided tours are held on Saturdays at 3pm and Sundays at 11am.

Hidden gem Take your time over Gustav Klimt's *Beethoven Frieze*. Created in 1902 for XIVth exhibition of the Association of Fine Artists of Austria Secession, it was later detached and sold. In 1985 it returned to the Secession and is now housed in a specially constructed room in the lower ground floor. In this monumental work, 34m (111 feet) long and 2.20m (7 feet) high, Klimt interprets Beethoven's *Ninth Symphony* as a journey through illness and suffering to pure love.

4 Karlskirche

From the start this grandiose place of worship was conceived as a powerful symbol. It is an unmistakable sign of the universality of the claims of Church and Empire. The cross on the dome lantern stands for the omnipotence of God, the crowns and eagles on the two triumphal columns for the power of the emperor.

Strictly speaking, the Karlskirche is a votive church. In 1713, when the plague cost the lives of almost 10,000 Viennese, Emperor Karl VI vowed to build a church dedicated to the patron saint of plague victims, St Carlo Borromeo. In 1714, against stiff competition, Johann Bernhard Fischer von Erlach won the commission to build the church in wooded meadows beside the as yet unregulated Wien River. He, and after his death his son Joseph Emanuel, created with their budget of 300,000 guilders a unique work of art, a church which is 80m (260 feet) long and 60m (200 feet) broad and which can be seen from far away in the city centre, down Herrengasse and Augustinerstrasse.

Imposing columns adorn Fischer von Erlach's baroque masterpiece

Resplendent from Outside...

In front of the central edifice, dominated by its green dome, is a porch in the form of a Greek temple, whose **Giebelrelief** (Pediment Relief) depicts scenes from the plague epidemic. St Borromeus stands on the pediment surrounded by allegories of the four virtues of contrition, mercy, prayerfulness and religion, all by Lorenzo Mattielli.

The building is flanked by two **Triumphsäulen** (Triumphal Columns) decorated with reliefs, which reach almost as high as the dome. Created by Mader and Matielli, they represent the empire's Pillars of Hercules. Beside them are two **Glockentürme** (Bell-towers) with a faint resemblance to pagodas. On each side of the **Freitreppe** (Stairway) is the mighty figure of an angel, the work of Franz Caspar.

...and from Inside

On the inside "Vienna's Hagia Sophia", as the largest baroque cathedral north of the Alps was soon called, is no less impressive. The oval **Hauptraum** (Central Hall) is crowned by the 72-m (235-foot) high dome, which looks even more imposing due to Gaetano Fanti's *trompe-l'oeil* perspective paintings on the lower edge.

The **Kuppelfresko** (Dome Frescoes) were done in 1725–30 by the then renowned ceiling painter Johann Michael Rottmayr. They show St Borromeo imploring the Holy Trinity for release from the plague. Rottmayr's numerous smaller paintings on the vault of the choir, in the chapels and above the organ all convey the impression of baroque opulence, as does Albert Camesina's over-lavish stucco. Johann Bernhard Fischer von Erlach's high altar, with Borromeo rising through clouds to the divine light, also makes its contribution.

TAKING A BREAK

In **Otto Wagner's Pavillon** in Karlsplatz, a Stadtbahn station converted into a café, you can enjoy a snack in fine Jugendstil surroundings.

🞢 193 D1 ✉ Wien 4,
Kreuzherrengasse 1 ☎ Mon–Sat
9–12:30, 1–6, Sun 1–6
Ⓤ Karlsplatz 🚋 Tram 62, 65, Bus
4A, 59A Karlsplatz 🅼 Moderate
❓ www.karlskirche.at

KARLSKIRCHE: INSIDE INFO

Top tips During the restoration work (due to finish in 2006), a lift takes visitors to the frescoes in the dome. The **panorama windows** at the top have a magnificent view of Vienna.

• The **Borromeus Museum** on the first floor has interesting items from the history of the Karlskirche and the life of St Borromeus.

Hidden gem Don't miss **Henry Moore's modern sculpture** *Hill Arches* in the pool in front of the church. After all the baroque extravagance inside the church, its sober simplicity is a pleasure to look at.

At Your Leisure

5 Wien Museum

From the outside the Wien Museum (Vienna Museum, formerly Historisches Museum der Stadt Wien) in Karlsplatz, is rather off-putting with its late-1950s steel framework, but inside it has much to offer. Extensive collections document the history of the city from the Celts onwards. Of particular interest are the original stained-glass and sandstone statues from the Stephansdom, objects from the two Turkish sieges and baroque, Biedermeier and Jugendstil exhibits.

193 D1 · Wien 4, Karlsplatz · (01) 505 87 47 · Tue–Sun 9–6 · Karlsplatz · Tram 62, 65, Bus 4A, 59A Karlsplatz · Moderate

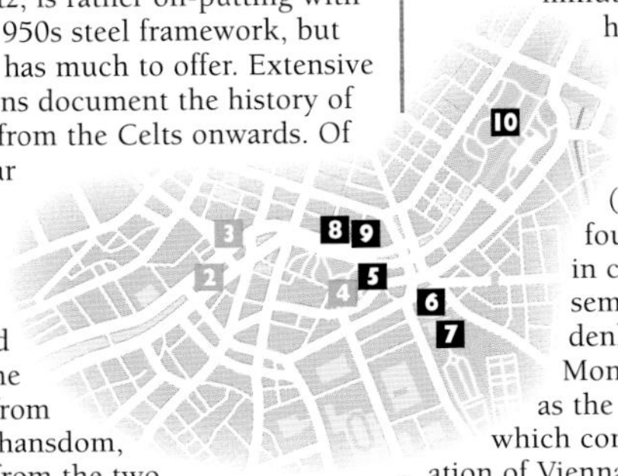

6 Hochstrahlbrunnen

The new Hochstrahlbrunnen (High-jet Fountain) was meant to spring into action on 24 October, 1873, in the presence of the emperor and all the civic dignitaries, to celebrate the completion of the First High Mountain Water Conduit. It caused some anxiety to its builders – it simply refused to work. After fraught minutes of waiting, however, the high column of water shot up into the sky – and since then it has carried on working (➤ 30). In summer the fountain is illuminated in colour. Behind it is the semi-circular Befreiungsdenkmal (Liberation Monument), also known as the Russian Memorial, which commemorates the liberation of Vienna at the end of World War II by the Red Army (➤ 181).

193 E1 · Wien 3, Schwarzenbergplatz · Karlsplatz · Tram D Gusshausstrasse

7 Palais Schwarzenberg

Schwarzenberg Palace, which is now practically in the middle of the city, was originally built as a garden palace on ground outside the city

Caryatids in the Goldener Saal of the Musikverein

walls, with a beautiful view of the fortified inner city. In 1697 Prince Mansfeld-Fondi commissioned Johann Lukas von Hildebrandt to build it. In 1716 Prince Adam Franz von Schwarzenberg took over the site and gave the work to Johann Bernhard Fischer von Erlach. After the latter's death in 1723 it was completed by his son Joseph Emanuel. The most interesting part of the palace, which is still owned by the Schwarzenberg family, is its nicely structured façade facing the city. Today it houses one of Vienna's finest luxury hotels, whose restaurant is also recommended for non-residents.

🚇 193 E1 ✉ Wien 3, Schwarzen-bergplatz 9 Ⓜ Karlsplatz 🚋 Tram D Gusshausstrasse

Johann Strauss competes with the sun for splendour

musicians have appeared in this house with its almost unbelievably good acoustics. In 2004 four new auditoria were added to the Musik-verein. As well as the world-famous Goldener Saal, from which the New Year's Concert is broadcast inter-nationally, it now has the Gläserner (Glass), Metallener (Metal, for young audiences), Hölzerner (Wooden) and Steinerner (Stone) halls.

🚇 193 D1 ✉ Wien 1, Bösendorfer-strasse 12 ☎ (01) 505 81 90, Infoline (01) 505 13 63 🎫 Box office Mon–Fri 9–7:30, Sat 10–6 Ⓜ Karlsplatz 🚋 Tram 62, 65, Bus, 4A, 59A Karlsplatz ❓ www.musikverein.at

8 Künstlerhaus

The Artists' House was built in 1895–68 in the style of the Italian Renaissance as an exhibition and meeting house for the "Genossen-schaft der bildenden Künstler Wiens" (Association of Viennese Artists). Eight marble statues stand on its façade: Dürer, Michelangelo, Raphael, Rubens, Leonardo da Vinci, Velázquez, Bramante and Titian. In the recent past the Künstlerhaus has staged spectacular and large exhibitions. It is now being completely renovated.

🚇 193 D1 ✉ Wien 1, Karlsplatz 5 ☎ (01) 587 96 63 Ⓜ Karlsplatz 🚋 Tram 62, 65, Bus 4A, 59A Karlsplatz

9 Musikverein

This building was constructed to Theophil Hansen's design in 1867–9 for the Musikverein (Music Society), which was founded in 1814. The landlords are the Viennese Phil-harmonic. Apart from the orchestra, virtually all famous international

10 Stadtpark

The lovingly tended Stadtpark (City Park) occupies part of what was open ground outside the city walls. It was laid out in 1862 to the design of Josef Selleny and Rudolf Siebeck in the English landscape style. Seen from here, the view of the Wien River is particularly interesting. After an underground passage of 2km (1.2 miles) it re-emerges through a Jugendstil gateway, flanked by walls, steps and pavilions. Many memorials commemorate notables like Schubert and Lehar. A major attraction and probably the most photographed object in Vienna is the marble and gold statue of Johann Strauss.

🚇 193 E/F2/3 Ⓜ Stadtpark

Where to...
Eat and Drink

Prices

Prices given are for one person, excluding drinks.
€ under 12 euros **€€** 12–25 euros **€€€** over 25 euros

Restaurants

Collio €€€

This restaurant in the Das Triest Hotel specializes in north-eastern Italian cooking; like the Silver Bar in the same location, it was excellently designed by Sir Terence Conran. Fresh fish is always on the menu, barbecued outside in summer. The wine list has an extensive range of Austrian, Italian and French wines.

🖶 194 B1 🖂 Wien 4, Wiedner Hauptstrasse 12 ☎ (01) 589 18–133 🕒 Mon–Fri noon–2:30, 6:30–10, Sat 6:30 pm–10 pm 🚊 Karlsplatz 🚋 Tram 62, 65 Paulaner Kirche

Hietzinger Bräu €€

This is by far the best restaurant in the elegant residential district of Hietzing. It belongs to the Plachutti family and, like their eatery in Wollzeile 1, specializes in truly outstanding beef dishes. Everything from *schulterscherzel* (top of shoulder) to *tafelspitz* is served in beef broth, accompanied by a delicious selection of vegetables.

🖶 198, west of the A3 🖂 Wien 13, Auhofstrasse 1 ☎ (01) 877 70 87 🕒 Mon–Fri 11:30–3, 6–11:30, Sat–Sun 11:30am until midnight (hot food until 2:30 pm and 10:30 pm) 🚊 Hietzing-Tiergarten 🚋 Tram 58, 60 Dommayergasse

Palais Schwarzenberg €€€

Seating only 35 people, this restaurant in the garden of Palais Schwarzenberg is one of the most elegant in the city. It has a superb view of the Schwarzenberg Park through the large glassed-in terrace windows, which can be opened wide in summer. The cuisine is modern Viennese. After your meal, enjoy a drink in the cosy and stylish Fireplace Room or in the Palais Bar, one of Vienna's finest.

🖶 193 E1 🖂 Wien 3, Schwarzenbergplatz 9 ☎ (01) 798 45 15–600 🕒 Daily noon–2, 6–10 pm, Palais Bar daily 10 am–1 am 🚊 Karlsplatz 🚋 Tram D Gusshausstrasse

ra'mien €€

A particularly interesting modern Asian restaurant, brightly decorated in grey and white. The red-painted cocktail bar provides a colour contrast; in the noodle bar the noodles are hand-made in front of the diners. The noodle soups (known as ramen) and rice dishes served at lunchtime are a real delight. In the evening there's a wide range of Thai, Japanese, Chinese and Vietnamese dishes. There's the Dance Lounge in the cellar, where on some nights throwing the die decides how much you pay for a drink.

🖶 192 B1 🖂 Wien 6, Gumpendorfer Strasse 9 ☎ (01) 585 47 98 🕒 Tue–Sun 11 am–midnight, Bar Tue–Wed, Sun 8 pm–2 am, Thu–Sat until 4 am 🚊 Museumsquartier 🚋 Bus 57A Köstlergasse

Schwarzer Adler €€

This rustic restaurant has long been known for its excellent traditional Viennese dishes, including hors d'oeuvres and some delectable fish dishes. The interior features wood panelling, cast-iron features and a tiled stove. The impressive wine list embraces numerous excellent Austrian and international wines.

🚹 194, southwest of the A1
🖂 Wien 5, Schönbrunner Strasse 40
☎ (01) 544 11 09 ◉ Tue–Sat 11–2:30, 6–11, Jul–Aug also Mon 6 pm–11 pm (hot food until 10:30pm) Ⓜ Pilgramgasse
🚍 Bus 12A, 13A, 59A Margaretenplatz

Silberwirt €€

This restaurant is the epitome of a superior Viennese pub. The menu lists traditional dishes like *schulterscherzel*, Wiener schnitzel and roast chicken, but also Italian pasta dishes. An inexpensive two-course set meal is available at lunchtime. The Silberwirt and neighbouring *schlossquadrat* (Castle Square), pledged to maintain high standards of food, wine and ambience.

🚹 194 A1 🖂 Wien 5, Schlossgasse 21 ☎ (01) 544 49 07 ◉ Daily noon–midnight (hot food noon–10:30 pm) Ⓜ Pilgramgasse 🚍 Bus 12A, 13A, 59A Margaretenplatz

Zu den 3 Buchteln €

This friendly wood-panelled restaurant specializes in Viennese and Bohemian cuisine from grandmother's days. It's not a place to start counting calories, especially if you try one of the wonderful hot desserts – which you certainly should do at least once in Vienna!

🚹 194 A1 🖂 Wien 5, Wehrgasse 90 ☎ (01) 587 83 65 ◉ Mon–Sat 6 pm–midnight (hot food until 11 pm), Closed Jul Ⓜ Pilgramgasse 🚍 Bus 12A, 13A, 59A Margaretenplatz

Zur Goldenen Glocke €€

Two wall-paintings with a total length of 12m (40 feet), depicting the famous names of late 19th-century Viennese operetta and theatre, make the garden of this traditional old-Viennese restaurant perhaps the most beautiful in the city. Even when it rains you can sit outside, under a huge awning. The menu is also impressive: superior Viennese and Austrian cooking, both of traditional dishes using

beef, offal and other meats, and imaginative creations. There are also speciality weeks.

🚹 194 B1 🖂 Wien 5, Kettenbrückengasse 9 ☎ (01) 587 57 67 ◉ Mon–Sat 11–2:30, 5:30–midnight Ⓜ Kettenbrückengasse 🚍 Bus 59A Kettenbrückengasse

Naschmarkt

The Naschmarkt is increasingly known as a place to eat really well. At its top end and on the Linke Wienzeile side some interesting restaurants have opened, where you can go on a culinary cruise around the world. **Calamari** and **Strandhaus** (Stand 1–5, Mon–Fri 9:30–7:30, Sat until 4:30 pm) are two restaurants of the Nordsee fish-food chain, offering quite excellent fish and shellfish dishes at usually moderate prices. The same goes for the Turkish-run **Umar Fisch** (Stand 76, Mon–Sat 11–11), where you may feel you're in a Mediterranean beach bar. It now counts as one of

Vienna's best fish restaurants. The **Indian Pavillon**, also a take-away, is filled with the delicious aromas of curry mixes and coriander from its Indian specialities (Stand 74–75, Mon–Fri 11–6:30, Sat until 5). Both **Take-Nudel** (Stand 87, Mon–Sat 10:30–10), and **Mr Lee** (Stand 278–280, Mon–Sat 10:30–10), serve oriental delicacies from the wok and aromatic noodle dishes. The two coolly stylish **TokoRi** restaurants are a little piece of Japan in Vienna, with splendid sushi, teriyaki and sashimi (Stand 261–277 opposite the Theater an der Wien, Mon–Sat 11–11pm, Stand 177–178, Mon–Sat 9:30–7). They also do a take-away lunchbox. The **Naschmarkt Deli** (Stand 421–436, Mon–Fri 7 am–10 pm, Sat until midnight) makes use of fresh, seasonal market produce, serving delectable little vegetable dishes and crisp salads. Its breakfast specialities are very popular, as is the coffee from a small Italian roasting house. There's jazz on Thursdays.

Cafés

Dommayer

This elegant coffee-house has a long musical history. Founded in 1787, it changed its name in 1833 to Kasino Dommayer and became the centre of Biedermeier social life. Both Johann Strauss the Elder and the Younger played here, as did Lanner. The Millefleurs Balls and "Rosenfeste" were legendary, and in the 1930s Viennese films were shot here. Today the Dommayer is as smart as the Hietzing district surrounding it. The *torten* served here are top quality, as is all the food, including classics such as goulash. On Saturday afternoons Dommayer concerts (2 pm–4 pm) and from May until September plays are performed on the garden stage (from 5:30 pm).

✚ 198, west of the A3 ⊠ Wien 13, Auhofstrasse 2 ☎ (01) 877 54 65 ◷ Daily 7am–midnight (hot food until 11 pm) Ⓤ Hietzing-Tiergarten ▤ Tram 58, 60 Dommayergasse

Drechsler

It's not beautiful or elegant, but this Viennese institution has a lot of character – and it opens really early. That's why the very likeable Drechsler, within the same family for three generations, is a popular place for night-owls after the night's exertions. Before 7 am you pay slightly elevated "night prices", but they really aren't very high.

✚ 194 B2 ⊠ Wien 6, Linke Wienzeile 22 ☎ (01) 587 85 80 ◷ Mon–Fri 3 am–8 pm, Sat until 6 pm Ⓤ Kettenbrückengasse ▤ Bus 57A Köstlergasse

Gloriette

The view from this café above Schönbrunn Palace is spectacular – the park and the palace are right before your eyes, and beyond them stretches the whole sweep of the city. Make sure you bring your camera! From 9 am at weekends you can breakfast royally at the buffet to the sound of classical music.

✚ 198 B2 ⊠ Wien 13, Schlosspark Schönbrunn, Gloriette ☎ (01) 879 13 11 ◷ Daily 9 am until an hour before the park closes Ⓤ Schönbrunn ▤ Tram 10, 58, Bus 10A Schloss Schönbrunn

High Tea

This is a special sort of tea-house, combining high tech with a living-room atmosphere. In one room you can settle down on comfortable old-world sofas. In another, two inter-net workstations and two lap-top web connections can be used free of charge.

✚ 194 C2 ⊠ Wien 4, Paniglgasse 17 ☎ (01) 504 15 08 ◷ Sep–Apr Mon–Fri 9 am–10 pm, Sat until 6:30 pm; May–Aug Mon–Sat 9 am–6:30 pm; closed first three weeks in Aug Ⓤ Karlsplatz ▤ Tram 62, 65 Paulaner Kirche

Museum Café

Designed by Alfred Loos, the café Museum opened in 1899. All was set out in his strict purist style. The decor is simple and free of ornamentation – and so the café soon became known as the "Nihilism Café". In 2003 it was thoroughly renovated and now, stripped of even its coffee-house patina, it looks more nihilist than ever, but it's a popular, central meeting-place.

✚ 192 C2 ⊠ Wien 1, Operngasse 7 ☎ (01) 586 52 02 ◷ Mon–Sat 8 am–midnight, Sun 10 am–midnight Ⓤ Karlsplatz ▤ Tram 62, 65 Bus 4A, 59A Karlsplatz

Sperl

This famous coffee-house has retained its fine old character, thanks to careful renovation. Around 1900 the spacious café was the haunt of artists and high-ranking officers. Now it's a popular hangout for artists, intellectuals and romantics.

✚ 194 B2 ⊠ Wien 6, Gumpendorfer Strasse 11 ☎ (01) 586 41 58 ◷ Mon–Sat 7 am–11 pm, Sun 11 am–8 pm, Jul–Aug closed Sun Ⓤ Museumsquartier ▤ Bus 57A Köstlergasse

Where to... Shop

The Wiental between Secession and Kettenbrückengasse is the best place to shop. The flea-market and the Naschmarkt offer all sorts of opportunities to acquire something interesting.

The **Flohmarkt** (flea-market) is very busy every Saturday (6:30 am– 6 pm). The traders, some of whom are professional dealers, arrive in the early hours to unpack their treasures. You can then rummage through them all day to your heart's content. The choice ranges from old glasses through china, books, records and furniture to – if you're lucky – genuine (or almost genuine) Jugendstil lamps and antique linen. With any luck there's always the chance of picking up something special.

Naschmarkt is a paradise for shopaholics. At one end you can buy seasonal fruit and vegetables. The choice of exotic fruit from across the globe is extraordinary – this is where Vienna's many foreign residents, who work in international organizations such as the United Nations, buy their food.

For many years **Strmiska** (Stand 248) has been known for the best sauerkraut and delicious pickled gherkins in the city. **Der Urbanek** has also long been a focal point; the tiny delicatessen (Stand 46), which sells marvellous ham, cheese and wine, is often overflowing with the whole Viennese "in-crowd".

The top end of Naschmarkt is specializing more and more in luxury foods. **Pöchl** (Stand 168) has excellent breads, salami, olive oil and pasta, as well as one of the best hams in Vienna. **Käseland** (meaning cheese-land, Stand 172) has a large selection of cheeses from around the world including unusual ones such as Vorarlberg mountain cheese and "Wilder Kaiser". Right next door is **Kurkonditorei Oberlaa** (Stand 175), a small, elegant shop with great *torten* and confectionery. Buy a picnic here and enjoy it in one of Vienna's beautiful open areas. **Gegenbauer** (Stand 111–114), on the other hand, is the place for perfect vinegar: it has rarities such as blackcurrant vinegar, balsamic quince vinegar, matured for five years in oak, or "Edelsaurer", a drinking vinegar.

The side of Linke Wienzeile opposite Naschmarkt is also of great culinary interest. **Piccini** (Linke Wienzeile 4) has specialized for many years in Italian delicatessen: mortadella, *prosciutto*, pasta and *antipasti*. If you want a tasty Italian snack to eat on the spot, go to **Piccolo Gourmet** next door (Linke Wienzeile 4, Mon–Fri 11 am–7:30 pm, Sat 9:30 am–2 pm). This shop-bar with a Jugenstil courtyard prides itself on its *antipasti* – it has an astonishing selection of 60 in the window!

Where to be... Entertained

In this part of the city the wine is excellent, and there are quite a few bars featuring an eyecatching modern design.

Bars

Aux Gazelles (Rahlgasse 5, tel: 01/585 66 45) is one of the most beautiful and interesting bars in the city. Its 2,000sq m (2,400 square yard) space offers all sorts of delights with a North African touch. The café/delicatessen (Mon–Thu 8 am–2 am, Fri-Sat 8 am–4 am, Sun 10 am–9 pm) provides a variety of breakfasts, a set lunch menu, Mediterranean specialities and oriental salads (also take-out). The elegant Caviar & Oyster Bar is attached (Mon–Sat 8 am–2 am, Sun 2 pm–1 am).

The Brasserie (Mon–Fri noon–3, 6–11 pm, Sat 6–11 pm) is separated from the kitchen by a courtyard; it serves French and North African specialities. The Club Bar (Mon–Thu 9 pm–2 am, Fri–Sat 9 pm–4 am) with its oriental feel is strikingly beautiful, and varied programmes of music go from soul to oriental beat. The absolute hit at Aux Gazelles is its large "hammam" (Tue–Fri 3-11 pm, Sat–Sun 11 am–10 pm), an oriental steam-bath with three temperature zones and a wonderful tea-room next door, where you can relax in style afterwards.

The chic and elegant **Theater-café** (Linke Wienzeile, tel: 01/585 62 62, Mon–Sat 9:30 am–2 am, Sun 3 pm–1 am) next to the Theater an der Wien quickly became the place to be seen for famous painters and musicians, as well as for would-be celebrities. At lunch, superior Viennese cooking is served, in the evenings the Viennese "in crowd" meet in the long cool bar. And if

evening stretches until early morning, there's nothing lost – Café Drechsler (▶ 134) is only a few steps away.

Vinissimo (Windmühlgasse 20, tel: 01/586 48 88, Mon–Sat 11 am–11 pm) is a successful combination of wine-bar and bistro. It has a small garden in Raimundhof, which leads up to Mariahilfer Strasse. The wine list is long, the menu features mainly Italian and Spanish special-ities, as well as typical Austrian delicacies, and many dishes are suitable for vegetarians.

The **Wein & Co** bar (Getreide-markt 1, tel: 01/585 72 57, Mon–Fri 10 am–midnight, Sat 9 am–midnight, Sun 11 am–midnight) is a must for wine-lovers. An enormous selection of Austrian and international wines is sold in the bar. And because of the attached restaurant, the shop stays open while others close. With your wine you can eat small snacks or Mediterranean specialities from the cold buffet. Sundays 11 am–4 pm is "Happy Sunday", when house wines are half price.

The **Silverbar** in Das Triest hotel (Wiedner Hauptstrasse 12, tel: 01/589 18-133, Mon 6 pm–2 am, Tue–Sat 7 pm–3 am, Sun 3:30 pm–midnight) is worth a visit simply for its elegant and unusual design, for which no less a person than Sir Terence Conran was responsible. The award-winning bar has an interesting selection of cocktails, and for entertainment there's jazz, Latino and soul. A good place to chill out.

The modern **Schikaneder** bar in the former lobby of the old reper-tory cinema of the same name (Margaretenstrasse 22–24, tel: 01/585 58 88, daily 6 pm–4 am, or 30 minutes before the film starts) is quite special. The unusually long bar, and equally long seating opposite, make for an atmosphere with flair. They mix some interesting cocktails.

MUSIC

This part of the city has the two institutions which, together with

the Staatsoper, form the basis for Vienna's reputation as world capital of music and in which the famous "Viennese style" was created. The **Konzerthaus** (Lothringerstrasse 20, tel: 01/242 00, information on 01/24 20 01 00, box office Mon–Fri 9 am–7:45 pm, Sat until 1 pm), which houses in its west wing the School of Music and Performing Arts, is home to the Wiener Symphoniker orchestra, while the **Musikverein** (▶ 131) has the Philharmoniker orchestra.

The **Kursalon Hübner Wien** Wien, in a beautiful Italian Renaissance building, provides an imperial stage for Viennese music, which is particularly appreciated by visitors. Operetta and waltz music is played from midday in the Johann Strauss restaurant (Johannesgasse 33, tel: 01/512 57 90, daily 11:30 am–midnight) and from 3 pm on the terrace. In the evenings the palm court orchestra Alt-Wien plays Strauss melodies (10 Apr–31 Oct 10:30 pm, otherwise 7:30 pm).

Belvedere, Prater and Danube

Getting Your Bearings

This area of the city, with both Belvedere Palace and the stunning buildings by Friedensreich Hundertwasser, has exciting architecture of very different styles. The Prater and the banks of the Danube are Vienna's great relaxation and recreation grounds.

The Belvedere, Prince Eugene's palace, is a grandiose baroque edifice set in a magnificent park. And the architect Friedensreich Hundertwasser, with his colourful, adventurous buildings, created structures way beyond the expected. With its vast stretches of wood and meadow, the Prater simply invites you to take a walk, simply relax in the sun or play sport. One part of "Vienna's green lung", however, the Wurstelprater, is reserved for fun unlimited: for a long time now, the fun fair with dodgem cars, ghost ride and hall of mirrors has provided the Viennese with entertainment and been good for a real laugh.

Page 137:
One of Vienna's landmarks: the Riesenrad (Giant Ferris Wheel)

Thanks to the Danube, Vienna has a beach. The Gänsehäufel (a bathing beach), the Old Danube and Danube Island are the places where the Viennese can play sport and enjoy a bathe – otherwise it would have to be the Adriatic. And on Copa Cagrana it's holiday-time all summer, with the wonderful aromas of multiethnic food and resounding with the music from distant lands.

On Danube Island you'll know you're on holiday

★ Don't Miss

- **1** **Belvedere** ➤ 142
- **2** **KunstHausWien** ➤ 144
- **4** **Riesenrad** ➤ 146
- **5** **Prater** ➤ 148

At Your Leisure

- **3** Hundertwasser-Haus ➤ 152
- **6** Gänsehäufel ➤ 152
- **7** Alte Donau ➤ 153
- **8** Donauinsel ➤ 153

First you'll immerse yourself in baroque architecture and works of art, as well as the eccentrically colourful world of Friedensreich Hundertwasser. The rest of the day is devoted to pure pleasure: in the Prater and along the Danube, fun entertainment and relaxation are the order of the day.

Belvedere, Prater and Danube in a Day

9:00 am

This starts with the **1** **Belvedere** (➤ 142). In the Upper Belvedere you'll find the splendid baroque architecture of the palace and the magnificent paintings of Klimt, Kokoschka and Schiele. Before you walk through the park to the Lower Belvedere (below), stop to take in a view of the city, which is spread out before you. Then you'll understand the name of the palace: Belvedere – beautiful sight.

11:00 am

Friedensreich Hundertwasser's **2** **KunstHausWien** (➤ 144)) is as demanding on your feet as on your eyes. The undulating floor forces you to tread carefully, and you also have to cope with the abundance of colours and forms that crowd in on you. But as you make your way

through the exhibition halls, you'll find that the surroundings take less getting used to than you first thought – and that in the end you don't really want to leave. But you don't have to, because there's a café with a beautiful garden where you can go on absorbing the unique atmosphere.

12:30 pm

After a visit to the multicoloured world of Hundertwasser the reality outside looks rather grey. But this impression soon vanishes in the

5 Prater (above; ➤ 148) Here everything is colourful and noisy. Try the **4 Riesenrad** (➤ 146), and then plunge into the throng. Want a shot of adrenalin? Try the wild Volare (big dipper), then take a ride on the Liliput railway and go on to lunch at Stelze (try the pig's trotters) and beer in the Schweizerhaus (➤ 155).

3:30 pm

Drink your coffee in the peace and calm of the Lusthaus (left; ➤ 155) After all the turmoil a breathing space is called for – you still have things to do by the Danube.

5:00 pm

A bit of jogging or a refreshing bathe in the river? You can do either on **8 Donauinsel** (Danube Island, below; ➤ 153) but be careful to reserve enough energy if you plan to pub-crawl on the Copa Cagrana (➤ 158) or to enjoy the sunset.

7:30 pm

You could carouse into the small hours on the Copa Cagrana, dancing to the sounds of sirtaki or salsa, and quite likely you will want to, but there are many alternatives. One would be to spend the evening in the Tribüne Krieau open-air cinema (➤ 18).

1 Belvedere

The Belvedere complex, with its magnificent gardens, represents the apex of perfection in baroque architecture. This world-famous palace, which lies on a low hill outside Vienna, houses great works of art. It also offers the visitor an incomparable view of the city.

Prince Eugene of Savoy (1663–1736) was anything but handsome. Small and not very sociable, he wasn't the image of a dazzling hero. And yet the prince, who was born in Paris, became the most important military commander of his day. It was thanks to his strategic skill that Austria defeated the Turks and won significant victories in the War of the Spanish Succession (1701–14).

These victories paved the way for the Habsburgs' rise to power, and for that they didn't mind spending a bit. The size of Prince Eugene's reward can be guessed by looking at the Belvedere: the prince spared no expense, when in 1714–23 he commissioned Johann Lukas von Hildebrandt to build his summer palace, which is really two palaces.

Oberes Belvedere

The Upper Belvedere is the more sumptuous of the two palaces. From the start it was only intended for grand events, and was furnished accordingly. The façade alone conveys the feeling of baroque luxuriance. This impression is reinforced inside the palace by Santino Bussi's white stucco in the **Sala terrena** and Carlo Carlone's frescoes in the **Gartensaal** (Garden Room) and **Marmorsaal**.(Marble Room). Prince Eugene never lived in his grand palace, but later it housed some famous personalities. In 1896 the composer Anton Bruckner spent the last year of his life here. Afterwards, it was the residence of the heir to the throne, Franz Ferdinand. After his assassination in 1914 in Sarajevo the palace stood empty for years. In 1955 it saw a historic

The Upper Belvedere, a showcase palace

The Marmor-saal is the centrepiece of the Lower Belvedere

event: in the Marmorsaal the Allies' foreign ministers signed the Austrian Treaty, and Chancellor Leopold Figl spoke the legendary words: "Austria is free!" from the balcony.

The Upper Belvedere now houses the Austrian 19th and 20th Century Gallery, an important collection of Austrian art. The highlights include paintings by Klimt (*The Kiss* hangs on the first floor in Room 4), Schiele, Kokoschka and Waldmüller.

Unteres Belvedere

The way to the Lower Belvedere leads through an extensive park with a view over Vienna. From the outside, the palace looks almost modest, but the rooms are really something. Here too the centrepiece is a frescoed **Marmorsaal**, but the **Goldkabinett** and the **Marmorgalerie** (Marble Gallery) are no less sumptuous. The baroque Museum is here, and the Museum of Mediaeval Art is in the Orangery.

TAKING A BREAK

Have a piece of Belvedere *torte* in the café-restaurant **Schloss Belvedere** (➤ 157).

🞥 195 D1 ✉ Oberes Belvedere: Wien 3, Prinz-Eugen-Strasse 27; Unteres Belvedere: Wien 3, Rennweg 6 ☎ (01) 795 57-0 🕐 Tue–Sun 10 am–6 pm
🚇 Oberes Belvedere: Tram D Schloss Belvedere, Tram O, 18, Bus 13A Südbahnhof; Unteres Belvedere: Tram 71 Unteres Belvedere 🖐 Expensive
❓ www.belvedere.at

BELVEDERE: INSIDE INFO

Top tip "Einblicke" (Insights) is the name of the 30-minute guided tour which takes you round the **gallery's highlights** (Fri–Sun and during school holidays Tue–Sun 11 am).

Hidden gem If you're thinking of getting married in Vienna, the palace chapel in the Upper Belvedere provides a suitably grand setting for your vows.

② KunstHausWien

This building, designed by Friedensreich Hundertwasser, is a museum that obeys none of the accepted norms. Colourful, curving and cheerful, it's a modern architectural adventure, striving to unite the creativity of nature and the creativity of man, an extraordinary experience for eyes and feet.

When at the end of the 1980s an appropriate home was being sought for the Austrian painter Friedensreich Hundertwasser's (1928–2000) extensive work, Vienna's third district offered the former furniture factory (1892) of the Thonet Brothers, near the Danube Canal. It took two years (1989–91) to adapt the site, making two houses into one. When it was opened in April 1991 it was a sensation.

A Bastion Against the False Dominance of the Straight Line

The master-architect oversaw the design of the museum himself. "The architecture of KunstHausWien is the first bastion against the dictatorship of the straight line, the ruler and T-square, a bridgehead against the grid system and the chaos of the absurd", he announced, and left not a stone standing. He added a porch on the street side and a staircase on the courtyard side. Within the house his treatment of every room on the four floors was highly unusual. Colourful pillars, curving lines, coloured window-frames and bright tiles make it into a fantastic Villa Motley.

The most important stylistic device is that in many areas the floors undulate in great irregular waves. You can't just wander through without watching where you put your feet. This is a quite new experience, for which Hundertwasser

Feast your eyes on Hundertwasser's colour-soaked paintings

Don't get confused!

Despite appearances, the Hundertwasser Haus and the KunstHausWien are not one and the same. The former was built by Hundertwasser as a private residence to a commission from the city of Vienna (left; ► 152), and the latter, also built by Hundertwasser, is the museum described on these pages.

evolved his very own theory: "An uneven and animated floor restores the human dignity, which has been violated in our levelling, unnatural and hostile urban grid system." The asphalted floors beloved by his contemporaries, he felt, were alienating man from his relationship with nature.

Hundertwasser and Other Artists

KunstHausWien is privately financed, with no public subsidies or taxpayers' money. It has a total exhibition space of around 4,000sq m (4,780 square yards). The ground floor houses the ticket-counters, cloakrooms, museum shop and a café-restaurant. The first and second floors house a permanent exhibition with a wide cross-section of Hundertwasser's work: paintings, drawings, tapestries and architectural models. The third and fourth floors are reserved for changing international exhibitions, including for example the photographic work of Cecil Beaton and Lord Snowdon. The exhibitions' high standard generally attracts a large public.

TAKING A BREAK

If after touring the museum you can't yet tear yourself away from the bright colours and curving lines, spend a while in the **KunstHausCafé** (► 157). Enjoy and marvel at the extraordinary atmosphere – you won't easily find its like anywhere else in the world.

Not of this world: the garden of the KunstHaus-Wien café

🚇 195 F4 ✉ Wien 3, Untere Weissgerberstrasse 13 ☎ (01) 712 04 91
🕐 Daily 10 am–7 pm Ⓢ Schwedenplatz 🚊 Tram N, O Radetzkyplatz
💰 Expensive ❓ www.kunsthauswien.com

KUNSTHAUSWIEN: INSIDE INFO

Top tip If you can, visit the museum on a Monday, the so-called **KunstHausMontag**, when there's a 50 per cent reduction of the admission price for each visitor (not on public holidays).

4 Riesenrad

After the Stephansdom, the second big emblem of Vienna is the Giant Ferris Wheel, visible from far and wide. The fact that it was rebuilt after World War II, at almost the same time as the Stephansdom and the "Steffl", shows how important it is to the Viennese, not least as a powerful symbol of the city's will to survive.

Emperor Franz Joseph's Golden Jubilee was what prompted Vienna, following the contemporary trend, to get itself a giant panoramic wheel. The commission went to the British engineer Walter Basset, who built it in 1896–97. Admittedly, his designs were not unique to Vienna: he also constructed similar panoramic wheels for London, Blackpool, Chicago and Paris.

Instant Success

From the outset the giant wheel was a hit with the public. The Viennese enjoyed looking down from one of the then 30 red cars on their town and on "Venedig in Wien" (Venice in Vienna; ► 149) at their feet. The technical data is also impressive. From the 1920s onwards the wheel was frequently used as a film location. Scenes from *The Third Man* (1949) by Carol Reed were shot here. In 1944 the mighty mechanism came to a halt; during World War II a fire damaged it badly. But it was soon repaired and in 1947 it started working again. From then on, for reasons of safety, the wheel operates with only 15 cars. Visitor numbers show how popular the leisurely

The giant wheel was an instant attraction

journey into the airy heights is: since the 1950s, some 30 million people have travelled on it. There are two luxury wagons – one in the style of 1892, the other in Jugendstil.

The Riesenrad today, as popular as ever

In the Course of Time

The Riesenrad doesn't just turn in a circle – it has recently experienced radical new additions. In 2002, eight cars that had been lost reappeared. They are now set up at the wheel's base, with lavish technical installations and a giant screen inviting visitors to take a virtual tour through 2,000 years of Vienna's history. And at night, thanks to installations by the British light-artist Patrick Woodroffe, it is bathed in different colours: the wheel shines a soft gold, while the pylons are in cool silver.

Technical data

- the highest point: 64.75m (212.43 feet) above ground level
- wheel diameter: 60.96m (200 feet)
- the axis of the wheel: 10.78m (35.37 feet) long, 0.5m (1.64 feet) thick, 16.3t (16.04 tons) in weight
- weight – entire structure: 244.85t (240.98 tons); all iron structures: 430.05t (423.26)
- speed: 0.75m/sec (2.46 ft/sec) = 2.7km/h (1.68 mph)

TAKING A BREAK

With its large terrace, the new, stylish **Café** by the entrance to the ticket-hall is a good place for some refreshments before or after your "trip aloft".

196 A5 Wien 2, Prater 20 (01) 729 54 30 Jan–Feb, Nov–Dec 10 am–8 pm; Mar–Apr, Oct 10 am–10 pm; May–Sep 9 am–midnight Praterstern Tram 0, 5, 21 Praterstern Expensive www.wienerriesenrad.com

RIESENRAD: INSIDE INFO

Top tips Make sure you see the Riesenrad by **night**, because after dark it becomes a clock-tower, sending out light signals instead of acoustic ones. Two minutes before each hour it starts to flash out the number of hours. If it flashes twice, you know it's two in the morning. And if it flashes three times, then the Viennese know it's time to hit the sack – it's 3 am.

• The Riesenrad's cars can also be **hired** – for small parties, press conferences, a romantic dîner à deux ... whatever. It costs 98 euros for half an hour and 196 euros for one hour in ordinary cars. For the privilege of riding in one of the two luxury cars you have to pay 260 euros for the first hour, 188 euros for the second and 116 euros for the third. Could there be a more romantic place to pop the question?

5 Prater

A quiet place to relax from the bustle of the city and a vibrant, noisy pleasure-ground – the Prater is both, which makes it Vienna's leisure Eldorado.

Once a real hit with the Viennese: the "Russian swings"

The history of the Prater is as varied as its attractions: once it was a swampy meadowland, then an imperial forest and hunting grounds, finally it became one of the world's first pleasure-gardens. Today the 6sq km (2.3 square miles) area contains old horse-racing tracks and the modern exhibition centre, idyllic avenues and thrilling fairground attractions.

From Water Meadow to Day-Trip Destination

For a long time the Prater was owned by various monasteries and aristocratic families, until in 1564 Maximilian II declared it to be a Habsburg hunting preserve. The populace was excluded from the attractive stretch of countryside until Emperor Joseph II opened the Prater to all Viennese. Soon

The Lusthaus was always a destination for romantic outings

Above left: the indestructible nostalgic chute "Tobogan"

after, pub landlords, coffee-brewers and gingerbread sellers set up their stalls at the western end, followed by swings, merry-go-rounds and skittle-alleys – the Wurstelprater (funfair) was born. In 1814 the Congress of Vienna was celebrated here in 40 inns, 50 skittle-alleys and several coffee-houses.

The "Volksprater" (People's Prater) became a European tourist site, whose fame reached its climax with the World Exhibition of 1873. That was when the fairground "Venedig in Wien" (Venice in

Above right: "Volare" is not for those with weak stomachs

Vienna) was unlike the **Riesenrad** (▶ 146) 1928 the **Liliputbahn**, a miniature steam loco, puffs its way from the Volksprater along the main avenue to the stadium and back. You'll find the railway station behind the giant wheel (www.liliputbahn.com; admission: moderate).

Above: you can drive off in style at the Freudenau golf club

The green Prater

The greater part of the Prater area is taken up by the "green Prater", broad stretches of natural country with meadows, woods and ponds. Here you'll also find the modern exhibition centre, a golf course, the Ernst Happel stadium and the stadium swimming-baths. The splendid chestnut avenue, almost 5km (3 mile) long, which leads from the Lusthaus to the Praterstern (star), was planted in 1537 by Emperor Ferdinand I. Here wealthy Viennese used to stroll, Napoleon's troops paraded here, and at the Congress of Vienna they danced in the coffee-houses

The Pratermuseum

In the planetarium near the Riesenrad, the Pratermuseum traces the spectacular history of the Viennese Prater. (Tel: 01/726 76 83 Tue–Fri 9–12:15, 1–4:30, Sat–Sun and public holidays 2–6:30 pm. Admission: inexpensive, Fri am and Sun: free.)

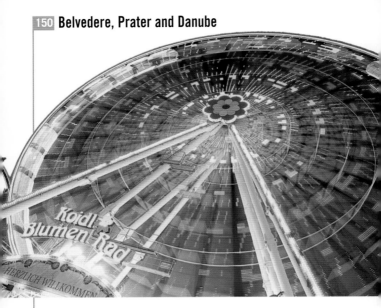

The view from the Blumenrad is tremendous

in the avenue. Today it's crowded with runners, cyclists and skateboarders, because since 1963 cars have been banned from the **Prater Hauptallee** (the Prater's main avenue). The **Jesuitenwiese** (Jesuits' Meadow) has the largest playing fields in Vienna, and here and in the numerous other playing fields and campsites there's ample space to play football or just do nothing. Right next to the **Lusthaus** (► 155) is the **Freudenau**, where the horse racing and the listed imperial lodge are very worth seeing.

Wiener Wurstelprater

This popular entertainment area takes its name from the Hanswurst (clown) who used to amuse the children in the puppet theatres. In the early years visitors were enticed into the Prater by sensational events such as waxworks, the Prater variety show, the vivarium or strange freak-shows. It always had the most modern attractions: the first steam carousel in 1844, the first cinema in 1896, the Riesenrad in 1897. After it was destroyed in World War II, the Wurstelprater was rebuilt from 1945 on, but on a smaller area. Every year it produces more amazing, faster, wilder and more breathtaking attractions. One of the newest challenges to daredevils eager for thrills is "Volare", a big dipper where you speed along lying flat, at

Who was Calafatti?

You'll come across his name again and again in the Wurstelprater. At one time, Basilius Calafatti, born in 1800 in Trieste, was the uncrowned king of the Prater. With his wife and nine children the small-time salami and cheese merchant built up a mini-empire, performed as a magician in front of the emperor and had the first steam carousel constructed. In the middle of this merry-go-round stood a 10-m (33-foot) tall figure with exotic features, the "Great Chinaman", which became the emblem of the Prater and was erected again after the war. From its position on Calafatti-platz it reminds us still of the Prater pioneer.

For Kids

In the vast area of **Kids Welt** (Kids' World) your children can, for a single entry fee, let off steam in many attractions while you relax at your table (Strasse des Ersten Mai 118, tel: 01/729 45 87; admission: expensive, www.kidswelt.com).

a height of 24m (79 feet), through a 420-m (460-yards) long jungle of rails (at Calafattiplatz). But some traditional activities have also stood the test of time, for example the 1887 Pony-karussell (opposite the Schweizerhaus), the wooden **Zwergerl-Hochschaubahn** (Miniature Railway, by the bike-hire) or the nostalgic chute »**Tobogan**«

from the 1950s. Antique attractions beside high-tech slot-machines, the chance of a win in the amusement arcades, rapid dodgem cars, a lot of music and still more fun – that's how the Wurstelprater presents itself today.

Top choice on the Schweizer-haus menu: *stelzen* (pig's trotters)

TAKING A BREAK

The **Meierei** (Dairy) can be found in the main avenue (May–Sep). In 1873 "American drinks" were served in the pavilion of the World Exhibition, later it was mineral water, from 1924 sweet and soured milk, and now there's the usual café-restaurant menu, with traditional Viennese and light, modern fare.

➕ 196 A–C 1–5 🎡 Attractions: Easter–Oct 10 am–1 am 🚇 Praterstern
🚋 Tram 0, 5, 21 Praterstern ❓ www.prater.at

PRATER: INSIDE INFO

Top tips Take a trip on the 35-m (115-foot) high **Blumenrad** (Flower Wheel), a smaller version of the Riesenrad. In the early evening the view from the revolving cars is spectacular!
• **Cycling** is a great way to explore the "green Prater". You can hire bikes by the Schweizerhaus, on the main avenue side (tel. 01/729 58 88, www.radverleih-hochschaubahn.com).

Hidden gem Behind the box-office of Europe's biggest and longest **Geisterbahn** (Ghost Train, Zufahrtstrasse 143) sits a Prater character: the producer and actor Hermann Molzer. He had theatrical pictures mounted along the track and is always ready with some nice stories about the Prater.

One to miss Beautiful though it is in daytime, the green Prater can be dark and distinctly **unpleasant at night**. At night-time it is therefore best avoided – stay on the illuminated roads!

At Your Leisure

🖪 Hundertwasser-Haus

The Hundertwasser House on the corner of Löwengasse and Kegelgasse is a colourful oasis in a grey urban desert. In a district where the buildings are mainly modest, so-called "period" houses or social housing, you suddenly come on a building with riotous shapes and brilliant colours. It consists of a jumble of windows of various sizes and with different frames, small balconies, bow-windows, strips of mosaic, onion towers and pillars, hanging gardens, and trees and shrubs sprouting out of terraces and from the roof. Friedensreich Hundertwasser designed this building with 50 apartments in 1983–85. The crazy "eco-architecture" is continued inside the house. Out of respect for the privacy of the tenants, many of whom knew the artist, the building can only be seen from the outside, but it's well worth it.

➕ 195 F3 ✉ Wien 3, corner Löwengasse/ Kegelgasse 🚊 Tram N Hetzgasse

Friedrich Stowasser

Friedensreich Hundertwasser was born Friedrich Stowasser in 1928 in Vienna. The *enfant terrible* of the artistic world, he developed a unique, very colourful pictorial language and carried out numerous architectural projects in Austria, Germany, Switzerland, California and Japan. New Zealand became his second home. He died in 2000, on the *Queen Elizabeth II* in the Pacific Ocean of a heart attack.

🖪 Gänsehäufel

The Gänsehäufel is something of a Viennese institution. Its history is closely linked to the rise of the workers' movement and the development of an independent culture of physical activity. In 1907 the city of Vienna took over the island in the Old Danube and constructed there the first civic bathing beach with changing rooms for 4,000 people. In 1926–27 the island was linked by a bridge to the "Viennese mainland".

During bombing raids in World War II the complex suffered 130 hits and was severely damaged. Rebuilding was a high priority for the city. This was quickly done,

One of the oldest bathing beaches the Gänsehäufel

On the other side of the Danube, high-rise residential and office blocks are creating a modern district

and thousands of Viennese could once again occupy their cabins and enjoy the summer on the Danube beach. With a total area of 33ha (82 acres) and a length of 1,000m (1,100 yards), the Gänsehäufel is now the biggest inland bathing beach in Europe.

🔟 197 F2/3 ✉ Wien 22, Moissigasse 21 ☎ (01) 269 90 16 🕐 In summer Mon–Fri 9 am–8 pm, Sat–Sun 8 am–8 pm 🚇 Kaisermühlen 🚌 Bäderbus (baths bus) from U-Bahn station Kaisermühlen 💶 Moderate

7 Alte Donau

The 1870–75 regulation of the Danube created in the north-east of the city the Old Danube, a lake no longer joined to the river. By 1900 it had already become a bathers' paradise, which it still is today. In summer the Viennese flock here to swim, sail and row. Between the New and the Old Danube lies the Danube Park. Formerly the site of the 1964 Viennese International Horticultural Show, it is now a leisure park with footpaths and cycle lanes. The 252-m (827-foot) high Donauturm (Danube Tower) which rises above the park has a revolving restaurant offering a splendid view. The mosque and minaret of the Islamic Centre on the nearby Hubertusdamm are also sure to catch your eye.

🔟 197 D5–F4 🚇 Alte Donau 🚌 Bus 20B Alte Donau

8 Danube Island

When in order to control flooding a second river bed was excavated in the 1970s, an island was created. 20km (12½ miles) long and 200m (220 yards) across, it became a leisure paradise for the Viennese. Cyclists, joggers, roller-bladers and walkers are undisturbed by traffic here. The Schotterstrände (gravel beaches), which are some 40km (25 miles) long, are great for sun-bathing and swimming, with a view of an exciting skyline. Surrounding UNO-City, which is shaped like a huge Y, an ultramodern district has arisen, with the Austria Centre, the Andromeda Tower, the residential park Donau-City and a series of glass-and-steel office tower-blocks. As a counterpoise, the Millennium Tower soars into the sky on the other side of the Danube.

🔟 197 D2/3–F1 🚇 Donauinsel

Where to...
Eat and Drink

Prices

Prices given are for one person, excluding drinks.
€ under 12 euros €€ 12–25 euros €€€ over 25 euros

Restaurants

Altes Jägerhaus €€

This inn with its four old-fashioned dining rooms and beautiful, large garden is immediately opposite the Lusthaus. The menu offers a wide range of interesting Viennese dishes, including the ever-popular Wiener Schnitzel, as well as many seasonal and fish specialities. The delicious pastries are made in-house, and the long wine list has Austrian and international wines.

🏠 196, east of C1 🖾 Wien 2, Freudenau 255 🕿 (01) 728 95 77 🕐 Daily 9 am–11 pm (hot food 11:30 am–9:30 pm); Oct–Mar closed Mon–Tue 🚌 Bus 77A Lusthaus

Amon €€

Refurbished from the bottom up, Amon specializes in traditional Viennese dishes like *wurzelfleisch* (meat with root vegetables) and *zwiebelrostbraten* (onion roast). It still puts on its popular specialities weeks, offering dishes from a particular region or country, but in a new setting. In the front-of-house, a wine and beer bar has been added, the conservatory and the gardens have been redesigned, and for children there's an indoor play area. In the "vinotheque" regular customers can settle in with wine boxes. House specialities are also available to take away.

🏠 196 B1 🖾 Wien 3, Schlachthausgasse 13 🕿 (01) 798 81 66 🕐 Mon–Sat 10 am–midnight, Sun 10 am–4 pm 🚇 Schlachthausgasse 🚋 Tram 18A Erdbergstrasse, Bus 74A, 77A, 79A, 80A, 80B, 83A, 84A Schlachthausgasse

Hansy €

Situated on one of the busiest traffic spots in the city, the corner of Praterstern and Praterstrasse, Hansy is everything that a good traditional Viennese inn should be. The bar is simple, the furnishings are simple and the garden is spacious. Good plain cooking and seasonal specialities are available all day – and they brew their own beer, "Hansy-Bräu", also available as a wheat or a strong beer.

🏠 195 E5 🖾 Wien 2, Praterstrasse 67 🕿 (01) 214 53 63 🕐 Daily 9 am–midnight 🚇 Praterstern 🚋 Tram 5, 21, 0, Bus 80A Praterstern

Kiang €€

Once you've made your way through the blue entrance cube, you'll find yourself in what seems like a germ-free lab. But the coolly minimalist styling of Kiang is complemented by one of Vienna's most interesting Asian menus. As well as sushi there are frequently changed chef's recommendations.

🏠 195 F2 🖾 Wien 3, Landstrasser Hauptstrasse 50 🕿 (01) 715 34 70 🕐 Daily 11:30–3, 6–11:30 pm 🚇 Rochusgasse 🚌 Bus 4A, 74A Rochusgasse

Lindmayer €€

This restaurant, idyllically situated on the Danube, specializes in fish and Thai dishes. In good weather food is served on the large terrace with a marvellous view of the river; a cool breeze blows here even on the hottest summer day. A five-minute walk along the river bank takes you to Vienna's only Buddhist pagoda, a still and peaceful place.

197, south of E1 ⊠ Wien 2, Lindmayer Strasse 1 (Hafenzufahrtsstrasse) ☎ (01) 728 95 80 🕒 Mid-Feb–Dec Tue–Sun 8 am–10 pm 🚋 Tram 21 Praterkai (15 minutes on foot), Bus 80B Fa. Elan (opposite the restaurant)

Lusthaus €€

This delightful pavilion at the end of the main Prater avenue has a long history. From 1560 on a small hunting lodge stood on this spot, the "Grünes Lusthaus". Emperor Joseph II commissioned the architect Isidore Canavale to remodel it, and in 1781–83 he converted the single-storey building to its present octagonal form, with eight columns and a balcony running right round it. As you drink your coffee on the little terrace or choose something in the restaurant from fine Viennese cuisine, you can still feel the atmosphere of the imperial era. The menu features truffles and stag, Barbary duck and pike-perch. The Lusthaus is a favourite place for functions like family celebrations or company functions. Booking is advisable for the evenings.

⊞ 196, east of C1 ⊠ Wien 2, Freudenau 254 ☎ (01) 728 95 65 🕒 May–Oct Mon–Tue, Thu–Sun noon–11 pm, Sat–Sun noon–6 pm; Nov–Apr Thu–Tue noon–6 pm 🚌 Bus 77A Lusthaus

Maestro €€€

The design of this restaurant in the Wiener Konzerthaus is elegant art deco. The menu, which features fine, imaginative Viennese cuisine, is designed in the same style. There is also a choice wine list.

⊞ 195 D2 ⊠ Wien 3, Am Heumarkt 6 ☎ (01) 714 89 11 🕒 Daily 5:30 pm–midnight, Sun and Wed from 11:30 am 🚋 Stadtpark 🚋 Tram 1, 2, 71, 0, Bus 3A, 4A Schwarzenbergplatz

Salm Bräu €

This traditional brewery tavern is in the cellars of the baroque Salesian monastery. The beers, brewed from historical recipes, are first-class. The food is simple, hearty and good, and during the week there's an inexpensive set menu.

⊞ 195 E1 ⊠ Wien 3, Rennweg 8 ☎ (01) 799 59 92 🕒 Daily 11 am–midnight (hot food until 11 pm) 🚋 Tram 71 Unteres Belvedere

Schweizerhaus €

Karl Kolarik's Schweizerhaus in the Prater is famous for serving the crispest *stelzen* (pigs' trotters) and the best-kept draught Czech Budvar beer in Vienna. But it has much more: it's also known for authentic Bohemian specialities such as *spiegelkarpfen* (mirror carp) and Szegedin goulash. The atmosphere in the enormous beer garden, with room for 1,300 people, is always great.

⊞ 196 A5 ⊠ Wien 2, Strasse des Ersten Mai 116 ☎ (01) 728 01 52 🕒 15 Mar–Oct Mon–Sat 10 am–11.30 pm 🚋 Praterstern 🚋 Tram 5, 21, 0, Bus 80A Praterstern

Seidl €

Seidl is a typical Old Viennese inn with cosy alcoves. The cooking is also Viennese, delicate but genuine and far removed from fashionable affectations. The roast chicken is said to be the best in town, and the roast liver and goulash are also a dream. The wine list is substantial, with a choice of 400 different wines. Once a month there's a set menu with wine.

⊞ 195 E2 ⊠ Wien 3, Ungargasse 63 ☎ (01) 713 17 81 🕒 Mon–Fri 10 am–11 pm 🚋 Tram 0 Neulinggasse

Stadtwirt €

This establishment has three parts: a bar with stand-up tables to the right of the entrance, an inn for light dishes and drinks to the left of the entrance, with a garden at the front, and a smart restaurant in the rear. The food is modern Viennese and first-class Burgenland/Upper Austria cuisine at affordable prices. The word has gone round, so it's always crammed full. Booking is essential for a table inside or out.

⊞ 195 E3 ⊠ Wien 3, Untere Viaduktgasse 45 ☎ (01) 713 38 28

⊙ Mon–Fri 9 am–midnight, Sat 4 pm–1 am (hot food until 11 pm), Sun 11 am–4 pm; lounge and bar Mon–Fri 9 am–1 am, Sat 4 pm–1 am, Sun 11 am–1 pm
Ⓜ Landstrasse/Wien Mitte 🚋 Tram 0, Bus 74A Landstrasse/Wien Mitte

Steirereck €€€
The Reitbauer family's legendary Michelin-starred Steirereck is one of the best restaurants in Austria. In 2004 it moved from Rasumofsky-gasse to the Stadtpark. In its new, romantic setting the standard of its "new Viennese cuisine" remains first-class, and the selection of breads, cheeses, wines and whiskies is outstanding.
✚ 195 D3 ⊠ Wien 3, Meierei im Stadtpark ☎ (01) 713 31 68 ⊙ Mon–Fri 7 pm–midnight Ⓜ Landstrasse/Wien-Mitte 🚋 Tram 0, Bus 74A Landstrasse/Wien-Mitte

Taverna Lefteris €€
The Greek owner comes from Crete, and his taverna is one of the best Greek restaurants in the city. The atmosphere is Mediterranean and welcoming, you feel on holiday. The bread is home-baked, and the choice of *mezes* is impressive. The owner strives to prove that he can serve more than the well-known classics, but nowhere else does a moussaka taste so tempting.
✚ 195 F3 ⊠ Wien 3, Hörnesgasse 17 ☎ (01) 713 74 51 ⊙ Mon–Sat 6 pm–midnight Ⓜ Rochusgasse 🚌 Bus 4A, 74A Rochusgasse

Wild €€
This typically cosy Viennese tavern on Radetzkyplatz specializes in regional cooking. The most popular dishes are classics, including offal, though prepared with imaginative additions. Try the roast liver, for example. For weekday lunch there are two menus, one vegetarian, one with meat. Neither at all expensive.
✚ 195 F4 ⊠ Wien 3, Radetzkyplatz 1 ☎ (01) 920 94 77 ⊙ Tue–Sun 10 am–1 am (hot food Tue–Sat 11 am–11:30 pm, Sun 11 am–10 pm) Ⓜ Landstrasse/Wien Mitte 🚋 Tram N, 0 Radetzkyplatz

Zum Alten Heller €
Tafelspitz, beef dishes and roasts in every possible variation – French, Spanish or "diabolo" – are served in this beautiful Viennese inn, which is also known for its garden shaded with large chestnut trees. Depending on the season, a selection of special chanterelle and asparagus dishes are also on offer. There's an inexpensive lunch menu.
✚ 195 E2 ⊠ Wien 3, Ungargasse 34 ☎ (01) 712 64 52 ⊙ Tue–Sat 10 am–11 pm (hot food 11:30 am–10 pm) Ⓜ Landstrasse/Wien Mitte 🚋 Tram 0 Ungargasse

Zur Steirischen Botschaft €
This traditional restaurant, whose name means literally "To the Styrian Embassy", has a garden planted with beautiful old walnut trees. The menu, as is to be expected, majors in Styrian (Central Austrian) food, but there are also international dishes. Salads are made with *kernöl*, the nutty pumpkin-seed oil which, because of its dark-green colour, is often mockingly called "Styrian axle-grease". And the numerous wines include the Styrian Schilcher. On weekdays there's a choice of three inexpensive lunch menus.
✚ 195 D2 ⊠ Wien 3, Strohgasse 11 ☎ (01) 712 33 67 ⊙ Mon–Fri 11:30 am–11 pm, Sun 11 am–3 pm (hot food until 2:30, 6pm–10pm) Ⓜ Landstrasse/Wien Mitte 🚋 Tram 0 Ungargasse, Bus 4A Neulinggasse

Cafés

Galerie Zum Hundertwasser-Haus
Besides coffee and cakes or snacks, such as mozzarella and tomato salad, this café offers great views of the stunningly colourful façade of the Hundertwasser-Haus opposite, so it caters for more than the stomach. In summer you can sit in the garden in front of the Hundertwasser-Haus, which belongs to the café.

🚃 195 F3 ⊠ Wien 3, Kegelgasse 37–39
☎ (01) 961 77 71 ⏰ Daily 9 am–11 pm
🚇 Tram N Hetzgasse

KunstHausCafé

The café is just as cheerful, colourful and eccentric as the rest of the Kunst-HausWien. A hundred different, brightly painted Thonet chairs are placed round tables, assembled from a variety of wooden boards. In summer the garden is sensational for its many wonderful exotic flowers. The food is less eccentric: traditional Viennese, with *schnitzel* and *tafelspitz*.

🚃 195 F4 ⊠ Wien 3, Untere Weissger-
berstrasse 13 ☎ (01) 712 04 97
⏰ Daily 10 am–11 pm 🚇 Schwedenplatz
🚇 Tram N, 0 Radetzkyplatz

Schloss Belvedere

The café in the Upper Belvedere, with its beautiful, large garden, is ideal for a short break after a visit to the palace. It serves home-made *torten* (Belvedere-Torte), pastries, snacks and its own ice cream, as

well as traditional Viennese dishes, such as *schinkenfleckerl* (a baked ham and pasta dish), or Italian pasta. So there's always something for the exhausted tourist.

🚃 195 D1 ⊠ Wien 3, Prinz-Eugen-
Strasse 27 ☎ (01) 798 88 88
⏰ Summer Tue–Sun 10 am–6 pm;
Winter Tue–Sun 9 am–5 pm 🚇 Tram D
Schloss Belvedere, Tram 0, 18, Bus 13A
Südbahnhof

Zartl

Zartl is one of the finest traditional Viennese coffee-houses with alcoves and a billiard table. The menu has mainly Viennese dishes, and breakfast is served until late. An unusual feature is the side-room, where the Viennese magicians hold their weekly meetings – though behind closed doors. On Sunday afternoons in winter there's live piano music. (3:30–6:30).

🚃 195 F3 ⊠ Wien 3, Rasumofskygasse
7 ☎ (01) 712 55 60 ⏰ Daily 8 am–
midnight 🚇 Rochusgasse 🚇 Tram N,
Bus 4A Rasumofskygasse

Where to...
Shop

Vienna's third district is well supplied with shops providing for both tourists and locals. Visitors to the city will strike lucky above all in the museum shops.

Landstrasser Hauptstrasse has been renewed in stages over the past few years. With its numerous businesses, it is the shopping street with the greatest turnover in District 3, with one interesting shop after another. There are boutiques, shoe shops, perfumeries and, of course, supermarkets. And dotted amongst them are cafés to satisfy the thirsty and hungry shoppers. At the start of the street, the market in the Wien-Mitte Centre provides an abundance of fresh groceries, meat and vegetables. For visitors, the greengrocers and delicatessens in

the **Rochusmarkt** are particularly inviting. **Arrigo's** wine-merchants (Rochusmarkt, Stand 33) stocks a superb selection of fine Italian, Spanish and Austrian wines and delicatessen items.

For imaginative presents for the children back home go to **Norbert Navara** (Austellungsstrasse 63). they have a wide range of wooden toys, hand puppets, old-fashioned toys and kaleidoscopes to please any child.

Museum shops are the place for unusual, pretty things. The shop in **KunstHausWien** is a treasure trove for diaries, mugs, wrapping paper, roller-pens, key-rings, silk scarves and posters with Hundert-wasser motifs. The shops in the Upper and Lower **Belvedere** have a similar selection of objects for all occasions, this time featuring motifs relating to the palaces, as well as Gustav Klimt's designs. There are shawls and scarves to umbrellas, as well as beautiful art books, diaries, jewellery and posters.

Where to be... Entertained

In this part of Vienna you can go out every evening. The name Copa Cagrana, which comes from the neighbouring district of Kagran, has become a synonym for fun, celebrations and long nights (and early mornings) by the Danube. On this part of Danube Island new pubs are always springing up, enhancing the holiday feeling, but there's plenty of other nightlife to discover.

Copa Cagrana

In the balmy summer months, from March to September night-owls and thrill-seekers, gourmets and lovers of multiethnic cooking flock to the open-air bars and pubs in this fun-filled district (take U-Bahn 1 to Donauinsel for Copa Cagrana).

Rembetiko (left bank, tel: 01/263 66 33, daily 10 am–2 am) is a Greek taverna, popular for its fish and lamb dishes.

The next-door **Ios** (left bank, tel: 01/263 35 04, daily 11 am–2 am) puts its customers in holiday mood with good plain Greek cooking, barbecued kebabs, retsina and ouzo aplenty plus obligatory sirtaki music.

Coccodrillo (left bank, tel: 01/263 71 71, Mon–Fri 10 am–2 am, Sat–Sun 10 am–4 am) has a large terrace right on the water's edge where it serves grills, spare ribs and a selection of salads.

All' Isola (the last bar on Copa Cagrana, tel: 06645/57 10 83, daily 10 am–2 am) has the finest Italian cuisine, really delicious *antipasti* (snacks), fresh fish and sophisticated pasta dishes.

Music

Since May 2004, top performers of jazz, pop and world music have appeared at **Birdland** (Am Stadtpark,

Hilton Vienna, tel: 01/21 96 39 15, Tue–Sun 7 pm–4 am) which belongs to the Austrian jazz legend and keyboard artist Joe Zawinul. The sophisticated jazz club is named after the legendary Birdland in New York, for which this club is meant to become a worthy counterpart. International cooking provides culinary pleasures to accompany the musical ones. Joe Zawinul's favourite dish, *paprikahendl* (chicken paprika), is always on the menu.

Bars

In **A bar shabu** (corner of Rotensterngasse and Glockengasse, tel: 0664/60 24 41, Tue–Sat 9 pm–4 am) not everything revolves around a high-alcohol green drink, but a lot does. A glance at its name will tell you that – this small bar in District 2 proudly bears the sub-title "Absinth Bar". It also frequently puts on exciting art projects.

If for nothing else, the small **Biedermeier-Bar** in the Mercure

Hotel (Landstrasser Hauptstrasse 28, tel: 01/71 67 15 28, daily 6 pm–2 am) is worth seeing for its beautiful early 19th-century surroundings in Sümnhof, which won the 1984 Europa Nostra Prize. It's fitted out in Biedermeier style, with cherry-wood furniture. Excellent classic cocktails are served, to pleasant live piano music.

More absinth drinks, plus a large selection of vodka, gin and whisky mixes, awaits all visitors to the **Hamburg Bar** (Neulinggasse 21, tel: 01/718 98 18, Mon–Sat and public holidays 8 pm–2 am, closed Sun), but there are also hangover drinks and non-alcoholic choices. The little American Bar plays jazzy background music, and sometimes there's live music and jazz.

The cocktail bar **Magic** in Vienna's third district (Marxergasse 14, tel: 0676/917 16 13, Mon–Sat 9 pm–4 am) has a small dance floor. There are snacks on offer, and for entertainment table football or a selection of party games.

Excursions

What would Vienna be without its Wienerwald and the Danube? Excursions to these famous destinations in the surroundings of the city will take you to see romantic villages brimming with ancient history, charming vineyards and precious treasures hidden behind monastery walls.

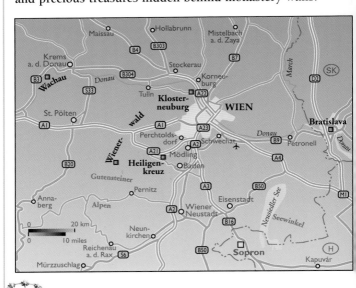

Klosterneuburg

The Augustinian abbey of Klosterneuburg is often likened to Spain's Escorial palace, not least because of its great size. It has become a world-famous site thanks to its art treasures – and, last but not least, due to the superb wines that are made here.

The abbey of Klosterneuburg was founded in the early 1100s by the Babenberg Leopold III. With his sanctification in 1485, the abbey became the national sanctuary, and later the treasury for the national crown. Karl VI began to extend Klosterneuburg in 1730. Abbey and imperial palace were to merge into one giant baroque complex. Ten years later, when the emperor died, only a quarter of these ambitious plans had been realized. And that's how it remained.

Page 159: the entrance to the imperial palace at Klosterneuburg

The Marian Column, an expression of profound piety

The medieval towers of the abbey church belong to the oldest part of the complex

A climb up the **Kaiserstiege** (Imperial Stairway) to the **Kaiserzimmer** (Imperial Room), where in fact Karl VI only stayed for a single night in 1739, will reveal the extent of the splendour and wealth here. It becomes even more obvious one floor higher up, when you see the valuable collections of the **Stiftsmuseum** (Abbey Museum). Its highlights are an 8-m (26-feet) long illustrated Babenberg family tree, panels by Rueland Frueauf the Younger and exquisite ivory carvings.

The fact that the baroque structure remained unfinished is not all bad for it meant that large parts of the medieval complex were preserved until today. The best Romanesque and Gothic vestiges can be seen on the external walls of the **Stiftskirche** (Abbey Church).

The baroque interior of the abbey and the most valuable treasures can only be seen with a guided tour. The tour takes you through the cloisters to the Leopold Chapel where the **Verduner Altar** (Verdun Altar) is kept. Created in 1181 as a pulpit face by goldsmith Nikolaus von Verdun, it has 45 enamel plaques depicting scenes from the Bible. In 1330, it was remodelled as a winged altar. A second Gothic winged altar, the **Albrechts-Altar**, is in the Sebastiani Chapel.

Fine Wines

A guided tour through the four-storey baroque cellars of Austria's oldest and largest wine-growing estate, including wine-tasting, is an experience not to be missed! (Rathausplatz 24, tel: 02243/ 411 548, Mon–Fri 9 am–6 pm, Sat until 5 pm)

A very different attraction is the late-Gothic **Binderstadl**, once the Abbey's bindery. This is where every year on 15 November (St Leopold's Day) the *fasslrutschen* takes place, when young and old slide over a 300-year-old barrel, the so-called "1,000-bucket-barrel".

✉ Klosterneuburg, Stiftsplatz 1 ☎ (02243) 411-212 🕐 Stiftsmuseum May–15 Nov Tue–Sun 10 am–5 pm; guided tours daily 10 am–5 pm 💶 Moderate ❓ www.stift-klosterneuburg.at

Directions: 12km (7.5 miles) north of Vienna; S40, bus 239 to Weidling or Kierling

Wienerwald

The Vienna Woods are often described as a "symphony in green". One of the largest mixed woods in Europe, they are typical of the Austrian countryside. This excursion will take you to the lower part of the woods, into the charming vineyards south of Vienna.

In the year 1002, the German emperor Heinrich II signed a deed of gift which made the area between Triesting and Liesing over to the Babenberg margrave Heinrich. This is how the history of the Vienna Woods began. For nearly 800 years the heart of the large wooded area remained a primeval forest. But at the beginning of the 19th century the Wienerwald was discovered as a romantic recreation ground by people in the city, and it became a popular destination for country outings and summer holidays.

Perchtoldsdorf

Vineyards have long been the dominant feature south of Vienna. One of the most picturesque wine villages is Perchtoldsdorf, where one wine tavern follows another, all featuring romantic vine arbours, flowering oleander and rustic wooden tables and benches. Before you settle in the first one, though, you should take a stroll through the village and visit the restored 14th-century **Herzogsburg** (Ducal Fortress), the Gothic **Hallenkirche** (Hall Church), the **Rathaus** (Town Hall) and the **Wehrturm** (Fortified Tower). The ancient walls withstood the Turkish siege in 1683.

Mödling

The neighbouring town of Mödling is today a pulsating commercial hub and an important centre for education. The middle of the Old Town with its well-preserved late-Gothic and Renaissance manor houses is still fascinating. A stroll here will seem like a journey back to the old days, when Mödling attracted many artists. Some of the streets and squares still look today as if any minute one of them might turn the corner – Schubert, Grillparzer, Waldmüller, or Beethoven, who spent the summers of 1818–20 here and in his usual manner moved four times. The **Beethoven-Gedenkstätte** (Beethoven Memorial) commemorates his years in Mödling.

Hinterbrühl and the fortress of **Burg Liechtenstein**, Austria's largest secular structure in the Romanesque style, are a favourite destination for

The charming village of Mödling, with its quaint Old Town

There are fabulous views in the Vienna Woods

The Vienna Woods are ideal for extensive rambles

excursions. The **Höldrichsmühle**, a mill, is said to have inspired Schubert's *The Linden Tree*, and the **Seegrotte** has Europe's largest underground lake.

From Gumpolds-kirchen into the Vineyards

Gumpoldskirchen has something very special to offer: its idyllic **Weinwander-weg** (Wine Walking Path), which leads up into the vineyards. You can smell the soil and the vines here, and illustrated information boards along the path explain all about viticulture and the grape varieties that are typical for Gumpoldskirchen, Rotgipfler and Zierfandler. A short way farther, a 19th-century stations of the cross leads up the hill, bearing witness to the piety of the vintners. During the half-hour walk you will get a series of beautiful views of the ancient village with its Renaissance estates and the Gothic parish church of St Michael, which is managed by the Deutscher Orden.

Baden – Chic Spa Town with an Imperial Touch

The lovingly tended small town of Baden possesses a unique ensemble of Bieder-meier-style houses – all thanks to a catastrophe! In 1812 a conflagration destroyed the entire town. It was rebuilt in pure neo-classical style. One of the most prolific architects was Josef Kornhäusel, who designed the **Rathaus** (Town Hall), the **Florastöckl** in Frauengasse, **Metternichhof** and the **Theresienschlössl**.

Early on, Baden became an elegant spa for those suffering from rheumatism, boasting generous parks, elegant hotels and beautiful villas. The atmosphere of the imperial age can still be felt with every step today, at a concert in the **Kurpark** (Spa Park), in the **Doblhoffpark** with its magnificent display of

roses and at the **Trabrennen** (Trotting Race). Numerous splendid villas remind us of the higher officials, officers and famous spa guests who used to visit here, including Mozart, Schubert, Nestroy, Raimund and Grillparzer.

While Baden may seem like a picture-book town, it has a very dynamic economy, having established itself as both a commercial and educational centre. A great attraction for visitors is the **Casino** in the Kurpark, Austria's first and largest.

The Baden Casino is more than a gambling house, it's also a venue for glamourous events

The **Römertherme** (Roman Baths) too, lavishly designed and covered by a giant glass roof, is well visited.

Baden is also proud of over 250 years of theatrical traditions. Both director Max Reinhardt and actress Katharina Schratt were born here, and every year the town hosts a popular operetta festival in its Summer Arena.

Hafnerhaus
✉ Mödling, Hauptstrasse 79
☎ (02236) 241 59 🕑 Mon–Wed 9–noon 💰 Moderate

Hotel-Restaurant Höldrichsmühle
✉ Hinterbrühl, Gaadnerstrasse 34
☎ (02236) 26 27 40 🕑 Daily

The Undine fountain in the Kurpark

11 am–10 pm 🚌 From Mödling station Bus 364 and 365 to Höldrichsmühle

Seegrotte
✉ Hinterbrühl, Grutschgasse 2a ☎ (02236) 263 64 🕑 Apr–Oct daily 8:30–noon, 1–5; Nov–Mar daily 9–noon, 1–3, Sat–Sun until 3:45 🚌 From Mödling station Bus 364 and 365 Seegrotte 💰 Moderate

Casino
✉ Baden, Kaiser-Franz-Ring 1 ☎ (02252) 444 96 🕑 Daily from 3 pm

Römertherme
✉ Baden, Brusattiplatz ☎ (02252) 450 30 🕑 Mon noon–10, Tue–Sun 10–1[

Directions: Mödling is 15km (9.3 miles), Gumpoldskirchen 20km (12.5 miles) and Baden 28km (17.4 miles) south of Vienna. S-Bahns S1 and S2 depart from Südbahnhof in the direction of Wiener Neustadt, stopping at Gumpoldskirchen, Mödling and Baden. Buses 364 and 365 leave from Mödling station to Hinterbrühl. From 2:20 pm to 3:15 am, the Casino Bus shuttles half-hourly between Wiener Oper and Casino Baden. Badener Bahn shuttles between Wiener Oper and Baden-Josefsplatz every 15 minutes (day), every 30 minutes after 8:12 pm

Heiligenkreuz

Heiligenkreuz Abbey lies in the hollow of a valley amidst the softly rounded hills of the Vienna Woods, surrounded by meadows and fields. For 850 years it has been a cultural centre and is now listed as a World Heritage Site.

Founded in 1133 by the Babenberg ruler Leopold III, the future patron of Lower Austria, the Cistercian abbey is still a place of harmony and beauty. Its name, meaning "Holy Cross" refers to a fragment of the Holy Cross, which Duke Leopold V brought back from his pilgrimage to Jerusalem and donated to the abbey in 1188. Today, the **Kreuzreliquie** (Relic of the Crucifix) can be see in the modern parish church.

Large parts of the abbey complex, which had always been intended to become the final resting place for the Babenberg rulers, date back to the Middle Ages. The long nave of the Romanesque buttressed church, the Gothic hall choir, the cloisters and the fountain house were built as early as the 12th and 13th centuries, and have been preserved in their original form. The outbuildings, the towers, the choir stalls (note the wooden sculptures) and the magnificent trinity column created by the Venetian sculptor Giovanni Giuliani, the

Gastronomic peak
Between Heiligenkreuz and Mayerling, you'll come across the beautifully styled Hanner hotel and restaurant (Mayerling 1, tel: 02258/23 78, Mon–Sat noon–2, 6–10, Sun noon–10pm). The cuisine has been awarded three chefs' hats by Gault-Millau!

The abbey church is adorned by choir stalls with beautiful carvings

Pure romance

From Heiligenkreuz Abbey, passing through the Wiener Tor, you will get to the baroque **Cloisters**, created by Master Giuliani. An avenue of winter-flowering lime trees takes you past the stations of the cross and statues of the saints on its way to the Chapel. Cross the road and you'll get to the wooded cemetery, where you'll find the **grave** of Mary Vetsera. Its inscription reads: "Like a flower a human being blossoms and is broken."

Joseph fountain, the library and the sacristy date back to the 17th century. All are splendid examples of the baroque style.

The **Klostergasthof** (Abbey Inn) is almost as old as the abbey itself. The best of traditional Austrian fare is dishes up in its vaults or in the shaded garden in summer, accompanied by wines from the abbey's own cellars.

Mystery and Tragedy

The small village of Mayerling, only 5km (3.1 miles) from Heiligenkreuz, became the scene of a tragedy that shook the entire country. On 30 January, 1889, Crown Prince Rudolf committed suicide in the Lodge, together with his mistress, Mary Vetsera, who was only 18 years old at the time. It has never been possible to establish for certain the reasons for this double suicide. Austria lost the heir to its throne and with him any hope for renewal and reform. The room where the lovers died is now a memorial church. Three further rooms in the Hunting Lodge have been transformed into a museum.

☎ (02258) 87 03-33 ⏰ Daily 8 am–8 pm, guided tours Mon–Sat 10, 11, 2, 3 and 4, Sun from 11 am 💰 Moderate ❓ www.heiligenkreuz.at

Jagdschloss Mayerling
✉ Mayerling 3, Karmeliterkloster ☎ (02258) 275 ⏰ Mon–Sat 9–12:30, 1:30–6, Sun from 10 am, in winter until 5 pm 💰 Inexpensive

Directions: 30km (18.6 miles) southwest of Vienna; Postbus 1140 from Baden station, Bahnbus 364 from Mödling station (► 164); stop at Heiligenkreuz, Badner Tor for Heiligenkreuz Abbey and Mayerling for the Jagdschloss (Hunting Lodge)

A River Cruise into the Wachau

For a very special Sunday adventure, take a river cruise on one of the most romantic stretches of the Danube, into the picturesque Wachau, a beautiful landscape steeped in history, legend and culture.

The large cruise ship leaves Vienna, gliding past the **Donauturm** (Danube Tower) and the modern skyline of Vienna on the right bank, and Kahlenberg and Leopoldsberg on the left bank. Shortly beyond the city limits, in **Korneuburg**, you'll see the green hills of Tullner Feld. At twice 470 horsepower, the *MS Admiral Tegetthoff*, flagship of the Danube River Cruise Company, chugs upriver to the flower-bedecked town of **Tulln**, past Zwentendorf, transporting its up to 600 passengers to **Traismauer**, a village with Roman and Nibelungen pedigree.

Above: Captain of the Danube up-river cruise

Romantic Wachau

The next stop for the boat is in the double town of **Krems-Stein**. Its more than 1,000 years of history is evident everywhere; you can even detect the signs from the boat. The superb Old Town was declared a World Heritage Site by UNESCO.

It is at Krems that the **Wachau** proper begins. This section of the Danube Valley guarantees an unforgettable experience in summer, from apricot blossom to the vine harvest. At a height of 449m (1,473 feet), **Stift Göttweig** (Abbey Göttweig) rises on the left bank of the Danube, a splendid Benedictine abbey that is often described as the Austrian Montecassino. The boat glides past the wildly romantic countryside, with steeply rising stone terraces where the Romans already cultivated vines, apricot trees, densely wooded hills and picturesque villages with beautiful, old churches.

Krems Old Town is an historical gem

Where Richard the Lionheart Languished

The **Dürnstein Ruin**, towering high above the Danube, is one of Wachau's

Vines have been grown in the Wachau since Roman days

DDSG Blue Danube Schiffahrt GmbH

The DDSG river cruises operate from April to October every Sunday on the stretch Vienna–Dürnstein–Vienna (day return: 25 euros).
Departure Reichsbrücke: 8:35 am, arrival Dürnstein: 2:30 pm
Departure Dürnstein: 4:40 pm, arrival Reichsbrücke: 9 pm
✉ Wien 2, Handelskai 265/Reichsbrücke
☎ (01) 588 80 (seats need to be reserved)
🕓 Mon–Fri 9 am–6 pm 🚇 Vorgartenstrasse
🚌 Bus 11A Vorgartenstrasse
❓ www.ddsg-blue-danube.at

emblems. Richard the Lionheart, King of England, was imprisoned here. As the legend tells it, he was found by Blondel, his loyal servant. While climbing up to the fortress, Blondel sang a song – and the second verse came from the dungeon. King Richard was freed in 1193, and part of his ransom made possible the extension of the fortress and lifted the village's fortunes.

From the boat, the church tower of Dürnstein is especially noticeable. Restored to its original blue and white, it is one of the most beautiful baroque towers in Austria. The tower is part of the **Augustinerchorherrenstift** (Augustinian Abbey), of which the impressive portal and the Abbey Courtyard are well worth seeing.

Almost too beautiful to be true: Dürnstein and the Augustinian abbey tower

The boat stops here for two hours, time enough for a pleasant stroll through Dürnstein. Apart from the former **Klarissinnenkirche** (Church of the Order of St Clare) and the **Stadttor** (Town Gate), you will discover romantic Renaissance courtyards, splendid manor houses and historical vintners' houses in the winding alleyways. In between you can fortify yourself with a Wachau speciality – Wachau ham and a glass of white wine – on the famous terrace of the hotel Schloss Dürnstein (tel: 02711/212, hot food served daily Apr–Oct 12–2, 6:30–9). Just make sure that you don't get distracted as you take in the local sights and delicacies, forgetting the 4:40 pm departure of the MS Admiral Tegetthoff back to Vienna…

Stift Dürnstein
✉ Dürnstein 1 ☎ (02711) 375 🕓 Apr–Oct 9 am–6 pm 💶 Inexpensive

Bratislava

Only a few generations ago, when great-grandmother wanted to nip across from Vienna to Pressburg, as the town was called at the time, she only had to hop on a tram. Today's Bratislava is not quite as easy to get to from Vienna, but this beautiful city is still within easy reach.

The two towns on the Danube, once so close thanks to their excellent road connections, were very far apart during the Cold War, separated by the Iron Curtain. In fact, for a long time it was impossible to get to Bratislava. Now that is in the past, although Austrian traffic planners did not prepare for the expansion of the EU in 2004.

Pulsating life in the street cafés of the Old Town

When Bratislava became the capital of the Slovak Republic in 1993, this city of 450,000 inhabitants quickly developed into a political, economic and cultural centre. No longer a sad and grimy town, Bratislava gives the impression of having been freshly spruced up.

The proud fortress of Bratislava, towering above the Danube

View from the Top

Before hitting the town, you should climb up the palace stairs to the **Burg** (Fortress). A former Roman outpost, it has been constantly remodelled since the 9th century, most recently in 1953–62. From the top you can see **Petrzalka** on the

right bank of the Danube, where one prefabricated tower block stands next to another, dating back to socialist days. Of all the central

Feasting as in grandmother's days

Delicious roasts with dumplings, accompanied by a beer can be enjoyed at the restaurant **U Zlatého Orla**/ Goldener Adler (Panská 14) or at the **Arkadia** (Zámocké schody/Schlossstiege) with views across the Danube.

European cities, Bratislava is the most densely populated.

Old Town and Magnificent Palace

Returning from the fortress hill, you will enter the **Old Town** via the Corvinus Gate. The Old Town is essentially grouped around three squares: Hauptplatz (Central Square), Franziskaner-platz and Primatialplatz. Much has been restored here in recent years, with great care and sensitivity. Thick ancient walls have been brought to life again, and often there is a charming hint of the former Austrian empire about the place. Start your exploration of the city at **Martinsdom** (Cathedral of St Martin).

Opera, Operetta and Ballet

The Slovak National Theatre is well worth a visit. You can buy tickets at the box office (Komenského námestie, tel: 0042 –17 – 533 38 90, Mon–Fri 8 am–6 pm, Sat 9 am–1 pm).

The Gothic church harbours evidence of the once close relationship between Vienna and Bratislava: the statue of St Martin (1734) was created by Raphael Donner, who also designed the Donner Fountain in Neuer Markt (► 30) in Vienna.

For the Hungarian aristocracy of the 17th and 18th centuries, a villa not just in Vienna and Prague but in Bratislava too was a *must have*. You can admire some of these palaces as you walk from Martinsdom along the Ventúrska and Michalská streets to **Michaelstor** (St Michael's Gate). On the way to the Old Town Hall you'll see the Archbishop's Palace, the largest of them all. At the

Beautiful historical buildings can be found near the Michaelstor

Primatialpalais (Primaciálny námestie, behind the Old Town Hall), the Treaty of Bratislava was signed in 1805 after Napoleon's victory at Austerlitz. The Municipal Museum inside the grand **Altes Rathaus** (Old Town Hall, Hlavné námestie, Tue–Sun 9–5) is worth a visit.

The Old Town is ideal for strolling. In between the lavishly restored historical buildings there are lively pedestrianized areas, shopping boulevards with expensive boutiques, street cafés and bars. The most famous "Viennese" coffee-house is **Mayer** (Hlavné námestie near the Old Town Hall).

Directions: 60km (37 miles) east of Vienna; express trains depart daily from Vienna's Südbahnhof, buses from Südtirolerplatz (seat reservation tel: 01/93 00 03 43 05); from May to 18 October the DDSG (► 168) also operates hydrofoil boats to Bratislava.

Walks & Tours

1 THROUGH THE DANUBE MEADOWS

Cycle Tour

The wildly romantic countryside of the Lobau is tailor-made for cyclists: well-marked cycle paths take you along even ground through the Viennese stretch of the Danube meadows. Cycle in the footsteps of Napoleon's army, and relax in the green spaces of Auwald.

DISTANCE: 16km (10 miles) **TIME:** 3 hours
START/END POINT: Bicycle hire Ostbahnbrücke ☎ (0664) 974 37 18
🚇 Kaisermühlen, then 🚌 Bus 91A Lobau

1,000 million kilowatt-hours of electricity a year. When you reach the Lobgrundtor, turn left into the Donauauen National Park.

2–3

In Lobgrundstrasse you'll soon see red-white-red signs for the first of six **Napoleonsteine**. These six memorial stones were erected in 1859 to commemorate the Battle of Aspern (1809). In this battle, Arch Duke Karl (▶ 106) defeated Napoleon for the first time, thus arresting his triumphal progress. The first stone, called **Am Brückenkopf** (at the bridgehead), dates back to the time when the Danube was still unregulated and the French could only cross it on pontoon bridges. Cycle along Lobgrundstrasse and reach **Ölhafen Lobau** (Oil Port Lobau) on your right. You'll pass impressive oil tanks and pipelines, which transport gas on suspension bridges across the river to the refinery at Schwechat. At Königsgraben, turn left onto the cycle path along the Danube-Oder-Canal.

3–4

As early as the 14th century, the **Danube-Oder-Canal** was meant to link Vienna with the Oder River, which flows some 3,000km (1,864 miles) away. In 1939–43 a short stretch of the artificial waterway was built in

Hire a bicycle next to Ostbahnbrücke

1–2

From the **bicycle rental outlet** your route takes you downriver on Danube Island, crossing the Steinspornbrücke to the Lobau; the path runs beside the New Danube, past **Kraftwerk Freudenau**, a power station producing over

FASANGARTEN
BIBERHAUFEN
ROTER HIASL
NAPOLEONSTRASSE
ESSLING

Lobau and Marchfeld. At the end of the Lobau section, in the middle of the woods, you'll find a refreshing **bathing spot**. Continue straight on to the next Napoleon stone, called **Übergang der Franzosen** (Crossing of the French). Here, the

French army crossed the Danube, 42 days after the Battle of Astern, before defeating the Austrians at Deutsch-Wagram.

around the Lobau, and you'll understand why its name means "water woods".

4–5

In the middle of the meadows, on the left, a short way from the cycle path, there are two more Napoleon stones: **Napoleons Pulvermagazin** (Napoleon's Magazine) and **Franzosen-friedhof** (French Cemetery), where 3,000 French are said to be lie buried in a mass grave. Now continue cycling in a large circle

Guided Tours and Bicycle Rental

The staff at the National Parks offer a free guided tours for groups of six people or more called "Through the Lobau by bicycle", reservation: 02249/23 53. Bicycles can be rented from the Radverleih Ostbahnbrücke (at reduced rates for those taking part in the guided tour). www.donauauen.at

When to go?

On a sunny weekend you will not be the only one making your way to the Lobau. You will find more peace during the week and you should definitely make sure to book any visits in advance. Note that on Mondays to Fridays the bicycle rental outlet opens at 11 am (Saturdays, Sundays and on holidays from 9 am).

Map labels

- Lobau
- OSTBAHN-BRÜCKE
- Radverleih
- **1**
- **8**
- RAFFINERIESTR.
- STEINSPORN-BRÜCKE
- Donauinsel
- Neue Donau
- Donau
- 0 1 km
- 0 1 mile
- Kraftwerk Freudenau
- RAFFINERIESTR.
- Panozza-lacke
- **7**
- Napoleons Hauptquartier 1809
- LOBGRUNDTOR
- LOR
- Am Brückenkopf
- **2**
- NAPOLEONSTR.
- Napoleonstein
- **6**
- Lobau-museum
- VORWERKSTR.
- Biber-gehege
- VORWERKSTR.
- OSTER-STEIG
- Wurzel-station
- GRUND STR.
- Ölhafen Lobau
- **3**
- Ölhafen
- Königs-graben
- Wildbade-stelle
- Demi-kreuz
- Franzosen-friedhof
- Napoleons Pulvermagazin
- Übergang der Franzosen
- **4**
- **5**
- ESSLINGER FURT
- Donau-Oder-Kanal
- Donau-Oder-Kanal

grounds became a national park. Continue along Vorwerkstrasse to the next **Napoleon stone**. This memorial stone marks the end of the road along which 96,000 soldiers and countless horses once made their way to the Aspern battlefields.

6–7

Return on Napoleonstrasse to Lobgrundstrasse, then along Stadtwanderweg 11 (Municipal Footpath 11) past the last Napoleon stone, **Napoleons Hauptquartier 1809** (Napoleon's 1809 Headquarters) to the idyllic **Panozzalacke**, a natural bathing spot and a vast meadow for games and sunbathing.

7–8

The footpath will take you back to the National Park entrance, and upriver from here is the cycle rental place.

A memorial commemorating Napoleon's main army

With a bit of luck you may spot a heron fishing in one of the ponds, or other rare birds among the willow and polar trees. The old tributaries, cut off from the main river for more than 130 years, seem unspoiled, just like the uncultivated fields. Continue along this unique nature reserve up to Esslinger Furt.

5–6

Turn left now and cycle up to Vorwerkstrasse. Here, in the heart of the Lobau, you'll come across a number of interesting sights: there's a **beaver enclosure** at the Förstersteig, for example, with

observed in the evening twilight. Or take a detour past the **Demlkreuz**, a cross commemorating Franz Deml, a policeman who was shot here in 1920. At the **Wurzelstation** (Root Station) you can admire the impressive roots of one of the water meadow trees; the teaching pond lets you explore the unique habitat of the water meadows; and the "Hohle Pappel" (hollow polar) is a giant tree which you can walk inside. Return on Vorwerkstrasse, and after Förstersteig you'll come across the **Lobaumuseum** on the right (open at weekends and by arrangement). This local museum has aquariums and educational slides to explain all about the wildlife in the water meadows. It

Top:
the fascinating
Lobaumuseum
Above: idyllic

2 GRINZING
Walk

Grinzing is Vienna's oldest and most famous wine tavern district. Situated in picturesque vineyards, it has preserved its charming village character. Here, mighty gateways open out into quiet drives and tiny gardens. The welcoming vintners' houses largely date back to the 16th and 17th centuries.

DISTANCE: 2km (1.2 miles) **TIME:** 1½ hours (or longer, depending on time at the wine tavern)
START POINT: Himmelstrasse Grinzing 🚊 Tram No 38
END POINT: Fernsprechamt Heiligenstadt 🚌 Bus No 38A

1–2

Tram No 38 is locally known as the "Heurigen-express", because it is the fastest way for the Viennese to get to the much-loved *heurigen*, or new-vintage wine taverns. From the terminus walk up Himmelstrasse on the left, past the 14th-century **Pöllinger Freihof** (Pölling Palace), used for a while in 1730 as Empress Maria Theresa's, to the late-Gothic Grinzing Church. Twelve vintner families built the **Kirche zum Heiligen Kreuz** (Church of the Holy Cross) in 1417–26, paying with their own money.

2–3

If you like, make a detour from the church along Managettagasse and Managettasteig to **Grinzing Cemetery**. It's the last resting place of Gustav Mahler, whose

Destination: *heurigen* wine taverns

modernist tombstone was commissioned by his widow Alma Mahler-Werfel, who is also buried nearby. Here are also the graves of the one-armed pianist Paul Wittgenstein, brother of the philosopher Ludwig Wittgenstein, as well as of the writers Heimito von Doderer and Thomas Bernhard.

3–4

Back at the church walk uphill on Himmel-strasse and turn right into Feilergasse, which leads to the **Altes Presshaus** (Old Presshouse,

Tip

Force yourself to climb up to the vineyard **Am Reisenberg** (Oberer Reisenbergweg 15, tel: 01/320 93 93, early May-end Sep Mon–Fri 4 pm–midnight, Sun noon–midnight). Your efforts will be rewarded with excellent wine and great views of Vienna.

Cobenzlgasse 15, tel: 01/320 02 03, daily 4 pm–midnight, closed Jan–Feb). The press-house, dating from 1527, is the oldest wine tavern in Austria. Apart from a 250-year-old wine press and giant vats, the impressive cellars also have the entrance to an under-ground path which, many centuries ago, was dug by the vintners as an escape route to Grinzing Church.

4–5
Now stroll back down Cobenzlgasse, past Grinzing's oldest house, the **Trummelhof** (Cobenzlgasse 30, tel: 01/328 90 61, Mon–Sat from 7 pm). It was built by the Babenberg rulers in 1150 on the site of a Roman settlement; today it is a bar. A few steps farther along it's worth stopping at the **Heuriger Reinprecht** (Cobenzlgasse 22, tel: 01320/ 14 71 0, daily 3 pm–midnight, closed mid-Dec–Feb). In the nearly 400-year-old vaults of this former monastery, some 150,000 litres (33,000 gallons) of wine are served every year. You can also admire the world's oldest and largest collection of corkscrews here, comprising well over 3,000 items.

5–6
Now continue along Cobenzl-gasse which, at the village end, leads into Sandgasse. Sandgasse eventually changes name to become Grinzinger Strasse. On the walls of **House No 64** a plaque commemorates Franz Grillparzer and Ludwig van Beethoven, who both spent several months of their lives here in 1808.

Taking a Break
The countless Heurigen restaurants offer a wide variety of foods, both cold and hot buffets in a typical atmosphere, usually with live music.
Feuerwehr-Wagner (Grinzinger Strasse 53, tel: 01/320 24 42, daily 4 pm–midnight) is famed for its *backhendl* (roast chicken); **Martin Sepp** (Cobenzlgasse 34, tel: 01/320 32 33-0, daily 11:30 am–midnight) specializes in seasonal foods; the elegant snack bar **Liebstöckl & Co** (Sandgasse 12, tel: 01/328 83 10, daily 11 am–midnight, hot food 11–11) serves traditional Viennese with a twist; in the **Neuland** tavern (Cobenzlgasse 7, tel: 01/320 00 63, Mon–Fri 4 pm–1 am, Sat–Sun 11:30 am–1 am) boasts a stylish ambience.

6–7
Turn left into Armbrustergasse. Opposite the former residence of **Bruno Kreisky**, the Austrian Federal Chancellor of many years, (Armbrustergasse 15), the tiny Probusgasse takes you towards the centre of the village. On uneven cobblestones you'll get to another **Wohnhaus Beethovens** (Beethoven Residence, Probusgasse 6, Tue–Sun 9–12:15, 1–4:30). A small staircase takes you up to his apart-ment where he wrote the *Heiligenstadt*

Music and merriment with wine

...esamen in 1802. Beethoven had hoped that his summer residence at Grinzing would bring relief from his hearing problems. When there was no noticeable improvement, he wrote a passionate and angry letter to his brothers, which however he never posted. The letter made history as the *Heiligenstadt Testament*.

7–8

Beethoven moved home more than 80 times in Vienna, and so it's not surprising that at the end of Probusgasse, on Pfarrplatz, there is yet another Beethoven House. In this mid-17th-century building, the composer worked on his Ninth Symphony in 1817. Today celebrities and wine lovers meet here at the Heuriger **Mayer am Pfarrplatz** (Pfarrplatz 2, tel: 01/370 33 61, Mon–Sat 4 pm–midnight, Sun 11 am–midnight). The façade of the romantic house is decorated with a statue of St Florian who is believed to have saved the house during a fire. Continue past **Heiligenstädter Jakobskirche** (Heiligenstadt Church of St Jacob), one of Vienna's oldest churches with structural remains dating back to the 2nd century AD. Via Nestelbachgasse you will get back to Grinzinger Strasse where there is a bus stop of route 38A, which will take you back to U-Bahn station Heiligenstadt.

In Sandgasse, where time seems to have stood still

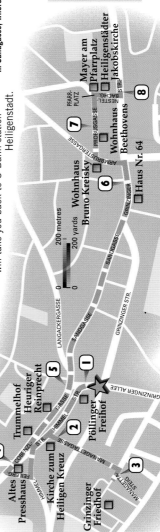

When to go?
The best time for your walk is the afternoon. It allows you to finish off the day over a pleasant glass of wine in one of the many Heuriger taverns.

3 ST MARX CEMETERY
Walk

No matter whether you're here in spring, when the lilac blossoms, or when the autumn mists hang between the rows of graves – the early 19th-century St Marx Cemetery is romantic during any season. In fact, it's no longer a cemetery but a park. Established in 1784, the cemetery was only in use until 1874, when Vienna's Central Cemetery was opened and the

DISTANCE: 1.5km (1 mile) **TIME:** 1 hour
START/END POINT: St Marx or Bus 18, 74A St Marx

mortal remains of the many famous dead were reburied there in memorial tombs. Only the tombstones remain in St Marx.

1–2
From **S-Bahn station St Marx** walk along Leberstrasse, away from the city centre. Soon you will see the A23 concrete bridge. The **cemetery entrance** is in front of the motorway bridge on the right,

just below the street level. As soon as you've passed through the red-brick entrance gate, you will feel enveloped by a special atmosphere of tranquillity and peace. A broad central avenue lined with chestnut trees leads straight ahead. Note the Angels of Death either side of the avenue.

2–3
Walk up the avenue, and step into one of the rows on the left. You'll spot many fascinating inscriptions on the tombstones. One says, for example:

The tombstone of one Josef März, with an unusual inscription

LEBERSTR.

S-Bahn-Station St. Marx

Michael Thonet

Eingang

0 100 metres
0 100 yards

The **"Mozartgrab"**, a lasting memorial

The entrance of St Marx Cemetery

"In memory of Herr Josef März, representative of the civilian salaried coachman and proprietor in Leopold-stadt No 138". Also on the left is the grave of **Ida Pfeiffer** (1797–1858, ▶ 34). As soon as her children had left home, this intrepid woman set out to travel around the world, all by herself. In the Biedermeier period, that was most unusual.

3–4

Where the rows of graves end, the former **grave shafts** begin. Here the dead were buried without much ado, as was typical of the time, in unmarked grave shafts holding up to six corpses. Wolfgang Amadeus Mozart was buried in such a pauper's grave. The **"Mozartgrab"** (Mozart's Tomb) was not built until 1859 and only roughly marks the spot where the composer was actually buried. The grave, featuring a broken column (a symbol of the freemasons) and the Angel of Grief is always adorned with fresh flowers. Continue strolling along the central avenue, and admire the romantic tombstones and angels.

Taking a break

In the vicinity of the cemetery there is **no place for refreshments**. Make sure therefore that you take a snack and a bottle of water along on your walk.

4–5

On your return, take a look at the graves to the right of the avenue. In the rear of the cemetery is the grave of **Moritz Michael Daffinger** (1790–1849), the most famous portrait and flower painter of his day. Near the common graves, but this time on your right, you'll see the grave of **Josef Madersperger** (1768–1850), the inventor of the sewing machine, and beyond it, quite close to the cemetery exit, the grave of **Michael Thonet** (1796–1871), a pioneering furniture maker who invented the world-famous bentwood furniture.

🗺 Wien 3, Leberstrasse 6–8
🕐 Nov–Mar 7 am until dusk; Apr–Oct 7 am–5 pm; May–Sep 7 am–6 pm; Jun–Aug 7 am–7 pm 🎫 Free

A 23

S 23

Josef Madersperger

Moritz Michael Daffinger

4

Schachtgräber

»Mozartgrab«

3

4 IN THE FOOTSTEPS OF *THE THIRD MAN*

Walk

The city walk in the footsteps of Carol Reed's famous film *The Third Man* (1949) takes you into the subterranean sewage system and through the streets of post-war Vienna, when the occupying Allies and the black market dominated the bombed-out city.

DISTANCE: 3km (2 miles) **TIME:** 2½ hours
START POINT: Stadtpark ⊞ 193 E2 Ⓜ Stadtpark
END POINT: Teinfaltstrasse ⊞ 192 B4 Ⓜ Herrengasse, Schottentor

Invitation for an organized Third-Man guided tour

the street. For the film, the pillar was rebuilt in another location, but more about that later. Now let's go down into the underworld!

2–3

You will enter the **Vienna Sewage System**, via a narrow spiral staircase – but you can only do this with a guided tour. The sewers measure 2,300km (1,429 miles) in length. After a cholera

The Story

Vienna 1948: The American writer Holly Martins (Joseph Cotten) wants to visit his friend Harry Lime (Orson Welles) in Vienna. He arrives too late, and Lime was injured in a car accident. Martins becomes embroiled in shady deals of penicillin smuggling; a witness claims to have seen a third man at the site of the accident. A spectacular chase through the Vienna sewage system ensues, leading to a dramatic final showdown...

You'd like to watch the film (again)?

Every Friday at 11:45 pm and every Sunday at 2:30 pm the Burgkino screens the film in its original English version (Wien 1, Opernring 21, tel: 01/587 84 06).

1–2

From **Stadtpark** walk down Lothringer Strasse to the **Litfasssäule** (advertising pillar) where Harry Lime disappeared into the world below. You are now between Beethovenplatz on the one side and the Konzerthaus on the other

epidemic in 1830, all the waterways within the city limits were covered over and two

3–4

Near the High-Jet Fountain, you'll see the **Heldendenkmal der Roten Armee** (Red Army Memorial). The nearly 12-m (40-feet) high figure representing a Russian soldier was unveiled on 19 August, 1945, at a parade of Soviet, American, English and French troops. From 1945 until 1955, Vienna was divided into four zones, the inner city was administrated by all four Allies together. Continue to Ringstrasse, where on your left you'll see the **Hotel Imperial.**

4–5

During Vienna's post-war occupation, the elegant hotel was the headquarters of the Russian secret service. From here

You'll need strong nerves for a visit down to the Viennese sewerage system

Into the pillar and down to the sewers

the Wien River were built. After the narrow stairs you'll get to listed tunnel vaults, designed by Otto Wagner and completed around 1900. This monumental structure banished the Wien River between Stadtpark and Naschmarkt from the surface. More than 100 years later, the intercepting sewers canals have become too small for the city of millions: a new canal is being constructed. For several years, because of the construction works, the subterranean part of

the guided tour will be restricted to this tunnel, where the exciting chase sequences with Harry Lime were filmed. Back in daylight, walk along Lothringer Strasse up to Schwarzenbergplatz.

continue along Ringstrasse, and then turn right towards the **Staatsoper** (▶ 98). Behind the opera house there's another secret film location, **Hotel Sacher**. The English forces were stationed in this hotel, built in 1860, among them Graham Greene, who wrote the novel, which the film is based on. In the hotel's files he found all the inspiration he needed to write his black-market thriller.

5–6

Immediately behind the hotel, at the **Café Mozart** (▶ 90), Graham Greene liked to drink a coffee, and he made the café's garden the location for some of the scenes. Philipphof, on Albertinaplatz, a multistorey residential block with a large air-raid shelter in the cellars, was completely destroyed in a bombing raid in 1945; some 300 people were buried alive. Today you can see the **memorial** by sculptor Alfred Hrdlicka here. Continue your tour down

Augustinerstrasse to Josefsplatz. Opposite Emperor Joseph II's equestrian statue you'll see the **Palais Pallavicini**, Harry Lime's home in *The Third Man* – with the legendary porter played by Paul Hörbiger.

6–7

From Reitschulgasse you'll reach **Michaelerplatz**, where Café Marc Aurel was reconstructed for the film. Via Kohlmarkt and Bognergasse the walk now takes you to the next famous film location: **Am Hof** (▶ 63) is where you'll find the famous advertising pillar by which Harry Lime enters the sewers. It was rebuilt in wood and shot using an effective wideangle technique.

7–8

Walk along Freyung and Teinfaltstrasse to **Mölkersteig**. Here is the archway of No 8 Schreyvogelgasse – another key location in the film: it is the spot where Holly Martins

Hotel Sacher was the base for the English Allied forces

Taking a Break

One of the best places to have a coffee before the start of your tour are the terraces of the **Kursalon Stadtpark** (Wien 3, Johannesgasse 33, tel: 01/512 57 90-30, in summer daily 11:30 am–midnight).

– and the spectators – first catch sight of Harry Lime's face.

8–9

If you've joined an organized tour, you will arrive at **Molly Darcy's Irish Pub** (Wien 1, Teinfaltstrasse 6) where the world-famous *Harry Lime Theme* will be played for you on the zither. You'll also hear amusing anecdotes about the composer, Anton Karas, and the production of the film.

Guided Tours

The Timmermann family organize guided tours all year round on Mondays and Fridays at 4 pm; no need to book. Meeting point is the U-Bahn station Stadtpark, exit Johannesgasse (www.viennawalks.com, tel: 01/774 89 01, expensive).

Practicalities

Websites
- www.wien.info.at
- www.info.wien.at
- www.jugendinfowien.at

In Austria
Wiener Tourismusverband
Obere Augartenstrasse 40
1025 Wien
☎ (01) 211 14-222

In the UK
Austrian National Tourist Office
9-11 Richmond Buildings
off Dean Street
London W1D 3HF
☎ (020) 744 03 842

BEFORE YOU GO

WHAT YOU NEED

	UK	Ireland	USA	Canada	Australia	France	Netherlands	Spain
● Required / ○ Suggested / ▲ Not required								
Passport/National Identity Card	●	●	●	●	●	●	●	●
Visa	▲	▲	▲	▲	▲	▲	▲	▲
Onward or Return Ticket	▲	▲	▲	▲	▲	▲	▲	▲
Health Inoculations (tetanus or polio)	▲	▲	▲	▲	▲	▲	▲	▲
Health Documentation (▶ 188)	●	●	●	●	●	●	●	●
Travel Insurance (▶ 188)	○	○	○	○	○	○	○	○
Driving Licence (national)	●	●	●	●	●	●	●	●
Third-Party Car Insurance Certificate	●	●	n/a	n/a	n/a	●	●	●
Car Registration Document	●	●	n/a	n/a	n/a	●	●	●

WHEN TO GO

Vienna

High season — Low season

JAN	FEB	MAR	APR	MAY	JUN	JUL	AUG	SEP	OCT	NOV	DEC
1°C	3°C	8°C	14°C	19°C	22°C	25°C	24°C	20°C	14°C	7°C	3°C

☀ Sunny ☁ Cloudy 🌧 Rainy ⛅ Changeable

The temperatures indicated are the **average daytime temperature** in the respective months. Vienna has a continental climate, with cold winters, hot summers and rainy periods in the spring and autumn. The Danube ensures a good supply of fresh air. Although Vienna is always in season, the most beautiful period to visit the city is from May, when the lilacs are in flower, to October, when the leaves in the vineyards surrounding Vienna start to change colour. Throughout the year there is an impressive programme of cultural events: theatre, music and numerous museums make it possible for you to enjoy yourself even when the sun isn't shining. More recently, a visit in the time before Christmas and around New Year has became more attractive. Thousands of visitors come to shop at the Christmas markets and for the New Year's Eve festivities, taking place all over the city.

GETTING THERE

By Plane Vienna International Airport Wien-Schwechat is about 15km (9 miles) southeast of the city centre. It is served by 60 airlines, flying to Vienna from 140 destinations in 59 countries. Schwechat is also served by charter flights.

Ticket Prices Ticket prices vary considerably. If you're lucky you may get a bargain because there is so much competition. The so-called "Red Ticket" of Austria's national airline AUA is generally good value; they also have tickets at permanently low prices and changing specials. Check the internet under www.aua.com or with your travel agents for current offers. The no-frills airline Air Berlin offers cheap flights between London Stansted and Vienna.

By Train Vienna can be reached by IC, ICE, Eurocity and regional trains. Trains from the West (Germany and Switzerland) arrive at **Westbahnhof**, trains from the south (Italy and Slovenia) at **Südbahnhof**. Regional trains to northern Austria depart from **Franz-Josefs-Bahnhof**. Information on trains is available on the internet under www.oebb.at.

By Car The A1 Westautobahn (western motorway) links Vienna with Salzburg and Linz, the A2 Südautobahn (southern motorway) links Vienna with Klagenfurt and Graz.

TIME

Vienna is in the Central European time zone (MEZ), i.e. one hour ahead of Greenwich Mean Time (GMT). From the end of March until the end of October clocks are adjusted one hour forwards for summer time (GMT + 1).

CURRENCY AND FOREIGN EXCHANGE

Currency Austria is one of the European countries to use the single currency, the **euro**. The official abbreviation for the euro is EUR. Euro notes are available in the following denominations: 5, 10, 20, 50, 100, 200 and 500 euros; coins to the value of 1, 2 and 5 euro cents (bronze-coloured), 10, 20 and 50 euro cents (gold-coloured), and the two-coloured 1 euro and 2 euro coins are available.
An **exchange rate calculator** is available on the internet: www.oanda.com.

Exchange Exchange bureaux can be found in the railway stations and at the airport. **Travellers' cheques** can be cashed at all banks, whose branches are plentiful throughout the city. Outside of bank opening hours, **ATMs** (Geldautomaten) are available in many locations.

Credit cards are accepted in almost all hotels, restaurants and shops. VISA and MasterCard cards with four-digit PINs can be used at most ATMs.

GMT	Vienna	Paris	New York	Los Angeles	Sydney
←			←	←	→
12 noon	1 pm	1 pm	7 am	4 am	10 pm

WHEN YOU ARE THERE

CLOTHING SIZES

UK	Austria	USA	
36	46	36	Suits
38	48	38	
40	50	40	
42	52	42	
44	54	44	
46	56	46	
7	41	8	Shoes
7.5	42	8.5	
8.5	43	9.5	
9.5	44	10.5	
10.5	45	11.5	
11	46	12	
14.5	37	14.5	Shirts
15	38	15	
15.5	39/40	15.5	
16	41	16	
16.5	42	16.5	
17	43	17	
8	36	6	Clothes
10	38	8	
12	40	10	
14	42	12	
16	44	14	
18	46	16	
4.5	36	6	Shoes
5	37	6.5	
5.5	38	7	
6	39	7.5	
6.5	40	8	
7	41	8.5	

HOLIDAYS

1 Jan	New Year's Day
6 Jan	Three Kings Day
Mar/Apr	Good Friday, Easter Sunday and Monday
1 May	Labour Day
May/June	Ascension Day, Whit Sunday and Monday, Corpus Christi
15 Aug	Assumption
26 Oct	National Holiday
1 Nov	All Saints' Day
8 Dec	Immaculate Conception
25 Dec	Christmas Day
26 Dec	St Stephen's Day

OPENING HOURS

○ Shops   ● Post Offices
● Offices   ● Museums/Monuments
● Banks   ● Pharmacies (Apotheke)

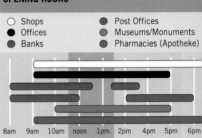

8am 9am 10am noon 1pm 2pm 4pm 5pm 6pm

□ Morning   □ Midday   □ Evening

Shops The liberalization of shop opening hours is currently much debated. Generally, most shops in the centre are open Monday to Friday from 9 am until 6:30 pm and on Saturdays from 9 am until 6 pm. Many supermarkets and shops in main shopping areas stay open later on Thursday and Friday evenings.

Banks Bank opening hours are Monday to Friday 8 am until 12:30 pm and 1:30 pm until 3 pm, Thursdays until 5:30 pm.

Museums Opening hours vary considerably from one museum to another.

EMERGENCIES:

POLICE 133

FIRE (and ambulance) 122

RESCUE SERVICES 144

PERSONAL SAFETY

Vienna has always been considered a relatively safe city. Recently, however, there has been a sharp rise in property crime. Car break-ins and handbag theft are particular problems for visitors. Make sure you keep your handbag well closed. Do not make life easy for thieves – firmly hold on to your bags and keep an eye on your valuables at all times.

- The U-Bahn is a favourite hunting ground for pickpockets. Always be aware of what is happening around you.
- Especially at night you are advised to avoid Karlsplatz and nearby U-Bahn exits as many drug dealers and users tend to congregate in this area.

Police assistance:
 133 from any phone

TELEPHONES

The ubiquitous mobile phone has made public phones almost unnecessary, but some still exist. To phone, you need coins or a phonecard, which can be bought at post offices or newsagents. To phone another country, leave out the initial 0 after the country code.

International Dialling Codes:

UK:	00 44
Ireland	00 353
USA/Canada	00 1
Australia	00 61

POST

There are post offices in all districts. Smaller offices open Mon–Fri 8–noon and 2–6, larger offices do not close at lunchtime. The central post office is open around the clock (Wien 1, Fleischmarkt 19). The post offices inside the stations (Westbahnhof, Südbahnhof and Franz-Josefs-Bahnhof) are open from 7am until 10pm. Post offices also sell a range of stationery items.

ELECTRICITY

The power supply in Austria is 220 volts. Sockets take two round-pin plugs. Travellers from outside continental Europe should use an adaptor.

TIPS/GRATUITIES

Generally, restaurant, drinks and taxi bills are rounded up generously. 5 per cent is a good general rule.

Hotel porters	1–2 euros
Chambermaids	1–2 euros
Tour guides	on own discretion
Lavatory attendants	30 cents

EMBASSIES AND CONSULATES

UK
☎ (01) 71613-0

USA
☎ (01) 31339-0

Australia
☎ (01) 506 740

Canada
☎ (01) 53138-3325

Ireland
☎ (01) 715-4246

HEALTH

Insurance: Special travel health insurance is recommended, particularly for visitors from non-EU countries. Nationals of EU countries can obtain medical treatment at reduced costs with the relevant documentation (for Britons form E111 in 2005 and an international health insurance card thereafter). Doctors are listed in the yellow pages of the phone book. The medical emergency service (Ärztlicher Bereitschaftsdienst) can be reached on tel: (01) 531 16-0.

Dental Services: Dental treatment for non-Austrian visitors can be expensive. The dental emergency service (Zahnärztlicher Notdienst) can be reached on tel: (01)512 20 78. Addresses and telephone numbers for dentists are listed in the phone book's yellow pages.

Weather: In the middle of summer it can be hot in Vienna. Take care to protect yourself against sunburn and drink plenty of fluids.

Drugs: There are many pharmacies (Apotheke) selling prescription and non-prescription medicines. Find out in the daily papers or from the Apotheken-Bereitschaftsdienst (pharmacy emergency service) tel: 15 50 (recorded message) which pharmacy is open outside normal opening hours.

Safe Water: Tap water is suitable for drinking, but the water from public wells throughout Vienna has been treated with chemicals – watch out with dogs, too!

CONCESSIONS

Reduced admission tickets to sights are usually available for senior citizens, the disabled and soldiers, on presentation of the appropriate ID. Concessionary tickets are also usually available for children, young people and school groups.
The **Wien-Card** is good value for money. At 16.90 euros it entitles to 72 hours unlimited travel on U-Bahn, trams and buses. In addition you will pay lower ticket prices at many museums and sights. You can buy the card at over 200 hotels and the Tourist-Infos (► 38).

TRAVELLING WITH A DISABILITY

Trams and buses are mostly difficult to access by wheelchair. The exception are the buses of the following lines which have lower floors: 5A, 7A, 8A, 13A, 57A, 63A, 77A, 83A and 84A. **U-Bahn stations** are better equipped for disabled visitors. A plan of **U-Bahn stations for sight-impaired visitors** is available from the Wiener Linien (tel: 01/79 090). Detailed information on access for disabled visitors at restaurants, museums and sights is available on the internet at www.info.wien.at. Click first on your language, then "Specials" and finally on "Vienna for Visitors with Disabilities".

CHILDREN

Children are welcome almost anywhere. Children's theatre and special kids' programmes in museums are the norm. For detailed information see www.kinderinfowien.at.

LAVATORIES

Public lavatories can be found in the stations and near all major sights.

LOST PROPERTY

Zentralfundamt Wasagasse 22, Wien 9, tel: 01/ 313 46. For public transport tel: 01/4 35 00; railway tel: 01/5800 356 56.

VIENNA PLACE NAMES

For ease of use this guide uses "ss" instead f *ß* in all cases. You may however find the correct German spelling on street signs, for example in "Straße".

The following German terms have been used throughout:
U-Bahn underground railway (subway)
S-Bahn overground (often overhead) local and regional railway

SURVIVAL PHRASES

Yes/no **Ja/nein**
Good day **Gruss Gott or Servus**
Good evening **Guten Abend**
Goodbye **Auf Wiedersehen, Auf Wiederschauen, Tschuss (informal)**
How are you? **Wie geht es Ihnen?**
You're welcome **Bitte schön**
Please **Bitte schön or Bitte sehr**
Thank you **Danke**
Excuse me **Entschuldigung**
I'm sorry **Es tut mir Leid**
Do you have ...? **Haben Sie...?**
I'd like ... **Ich möchte ...**
How much is that? **Was kostet das?**
I don't understand **Ich verstehe nicht**
Do you speak English? **Sprechen Sie Englisch?**
Open **Geöffnet** Closed **Geschlossen**
Push/pull **Drücken/Ziehen**
Women's lavatory **Damen**
Men's lavatory **Herren**

DAYS OF THE WEEK

Monday **Montag**
Tuesday **Dienstag**
Wednesday **Mittwoch**
Thursday **Donnerstag**
Friday **Freitag**
Saturday **Samstag**
Sunday **Sonntag**

OTHER USEFUL WORDS & PHRASES

Yesterday **Gestern**
Today **Heute**
Tomorrow **Morgen**
Could you call a doctor please?
Könnten Sie bitte einen Arzt rufen?
Do you have a vacant room?
Haben Sie ein Zimmer frei?
- with bath/shower
mit Bad/Dusche
Single room **Das Einzelzimmer**
Double room **Das Doppelzimmer**
One/two nights Eins/Zwei Nächte
How much per night? **Was kostet es pro Nacht?**

DIRECTIONS & GETTING AROUND

Where is...? **Wo ist...?**
- the train/bus station
der Bahnhof/Busbahnhof
- the bank **die Bank**
– the nearest toilets
die nächsten Toiletten
Turn left/right **Biegen Sie links ab/rechts ab**
Go straight on **Gehen Sie geradeaus**
Here/there **Hier/da**
North **Nord**
East **Ost**
South **Süd**
West **West**

NUMBERS

1 **eins**	13 **dreizehn**	31 **einunddreissig**	300 **dreihundert**
2 **zwei**	14 **vierzehn**	32 **zweiunddreissig**	400 **vierhundert**
3 **drei**	15 **fünfzehn**	40 **vierzig**	500 **fünfhundert**
4 **vier**	16 **sechzehn**	50 **fünfzig**	600 **sechshundert**
5 **fünf**	17 **siebzehn**	60 **sechzig**	700 **siebenhundert**
6 **sechs**	18 **achtzehn**	70 **siebzig**	800 **achthundert**
7 **sieben**	19 **neunzehn**	80 **achtzig**	900 **neunhundert**
8 **acht**	20 **zwanzig**	90 **neunzig**	1,000 **tausend**
9 **neun**	21 **einundzwanzig**	100 **hundert**	
10 **zehn**	22 **zweiund-**	101 **einhunderteins**	
11 **elf**	**zwanzig**	102 **einhundertzwei**	
12 **zwölf**	30 **dreissig**	200 **zweihundert**	

EATING OUT

A table for ..., please **Einen Tisch für ... bitte**

We have/haven't booked **Wir haben/haben nicht reserviert**

I'd like to reserve a table for ... people at ... **Ich möchte einen Tisch für ... Personen um ... reservieren**

I am a vegetarian **Ich bin Vegetarier/in**

May I see the menu, please? **die Speisekarte bitte?**

Is there a dish of the day, please? **Gibt es ein Tagesgericht?**

We'd like something to drink **Wir möchten etwas zu trinken**

Do you have a wine list in English? **Haben Sie eine Weinkarte auf Englisch?**

This is not what I ordered **das habe ich nicht bestellt**

Could we sit there? **Können wir dort sitzen?**

When do you open/close? **Wann machen Sie auf/zu?**

The food is cold **das Essen ist kalt**

The food was excellent **das Essen war ausgezeichnet**

Can I have the bill, please? **Wir möchten zahlen, bitte**

Is service included? **Ist das mit Bedienung?**

Breakfast **das Frühstück**
Lunch **das Mittagessen**
Dinner **das Abendessen**

Starters **die Vorspeise**
Main course **das Hauptgericht**
Desserts **die Nachspeisen**

Fish dishes **Fischgerichte**
Meat dishes **Fleischgerichte**
Fruit **Obst**
Vegetables **Gemüse**
Dish of the day **das Tagesgericht**
Wine list **die Weinkarte**

Salt **das Salz**
Pepper **der Pfeffer**

Knife **das Messer**
Fork **die Gabel**
Spoon **der Löffel**

Waiter **der Kellner**
Waitress **die Kellnerin**

MENU A–Z

Äpfelstrudel Apple pudding
Apfelsaft Apple juice
Apfelsinen Oranges
Aufschnitt Sliced cold meat
Austern Oysters
Belegte Brote Sandwiches
Birnen Pears
Blumenkohl Cauliflower
Brathähnchen Roast chicken
Bratwurst Fried sausage
Brokkoli Broccoli
Brötchen Bread roll
Eintopf Casserole
Eisbein Knuckle of pork
Ente Duck
Erbsen Peas
Erdbeeren Strawberries
Fasan Pheasant
Fenchel Fennel
Flunder Flounder
Forelle Trout
Frittatensuppe Beef broth
Frühstücksspeck Grilled bacon
Gans Goose
Gekochtes Ei Boiled egg
Gulasch Goulash
Fisolen Green beans
Heilbutt Halibut
Hering Herring
Himbeeren Raspberries
Honig Honey
Hummer Lobster
Kabeljau Cod
Kaffee Coffee
Kalbsleber Calf's liver
Karotten Carrots
Erdäpfel Potatoes
Käse Cheese
Käsekuchen Cheesecake

Kasseler Smoked pork loin
Kirschen Cherries
Knödel Dumplings
Krabben Shrimps
Kohl Cabbage
Konfitüre Preserves
Lachs Salmon
Lammbraten Roast lamb
Lauch Leeks
Mais Sweet corn
Milch Milk
Obsttorte Fruit tart
Obstsalat Fruit salad
Orangensaft Orange juice
Palatschinken Pancakes
Paprika Pepper
Pfirsiche Peaches
Pflaumen Plums
Pilze Mushrooms
Rinderbraten Roast beef
Rotkohl Red cabbage
Rührei Scrambled egg
Sachertorte chocolate cake
Schinken Ham
Scholle Plaice
Schokoladentorte Chocolate cake
Schweinebraten Roast pork
Schweinekotelett Pork chop
Seezunge Sole
Spargel Asparagus
Spinat Spinach
Stelze Pork shanks
Tomaten Tomatoes
Topfenstrudel Cream cheese pastry
Wiener Schnitzel Veal escalope
Wild Game
Zwiebeln Onions

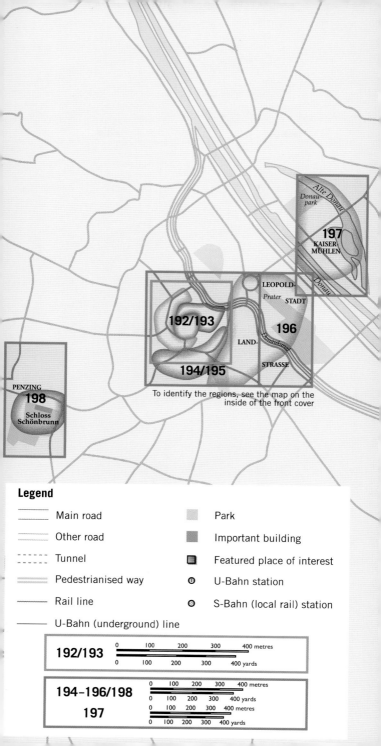

197
KAISER-
MÜHLEN

192/193

LEOPOLD-
STADT

196

194/195

LAND-
STRASSE

To identify the regions, see the map on the
inside of the front cover

PENZING
198
Schloss
Schönbrunn

Legend

———	Main road	▮	Park
———	Other road	▮	Important building
- - - -	Tunnel	◻	Featured place of interest
═══	Pedestrianised way	Ⓤ	U-Bahn station
———	Rail line	Ⓢ	S-Bahn (local rail) station
———	U-Bahn (underground) line		

192/193

0   100   200   300   400 metres
0   100   200   300   400 yards

194–196/198
197

0   100   200   300   400 metres
0   100   200   300   400 yards
0   100   200   300   400 metres
0   100   200   300   400 yards

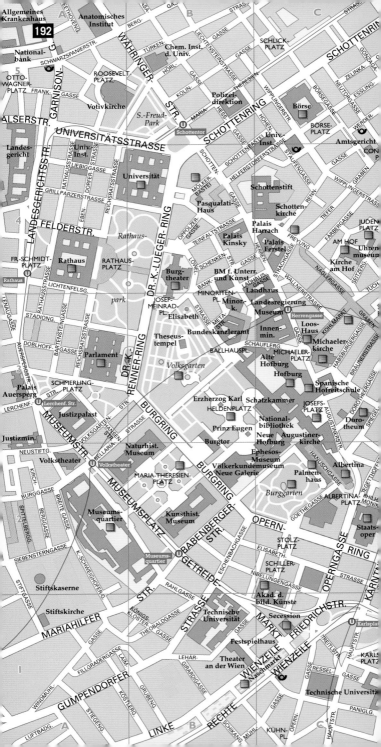

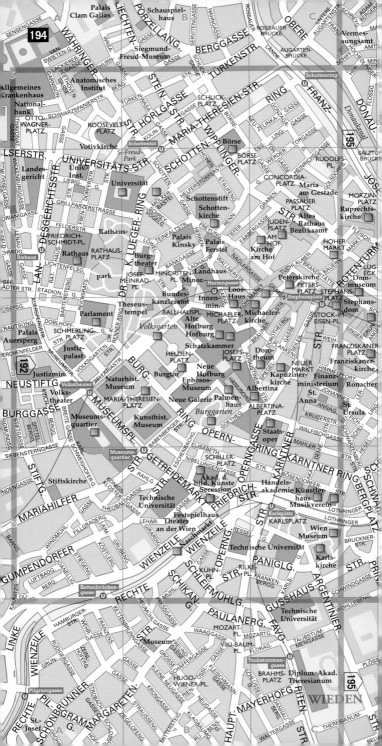

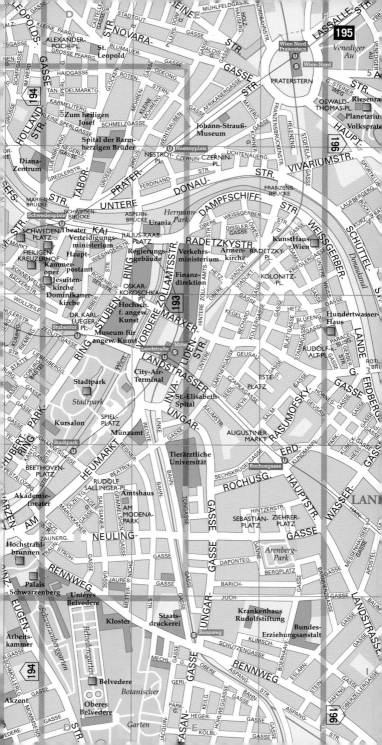

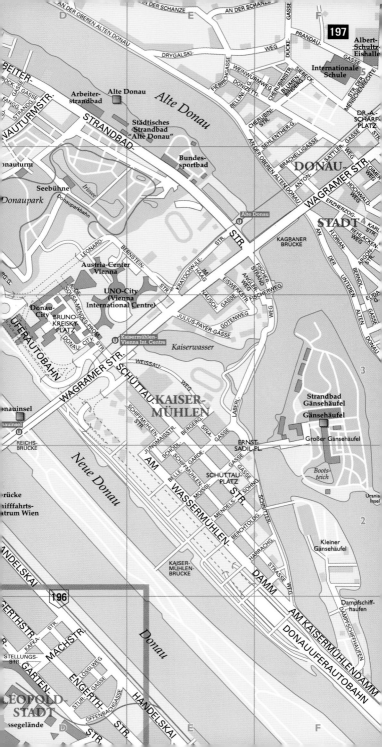

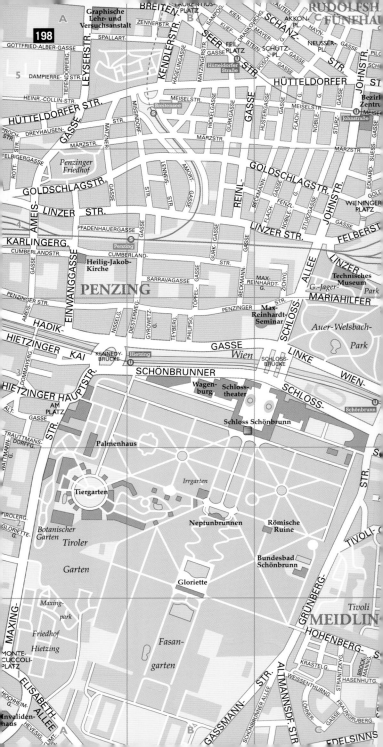

Streetplan index

Index

Picture credits

Abbreviations for terms appearing below: (t) top; (b) bottom; r (right); (l) left; (m) middle

Covers: (t) Werner Dieterich, (m) Rainer Hackenberg, (b) Ralf Freyer

AKG Images, Berlin: 12/13 background woodcut from drawing by Bartel Beham (1502–40), 12/13m illustration "The Relief of Vienna", around 1688 by Franz Geffels, 13tl "Die Entführung aus dem Serail" by Wolfgang Amadeus Mozart, 14tr "Maria Theresia", painting by Martin van Meytens the Younger, 15 "Die Thronbesteigung des Kaisers Franz Josef I", woodcut, 16bl "Kaiser Franz Joseph zeichnet die Generäle und Offiziere des Krieges von 1848 aus", painting by Anton Strassgeschwandthner, 16/17tr "Assassinat a Sarajevo", colour print from: Le Petit Journal, Suppl. Illust., 20bl Thomáš Masaryk, 20m reconstruction of the treatment room of Sigmund Freud in Berggasse 19 in Vienna after information from Freud's daughter Anna, 20r Sigmund Freud, 20mr sculpture by Johann Scherpe 1908, 22tm "Joseph Haydn", painting by Thomas Hardy, London 1792, 22ml "Beethoven mit dem Manuskript der Missa solemnis", painting by Joseph Karl Stieler, 22b potrait of Wolfgang Amadeus Mozart, painting by Barbara Krafft, 22mb watercolour by Richard Moser 1905, 23r "Joseph Lanner und Johann Strauss", painting by Charles Wilda from 1906, 28/29m "Cafe Griensteidl am Michaelerplatz", watercolour by R Völkel 1900, 121t "Der junge Mozart wird Kaiserin Maria Theresia durch Joseph II vorgestellt", painting by Eduard Ender 1869, 146 "Praterstern", picture postcard after a painting by Jindrich Tomec 1910, 148ml "Russische Schaukel" woodcut after an illustration by Leo von Elliot, 148br "Das neue Wiener Ringspiel im Prater", etching by Karl Postl; Werner Dieterich, Stuttgart: 2III, 2V, 3I, 3II, 3III, 10b, 18/19m, 19tr, 20ml, 20t, 21b, 24/25, 25t, 25b, 28b, 29t, 31t, 32ml, 32tr, 33t, 47, 48, 49, 50m, 50/51b, 51tl, 51m, 53t, 54, 56, 57tr, 57ml, 58, 59, 60t, 60br, 61m, 62tl, 63bl, 63tr, 72m, 76/77, 77t, 93, 94, 95, 96, 97t, 97b, 99, 100, 101tr, 101mr, 102ml, 102br, 103m, 103br, 104tl, 104bl, 104/105, 105tr, 106, 107, 108, 113, 123, 126, 127, 137, 145t, 159, 160, 161tr, 161ml, 163b, 165, 166, 169br, 179, 180/181, 187tl, 187tr, 187mr; Ralf Freyer, Freiburg: 3IV, 3V, 8t, 9b, 11tr, 13tr, 14bl, 27t, 28/29, 30t, 30lm, 31b, 33b, 70/71, 73br, 86, 128, 129, 140, 142, 148/149m, 149tl, 149tr, 150, 152, 153, 171, 172l, 172r, 174tl, 174ml, 174br, 175, 177tr, 178/179, 178r, 183; Rainer Hackenberg, Köln: 2II, 2IV, 6l, 6/7, 7m, 11br, 13mr, 19br, 21ml, 22/23 background, 26tm, 26lm, 26rm, 29b, 30mr, 32b, 35, 69, 71b, 72br, 74, 75t, 75b, 78, 79mr, 80, 81, 83t, 83b, 114tl, 116, 117t, 120/121m, 124bl, 125t, 125mr, 141t, 141m, 141br, 143, 144, 147t, 147m, 151, 164tl, 167tl, 167mr, 167bl, 168, 176, 180m, 181b; HB Verlag, Ostfildern: 9t, 10/11, 98/99m, 117b, 122, 130, 162/163, 163t, 164mr (Axel Krause); Peter Hautzinger, Wien: 2I, 5, 52/53, 55, 169tl, 170tr, 170ml; Thomas Stankiewicz, München: 182; Martin Thomas, Aachen: 6r, 7r, 8b, 10/11, 16/17 background, 18tl, 18bl, 22tl, 70b, 73t, 79tr, 82, 84, 85, 115, 118/119, 121br, 124t, 131, 139, 145mr; Schloss Schönbrunn Kultur- und Betriebsges.m.b.H.: 17b (E. Knaack)

Questionnaire

Dear Traveller

Your comments, opinions and recommendations are very important to us. So please help us to improve our travel guides by taking a few minutes to complete this simple questionnaire.

You do not need a stamp (unless posted outside the UK). If you do not want to remove this page from your guide, then photocopy it or write your answers on a plain sheet of paper.

Send to: The Editor, Spiral Guides, AA World Travel Guides, FREEPOST SCE 4598, Basingstoke RG21 4GY.

Your recommendations...

We always encourage readers' recommendations for restaurants, night-life or shopping – if your recommendation is used in the next edition of the guide, we will send you a FREE AA Spiral Guide of your choice. Please state below the establishment name, location and your reasons for recommending it.

_____

_____

_____

_____

_____

Please send me AA Spiral _____

(see list of titles inside the back cover)

About this guide...

Which title did you buy?

_____ **AA Spiral**

Where did you buy it? _____

When? m m / y y

Why did you choose an AA Spiral Guide? _____

_____

_____

_____

_____

Did this guide meet your expectations?

Exceeded ☐   Met all ☐   Met most ☐   Fell below ☐

Please give your reasons _____

_____

_____

_____

_____

continued on next page...

Were there any aspects of this guide that you particularly liked?

Is there anything we could have done better?

About you...

Name (Mr/Mrs/Ms) _____

Address _____

_____ Postcode _____

Daytime tel no _____ email _____

Please *only* give us your email address and mobile phone number if you wish to hear from us about other products and services from the AA and partners by email or text or mms.

Which age group are you in?

Under 25 ☐   25–34 ☐   35–44 ☐   45–54 ☐   55–64 ☐   65+ ☐

How many trips do you make a year?

Less than one ☐   One ☐   Two ☐   Three or more ☐

Are you an AA member? Yes ☐   No ☐

About your trip...

When did you book? mm/ y y   When did you travel? mm/ y y

How long did you stay? _____

Was it for business or leisure? _____

Did you buy any other travel guides for your trip?   ☐ Yes   ☐ No

If yes, which ones? _____

Thank you for taking the time to complete this questionnaire. Please send it to us as soon as possible, and remember, you do not need a stamp (unless posted outside the UK).